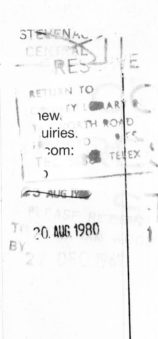

YEARS OF CONTENT
1858–1886

G.L.G.

1902

YEARS OF CONTENT
1858–1886

by

SIR GEORGE LEVESON-GOWER,
K.B.E.

LONDON
JOHN MURRAY, ALBEMARLE STREET, W.
1940

To

DEAREST CICELY

for whose counsel, encouragement
and help in commencing, continuing
and completing this book, I can
never find words to express my
deepest gratitude.

Printed in Great Britain by
Wyman & Sons, Ltd., London, Fakenham and Reading.

CONTENTS

CONTENTS

ILLUSTRATIONS

* In the possession of the author.

INTRODUCTION

I FEEL that some apology is due for presenting at the present moment of storm and stress, a record of earlier, happier and more gracious days. But yet, I cannot concur with the poet that "a sorrow's crown of sorrows is remembering happier things"; for surely the recollection and contemplation of a more tranquil, if less eventful, period brings respite and refreshment in these distressful times.

This book was not written for publication, but as a record for my wife and children. My friends, however, have induced me to publish it, as they are sanguine enough to hope that it may prove of interest to the public. I had no diary to refer to, having only kept a journal when travelling abroad, and have thus had to rely on my memory and a certain number of letters.

Whilst the book has a certain chronological thread running through it, it is not written with any strict regard to the sequence of events according to time. Rather it is of a discursive, some may perhaps think of a disjointed, nature, as I have spoken of people and places as suggested by the course of the narrative. If some should think that an undue proportion of space has been devoted to my childhood and boyish days I would plead that a childhood such as I spent is so unlike what any child is likely to spend in these days that it may have real value and interest. Moreover, owing to my being an only child constantly associated with a father who lived in really interesting political and social circles, I was privileged to have contacts with many well-known people whom I should not have met in the normal schoolroom life of a large family.

Although certainly without my will or knowledge, it is possible that some of my anecdotes are already known to the public. If so I hope that my offence may be forgiven, as purely involuntary. Tityrus, it may be remembered, observed, "*Sunt mihi castaneæ nuces et mitia poma*," and thus I hope that if there be any chestnuts they may be excused if some of the apples are adjudged to be mellow.

ix

INTRODUCTION

I have to thank Mr Albert Gladstone of Hawarden Castle for leave to reproduce some letters of his grandfather's.

My warmest thanks are also due to my wife, without whose invaluable help this book could hardly have been produced, and also to my daughters, Iris Palmer and Margaret Leveson Gower, for their assistance. Nor must I forget to mention the efficient help given me by Miss Sybil Davis.

For reasons, into which it is not worth while to enter, it was thought advisable not to prolong this narrative beyond the date of the General Election of 1886.

G. LEVESON GOWER.

The Lady Margaret Leveson Gower,
AT THE AGE OF 26, 1856

The Hon. Frederick Leveson Gower,
AT THE AGE OF 24, 1843

CHAPTER I

HAPPY CHILDHOOD

I was born on May 19, 1858, at 10 Stratton Street, then and for many years later a quiet cul-de-sac, running from Piccadilly on the western side of Devonshire House.

My Mother was Margaret, youngest daughter of the second Marquis of Northampton. She died a day or two after my birth. In her diary on April 23, 1856 she wrote: "The other day I heard, to my horror, a rumour that Devonshire House was to be sold for a large hotel. As we took this house for twenty years, just because of the large open space in front of it, and the pleasure of seeing green trees instead of sooty brick houses, I was in despair. I hear that an offer was made to the Duke of £400,000. Lucky for us that our good Uncle is rich enough to be able to turn calmly away from such temptation."

The sale of Devonshire House was thus postponed for sixty-nine years, whilst the price rose (if I am informed aright) from £400,000 to £1,000,000. I think that the late Duke was quite right to dispose of the site. Devonshire House, for all its historical associations, was not architecturally beautiful nor comfortable. The chief feature of the house was the great staircase which rose in two semi-circles from the ground floor. Maria, Marchioness of Ailesbury, said that she enjoyed the Devonshire House parties, because from the top of the staircase she could estimate the progressive advance of baldness amongst her friends and acquaintances.

My Father felt his bereavement so acutely that he never once trusted himself to speak to me of my Mother. He took me soon afterwards to Chiswick House, which had been left by his uncle, the sixth Duke of Devonshire, to his sister, my grandmother, the first Countess Granville, for her life. This was my home until she died when I was four and a half years old. I can well remember her in her big black bonnet and widow's weeds. To others she was rather alarming as she had a pretty wit to which she gave free play, as is seen in her extraordinarily amusing letters which were edited by my Father; but to me she was always kindness itself, possibly because of my being motherless.

Chiswick House, which Lord Hervey described as being "too small to live in but too large to wear on your fob," was in many ways an ideal home for a child whose father's parliamentary duties prevented his living far out of town. It was a Palladian villa, built in the 18th century, and here two great men passed away, Charles Fox in 1806 and George Canning in 1827. I remember the splendid cedars, the wide lawns sloping down to a small lake with reed-grown margins, the classic statues and stately avenues, the beautiful gates later removed to the front of Devonshire House and now re-erected on the Piccadilly side of Green Park.

During the season my uncle, Earl Granville, used to give garden-parties there, at one of which the Empress Eugénie was the principal guest. The day before, he had a rehearsal of my presentation of a bouquet to the Empress and showed me how I was to give it to her. When the Empress came the next day, I got confused, made my bow to my uncle, and as I presented my back to her and was dressed in a short white petticoat, the effect was unconventional.

Years afterwards, I think in 1877, when I was an undergraduate at Balliol, the Master took her and the Prince Imperial to see my rooms. What a contrast and what a change! From Empress of the French, at the zenith of her beauty, to a widow and an exile, and yet with what cheerful gallantry her spirit rallied beneath the strokes of adversity. Her son was of small compact figure, grey eyes in an eager and intelligent face. When the Master presented me she said: "Ah! but we know each other already, do we not? This time you have no bouquet for me, although" (with a smile) "you bow in a different way." To which I answered: "Madam, I hope that my bow has improved, but I am afraid that your Majesty will think that my bouquet is worse." I went into the Quad, and against all rules and under the Master's nose, gathered a few flowers and made them up into a rough nosegay.

In 1862 we lived for a few years at my Uncle Granville's house in Bruton Street, his wife having recently died. By her first husband she had a son, Sir John Acton, the distinguished scholar and historian, later created Lord Acton. Lord Granville always treated me with the same affection which he would have given to a son, and romped and played with me, and I loved him dearly. He used to have me up in his bedroom and one morning I was so indignant at the cession of the Ionian Islands to Greece, of which I had vaguely heard, that, although I could not tell what or where they were, I vented my patriotic feelings by pummelling him as he lay in bed, much to his amusement. It was his habit to have a light breakfast and he generally treated me to a rusk. One morning he forgot the customary offering, and to stimulate his memory, I observed, quite untruthfully, that I had had no breakfast. Instead of the hoped for rusk, to my dismay he jumped out of bed and hurried me up to the nursery.

"What is this, Mrs Page! George says that he has had no breakfast!"

"Oh, no, my Lord, Master George had an excellent breakfast; some bacon, three slices of bread and butter and some marmalade, besides the top of my own egg."

"How dare you tell me such a lie?"—this to me.

"I wanted you to give me a rusk."

"Instead of telling me a lie, why did you not say: 'Please, Uncle, may I have a rusk?'"

Whereupon, driven to my last defences, I said in despair: "And why did you not say: 'Please, George, would you like a rusk this morning?'"

If he was still sleeping I was strictly ordered to be very quiet so as not to wake him. The period of waiting sometimes grew tedious, and I beguiled the interval one morning by filling a long row of his Wellington boots with water from an ewer. There was a lot of unpleasantness over this.

Charles Greville, the well-known diarist, also lived with my uncle, and was known either as "The Lodger," or "The Gruncher." I included him in my round of morning calls, and he also occasionally presented me with some delicacy or other.

On my seventh birthday a children's party was given. A conjurer failed to turn up, and the party seemed to be rather flagging. The mothers and governesses started some silly game which began by the boys being all in one room and the girls in another. I had just been initiated into the early history of Ancient Rome, and a brilliant idea occurred to me, so I said to my guests: "I've thought of a much better game, the Rape of the Sabines!" "What's that?" I explained the rules. "I'll be Romulus; you'll be the Romans; we'll rush in, and we'll each grab the girl we want. They'll be the Sabines, you see, and they'll have to come with us to be our wives." "But suppose they won't?" "Oh, then we just drag them along; that's half the fun!" One small boy objected that he didn't want a Sabine, but was told not to be a silly. So in we burst upon the unsuspecting Sabines, whom we proceeded to hale about, according to plan, with dire results. My own particular Sabine put up a very vigorous resistance, and kicked me hard on the shin, whilst my companions were severally dragged off their prey, not without sundry boxes on the ear. When rebuked by "Pagey," my nurse, for my behaviour, I could only reply: "Well, it was better fun than waiting for a conjurer who didn't come."

When I was about six my Father took the lease of 14 South Audley Street, a house much too big for our requirements. Here had lived Mrs Delany, the celebrated 18th century blue-stocking, and later on Westmacott, the sculptor, whose studio was a long gallery. Here were a number of treasures bought for my Father in Japan by his old friend, Laurence Oliphant, who was on Lord Elgin's staff, the first English Minister accredited to that country. Oliphant was nearly killed by a sword-cut by a Samurai in an anti-foreign riot.

Here my Father lavishly entertained, giving big dinners which came to be regarded as some of the best in London, owing to the incomparable skill of his chef, Monsieur Béguinot. He had previously been second cook to the Duc de Morny, the powerful Minister and illegitimate half-brother of Napoleon III. I am afraid that in the exercise of his art he was not over-careful of my Father's pocket. He was justly celebrated for the lightness and excellence of his soufflés; if the service was not ready for one of these masterpieces, he invariably threw it away and started another and continued to do so until the exact moment for its presentation arrived.

Musson, the butler, remonstrated on the ground of economy, but Béguinot waived his objections aside:

"*Vous ne comprenez pas, Monsieur Musson, vous n'êtes pas artiste.*"

Béguinot afterwards transferred his services to Lord Granville, who was Foreign Secretary during the Franco-Prussian War of 1870-71. When called to the colours, he consulted my uncle whether he should go. Lord Granville answered that he must decide for himself. He asked for twenty-four hours' reflection and next day remarked:

"*J'y ai réfléchi, Milor, et me suis décidé à rester au service de Milor, car je préfère faire les entrées aux sorties.*" Excellent wit but indifferent patriotism!

From my uncle's service he passed to that of Lord Spencer, who assigned him two rooms at Althorp and asked him how he would like them decorated. Béguinot opted for dark red hangings and mahogany furniture in one room and for a scheme of white and light blue in the other. He explained that the former would help him if he had to compose the menu "*d'un grand dîner sérieux,*" whilst the latter would be "*plutôt propice pour quelque combinaison amusante et frivole.*"

He subsequently was chef to Lord Iveagh and finally bought a little restaurant, "Le Dîner Français," in Old Compton Street, Soho, which my Father as well as my family frequented as the food was remarkable both for quality and price. A dinner of four courses, beautifully and liberally served, cost 1s. 6d. before the war, and 2s. 6d. afterwards, including coffee. I asked him how he managed to make it pay, and he said: No music, no gilding, no marble, no velvet; the place always full; the fact that he bought everything himself wholesale, whilst whatever was left over, after his staff had been fed, was disposed of at a reduction to humbler restaurants. He further explained that I and my friends could always bring ladies there, "*puisque nous éloignons la société équivoque.*"

My aunt, Lady Georgiana Fullerton, a very devout Catholic, was dining on a Friday with my Father, which meant a "*dîner maigre.*" She asked whether she could have a recipe of the delicious soup. My Father noted a certain amount of stock amongst the ingredients. "*Ce n'est rien du tout, Monsieur,*" Béguinot explained, "*rien qu'un petit soupçon; cela se fait toujours à Paris,*" the last argument in a tone which indicated that it was conclusive. My aunt got the recipe minus the stock but said the result was disappointing.

Madame Béguinot continued to manage the Dîner Français for some years after her husband's death. She was an intelligent woman with charming manners, and during the war she continuously entertained as her guests five or six wounded or convalescent English officers at her farm near Rouen.

The mention of Béguinot recalls one or two other stories of cooks and their ways. My aunt, Lady Marian Alford, had a very good chef who could never get on with his kitchen-maids, to whom he either made violent love or violently abused. One day he chased two girls round the kitchen with a big knife in his hand, and they not unnaturally complained. His only defence was: "*Ce n'est que trop vrai, Miladi; je le regrette profondément; en effet j'ai manqué envers ces demoiselles.*"

Her Father, Lord Northampton, brought back to England two Italian servants, a coachman and a lady's maid. The former, Amadio by name, was much distressed at what seemed unjustifiable extravagance in the kitchen. One day a large joint was served for the servants' dinner. Amadio seized the carving knife, and metaphorically bestriding the joint, exclaimed: "*Questo coltello sara nella pancia del primo chi tocca al rosbif.*"[1] My grandfather could hardly keep his countenance when the butler came in to announce that "Mr Armadeer has been threatening us all with a knife, and carrying on something dreadful!"

He not unnaturally found the pronunciation of English names a difficulty. Once he was told to drive to two celebrated old oak trees in the Park called Gog and Magog, and answered: "*Si, si, Milordo, capisco, al Cocco e Micocco.*"[2]

Antonietta, the lady's maid, once received a letter addressed to "La Signorina Antonietta So-and-so, Caslasbi, Londra," which the postal authorities ingeniously deciphered as Castle Ashby, Northampton.

At one time my great-uncle, the Duke of Devonshire, found that he had been spending too much, so a committee of ways and means was appointed. About a hundred suits of clothes were found in the wardrobe, and the valet was asked whether some of these could not be disposed of, he answered: "His Grace must have a coat to his back."

The Duke's chef received a salary—it could hardly be called wages—of £300 a year. The Archbishop of Canterbury was dining with the Duke and, after some compliments as to the chef's skill, inquired not very tactfully as to how much he was paid. On hearing the amount, he heaved a sigh, and said: "Ah! to think that many a poor curate does not receive a third of that amount!" To which the Duke, slightly annoyed, answered: "Perhaps, but you must compare the value of his productions with that of the curate's activities, besides which," he added, "he occupies the same position in his profession as your Grace does in your own."

[1] "This knife shall be in the paunch of the first person who touches the roast-beef!"

[2] "Yes, my lord, I understand, to Gog and Magog."

On the occasion of this fiscal inquiry, it was proposed that the chef's wages should be *raised* from £300 to £500 a year, on condition that his books should be strictly audited and an exact account kept of the precise amount and price of everything that came into the kitchen. This offer was respectfully declined, as the chef said: "*Cela me ferait trop de tort,*"[1] in other words he confessed that his "perquisites"— not to use a more offensive term—exceeded £200 a year.

My Father, when we moved to South Audley Street, very sensibly engaged a French nursemaid, who proved, like a series of successors, a thorn in the flesh to "Pagey." She could not understand a word of French, so the maids not unnaturally were impertinent and insubordinate. One of them, Félicité, had a light blue parasol, of the very small size then fashionable, of which she was inordinately proud, so much so that when we were driving in the brougham one rainy day she insisted on opening it and holding it outside the window, pretending not to understand poor "Pagey's" remonstrances.

Mrs Page was a dear and life-long friend of all our family. She came as maid to my Mother in 1839, when the latter was only nine years old, remained with her until she died, and then became my nurse; my dear Mother having earnestly committed me to her care. Afterwards she was my Father's housekeeper and died in my house, 13 Seymour Street, in 1902, at the age of eighty-nine. She had gentle blood in her veins, and was of a most refined and thoughtful countenance; she was very pretty when young, so I have heard; her speech was cultivated and her manners perfect. She was deeply religious, tolerant, broad-minded and had a strong sense of humour. I never heard her speak ill of anyone, but she sometimes talked disparagingly of "*nouveaux riches,*" a class whom she could not endure. All my Oxford friends used to pay her a visit and sit and chat with her when they visited us at Holmbury, and won her heart by praising her marmalade, which she always made herself, a provision of which she insisted on my taking back with me at the beginning of each term.

My aunt, Lady Marian, had a lady's maid whose name was Mrs Ford, so Mrs Page and Mrs Ford became inevitably in her vocabulary "The Merry Wives of Windsor." "Though," as Mrs Ford observed, "why her ladyship should call us so I really cannot understand, as we have neither of us been married nor lived at Windsor."

When I was married at St Peter's, Eaton Square, on June 9, 1898,

[1] "I should lose too much by it."

my Father took "Pagey" on his arm up the nave and placed her next to him during the ceremony.

John Musson was Mrs Page's great friend and ally. When in Italy he had acquired the name of Giovanni, of which he much approved, and which Mrs Page rendered as "Javarny." They occasionally had oysters for supper, because they were so cheap, only a farthing each. Giovanni was a man of much character and considerable attainments. He resembled Abraham Lincoln, but clean-shaved with strongly marked and rather rugged features, a sallow skin with deep wrinkles and a thick crop of black hair, which to the end of his life only showed a thread or two of silver. When Lady Spencer, the Red Earl's wife, was staying at Holmbury, she said to her maid that she thought that he wore a wig, which the maid repeated to Giovanni; being a man of direct speech, he answered: "You can tell her ladyship that she can pull it if she likes."

The first time that my Father let his London house, Musson highly disapproved, not so much on the ground of trouble or inconvenience as of the indignity of the proceeding. "It used to be a gentleman's house, sir; now it will be nothing but a common lodging house!"

One day, when I was about fourteen, my great-aunt, Lady Elizabeth Scrase-Dickins, and her husband drove over from their home, Coolhurst, near Horsham, some twelve miles away, to visit my Father at Holmbury. He had gone up to town for the day, and I was alone there with a charming young French tutor, Maurice Vincens, a Protestant from La Rochelle, who afterwards joined the staff of the Crédit Lyonnais. My visitors were very old and I felt some embarrassment at entertaining them, particularly at luncheon, when I am sorry to say that I had a bad attack of giggling, not at all an uncommon thing with boys of that age. After the old people had left Musson severely reprimanded me for my discourteous behaviour. His rebuke showed how much he had at heart what he regarded as the honour of the house.

He always insisted on making the black coffee and mixing the salad, in both of which tasks he acquitted himself remarkably well.

Musson was with my Father for nearly forty years, having been with him before his marriage in 1853, and dying in his service in 1888. He not only read, but also talked and wrote fluently and correctly French, German and Italian; he affected a soft black felt hat with a wide brim and a black cloak flung in Italian fashion over the left shoulder. He

8

SARAH ANNE PAGE – "PAGEY"

FOR 68 YEARS THE DEVOTED FRIEND AND NURSE OF
MARGARET LEVESON GOWER AND OF HER SON, GEORGE
BORN 1813: DIED 1901

was an expert at fly fishing and a graceful dancer, which last accomplishment made him a favourite with the ladies downstairs. Once when we were at Castle Ashby, my uncle's butler, Ingram, came in and asked whether the date of the servants' ball could be changed.

"Certainly, but why?" "Because Mr Leveson will then be here, my lord." "But Mr Leveson is not going to dance at the ball." "No, my lord, but Mr Musson will, and it will make all the difference."

My uncle was for a day or two at Northampton House, now 145 Piccadilly, subsequently the home of King George VI when Duke of York. An old friend, Rin Macdonald, dropped in one Sunday morning. Ingram, when two glasses of sherry were ordered, looked embarrassed and said:

"It is the hour of divine service, my lord."

"I did not ask you about divine service, I asked for two glasses of sherry."

Hereupon Ingram had to whisper in his master's ear that there was no sherry in the cellar and that the public houses were closed during the hour of divine service.

Ingram was a rotund, jovial looking man with bushy whiskers, very like the typical English butler as depicted by Leech in the early numbers of *Punch*. He had a son of whom he was inordinately proud, who had emigrated to America, and whose letters he regarded as masterpieces. Whenever Ingram lingered longer than usual in the dining-room at the end of dinner, shifting decanters about, moving candlesticks, etc., it was a sure sign that a letter had arrived. My uncle knew these symptoms perfectly well, but always waited a little before asking: "Have you heard from Henry lately, Ingram?" "Only to-day, my lord," and whipping the epistle from his pocket: "Have I your lordship's permission?" "Fire away, Ingram." The letter would then be read, with admiring comments from the fond parent. I remember two gems. In one of his earliest letters Henry wrote: "Although I have been here only three weeks, I am already beginning to pick up the language." (Always a wonderfully bright lad, my lord!) In another letter Henry described Niagara. "It is remarkable, my dear Father, what a stupendous effect is produced by the combination of such ordinary materials as rocks and water." (He always had a great gift of expression, my lord.)

Mention should also be made of two other of my Father's old

servants, who entered his service when he married in 1853, both of whom came from Castle Ashby. William Robinson, the coachman, a spare and agile man, lived to a great age and must have been fifty years with my Father. He had a family of twelve, all of whom obtained excellent positions in different walks of life. Our stables in London had the singular advantage of being in a small mews of which there were no other occupants. They were at the back of our house in South Audley Street, and opened on to a little street, then known as Union Street. Chickens were kept in the yard which furnished us with the luxury of new laid eggs.

Caroline, the other servant from Castle Ashby, was with us for forty years, first as under and then as upper housemaid. She was a warm-hearted, impulsive girl and fell in love with an attractive but ne'er-do-weel footman of ours called Benjamin West, to whom she got engaged. This, however, did not deter him from seducing a younger housemaid, but instead of breaking off the engagement, she declared that it was all the other girl's fault, who had "led poor Benjamin on." My Father warned her and told her that he would probably spend all her savings in a year. The warning did not shake her resolve, and was only productive of a flood of tears, but it unhappily proved more than correct, as Benjamin only took six months to run through her savings when he deserted her, and she then returned to my Father's service. After her return she became in great request as a bridesmaid whenever one of her acquaintances was married, in spite of her being a grass widow, Benjamin having vanished into space. The sequel is even more curious. Years afterwards, when about fifty years old, she struck up a friendship with a butler next door during the dead time of the season, when she was left in charge of the house, for she never went to Holmbury. She subsequently announced her engagement. By an extraordinary coincidence I had received a few days previously a letter from an old friend, in which she told me that she had a gardener in her service of the name of Benjamin West who had previously been footman to my Father and who remembered me as a small boy. When my Father told Caroline that her good-for-nothing husband was still alive she said that the last that she had heard of him was that he had "gone for a soldier" and that she had been told by a comrade of his that he had seen him lying badly wounded in the hospital after the battle of Tel-el-Kebir, and that he was not expected to recover. She somewhat inconsequently remarked: "Even if he's not dead, it's a long time ago." In vain we tried to explain that in these cases there was no statute of limitation, and that they not only would run the risk of being tried for bigamy but also that of being blackmailed by Benjamin if her "re-marriage" came to his ears. To this she only answered: "I'm sure I don't know how he should hear of it; it won't be in the *Morning Post*." What finally roused her tearful indignation was an unfortunate suggestion of my Father's as a last resort that they should go into partnership without the marriage ceremony, especially as she was past the age of bearing children. I can see her now, weeping into her apron and sobbing out: "No, Master George, I never thought that Mr Leveson would have said a thing to me like that after having known me as a respectable woman all these years." So she and her butler went through the ceremony of marriage, and without either of the inconveniences, the possibility of which we had thought it needful to point out.

I am afraid that I got into a good many scrapes when I was a child, partly because having no or few playmates I was much thrown on my own resources.

Once at Belton, my cousin Lord Brownlow's place near Grantham, when I was very little, I took it into my head to hide in a thick clump of rhododendrons. When missed there was a hue and cry and I thoroughly enjoyed this novel form of hide and seek. They at last got seriously alarmed and were even thinking of dragging the ponds, when Tweedie, the groom of the chambers, a sharp little fellow, formerly a jockey, peering into the rhododendrons, caught a glimpse of my white frock (for it was before my promotion to knicker-bockers) and triumphantly dragged me out in a very grubby condition. Everybody was too much relieved to think of punishing me and when "Pagey" scolded me and asked me how I could be so naughty, I said: "I hoped Aunt Marian would think I was dead, like the babes in the wood, and would say, 'Alas! poor George!'" In fact I believe that the only person who was really put out was old Lady Caroline Cust, whose tea had been forgotten in the general commotion, and who, not altogether unreasonably, exclaimed: "Oh! I could shake that child!"

Lady Caroline as a rule contributed little to the conversation, her chief part in which consisted in repeating with much emphasis the concluding words of the person who had last spoken. Upon a description being given of the shortcomings of a young man, whose people had arranged to ship him off to South Africa, the person who was telling the incident ended: "But he somehow got away from the ship, at the last moment, after his luggage had been put on board, and his ticket taken for the Cape of Good Hope." "For the *Cape of Good Hope*!" echoed Lady Caroline with intense earnestness and pathos, as though it might be intelligible that a young reprobate should be able to withstand the lure of Canada or Australia, but most assuredly not that of "the Cape of Good Hope."

When I was about eight years old I conceived a *passion malheureuse* at Ashridge for a cousin of Brownlow's, a lovely child some four years older than myself called Flora Porcelli, who later became Mrs St George. I therefore entertained a quite mistaken, though none the less deadly, hatred for Brownlow's cousin and heir presumptive, a boy of about Flora's age, a certain "Buddy" Cust, whom I erroneously regarded as a rival in my affections. He was a shy and gawky lad who was, in reality, much more overpowered than attracted by Miss Flora. One afternoon Brownlow found me lurking behind the portière of a door, armed in the most melodramatic fashion with an Indian dagger which I had taken down from a trophy. "What on earth are you doing there?" "Hush! I'm waiting to kill Buddy." If I had not been disarmed and sent off in disgrace I really believe that I should have had a go at him if he had happened to pass by.

Brownlow's elder brother, who died of consumption whilst comparatively young, was my god-father, and we were very fond of each other. He was distressed by the fact that much of his land had, in pre-Reformation days, been ecclesiastical property and had expressed his wish to restore it, if possible, to the Church. My Father, however, dissuaded him not only by pointing out that, even if it were feasible, this would be very unfair to his heirs but that if such a transfer were to be made, the property should logically revert to the Catholic and not to the Anglican Church. He also wished to join the Liberal Party, but strong a Liberal though my Father was, he persuaded him to abandon the idea, for, as he said, one vote more or less in the House of Lords was not worth dissensions in a happily united family. Some six months after his death, when I was still very young, his brother called at South Audley Street and was naturally announced as "Lord Brownlow." I vividly remember how, for one wild moment, I thought that, by a miracle, my dear cousin had been brought back to life, and the subsequent bitter disappointment.

G.L.G. As An Infant

From A Water-Colour by Lady Marian Alford

He had a huge dog, half mastiff and half blood-hound, from which I was inseparable. When I heard someone wondering whether it was quite safe for me to be about with him, I answered: "It's all right, the animal's not afraid of me."

The mention of dogs reminds me of a sad tragedy in the Ashridge kennels. Truffles abounded in the Park, and a truffle-dog, who was trained to scent out these delicacies, arrived one day from France. He was put among the other dogs, a very motley lot, who promptly killed him the very first night, possibly on account of the traditional English suspicion of a foreigner.

Brownlow, the younger brother, once said that he would give me a pound if I put a pinch of salt on the tail of one of the fallow deer that used to lie about under the trees opposite the front door. I picked up a George I salt-cellar and spent a heated afternoon vainly trying to stalk them. When I reported my failure, and added that I had thrown away the salt-cellar in disgust, a commotion ensued.

During the American Civil War there was much talk of the "fili-busters," or gun-runners to the Confederacy. I thought that this was the word used when Lady Marian said one day at Ashridge: "The Philip Listers are coming to-day." I puzzled the company by remark-ing: "Are they? Well, if we can't take them prisoners, we must drive them off."

Another rather laughable incident occurred whilst I was a child at Ashridge. At luncheon I got rather more involved with an apple dumpling than was seemly, so my aunt ordered me off to wash my hands. My room was very far off and I realized that, long before I could return with hands duly washed, the delectable dumpling would, like Hans Breitmann's "barty," have been borne away into the "Ewigkeit." In the next room there was a Persian carpet with a thick pile into which I plunged my offending fingers and rid them of all traces of dumpling. My aunt remarked on the shortness of my absence and asked whether I had done as I was told. In imitation of the youthful Washington, I said: "Well, I haven't exactly washed them, but I have cleaned them all right." The process was described, with resultant disgust and indignation on my aunt's part. "Oh! it's all right," I said, "the apple won't show, I rubbed it well in."

I have mentioned Lady Marian Alford so often that a short descrip-tion of that charming and remarkable woman would not be amiss. She was left a young widow with two sons, by the early death of her husband, Lord Alford, before he succeeded to the Earldom of Brown-low. She was my Mother's only sister and some years her senior, and promised her on her death-bed to give me a mother's care and never was an engagement more scrupulously and abundantly fulfilled. Gifts of every sort were lavished upon me, her heart and her mind were always open to me as well as her homes. She was the ever ready and sympathetic confidante of all my youthful difficulties and troubles, and took me to Ashridge a month or so after my birth, and watched over me with the tenderest care, as is shown by her daily letters to my Father. Her generosity was unbounded, she loaded her many friends with gifts which, apart from their intrinsic value, were chosen with unerring comprehension of what would best please the recipient. Her public liberalities exceeded the measure of what her resources allowed. She was proficient in many of the arts of which she was a liberal and discriminating patron, and designed the beautiful house, opposite Prince's Gate, which for long after her death was called Alford House. Both there, throughout her later life, and at Ashridge and Belton during her son's minority, she exercised a wide and genial hospitality. Royalty, statesmen, artists, men of science and letters, eminent foreigners, in fact nearly everyone who was distinguished or interesting, were amongst her numerous guests. A number of brilliant fancy dress balls at Alford House were given, at one of which she and the Princess of Wales exchanged dominoes, and being of about the same height they succeeded in mystifying a number of her guests. Her gardens were nobly planned and beautifully kept. She travelled much, especially in Italy where she was born and which was to her a second home. Whilst a skilful painter in water-colours, her design and composition were better than her portraiture. She was well read in foreign literatures as well as in her own tongue, and had a gift of ready and witty repartee, informed with playful irony whilst free from bitterness. Although not strictly beautiful she was tall, exceptionally graceful and dignified, and was endowed with extra-ordinary charm. As the song has it, she was "merry and wise." No wonder that her society was eagerly sought and that she was beloved by all who knew her, rich or poor, small or great. She founded the Royal School of Art Needlework and wrote a standard *History of Needlework*, which was published when I was an undergraduate at Oxford and in which appear some translations in verse from Homer and Virgil, which I suggested to her and made at her request. Her sense of humour was keen, and I remember her describing a dinner which she gave, when Browning and the late Lord Houghton were on either side of her. "They both wanted to talk to me. When the poet thought that Dicky[1] had had his share he would seize me by the arm; when the peer thought that the poet had had his innings, he would intimate his opinion by digging me in the side with his elbow. By the end of dinner, my dear, I was black and blue."

The one virtue in which she was conspicuously deficient was that of thrift, her lack of which produced occasional financial crises. During one of these her brother remonstrated with her: "It is not as though, like most people, you had one or two hobbies. You spend on everything and on everybody. In short you are burning the candle at both ends." "How absurd you are, my dear Compton!" she answered. "Why, only just now you were urging me to make both ends meet; surely that is the quickest way to do it." As an instance of her extravagance, when she took a villa at Madeira for her elder son's health, hearing that there was no good mutton there, she imported a flock of fifty Southdowns, together with a shepherd, "to look after them, poor dears."

During her stay at Madeira she gave a big party at her villa to the leading members of the local society, but was distressed the next morning on finding that a number of trinkets had disappeared. She summoned the police and suggested that the homes of the waiters should be searched. The head of the police took no notice of this but asked to see a list of her guests which he punctuated with a series of notes. "Ah! Don Emilio lost heavily at baccarat last Tuesday." "Count —— is in love with Senhora ——, the actress." "The vines of the Marquis —— have been blighted this year." "Senhora —— has a big dressmaker's bill." He then departed with an assurance that the missing articles would be found and returned, which they were the next day. No further steps were taken, but neither were any more receptions given for the benefit of the indigenous and indigent society of Funchal.

Lady Alwyne Compton, together with her brother, Mr Anderson, accompanied her. He created some scandal and excitement by eloping with a Portuguese nun whom he subsequently married.

[1] The lines will no doubt be remembered:

> "He whom men call Baron Houghton
> But the gods call Dicky Milnes."

Lady Marian was so full of interest and intelligence that she "suffered bores gladly," in fact she did not know what boredom meant. My Father used to say with a sigh of resignation: "The bores all flock to her, as pieces of iron are drawn to the magnet."

She died in 1888, to my never ending regret.

My education in French was continued by a well-known French teacher, M. Antonin Roche, a little, round, dark man, rather stout and with quick black eyes, who certainly knew how to make his lessons interesting. He taught us History, Geography and Belles Lettres, without any admixture of English, and there I made the acquaintance of various classical celebrities, under the strange guise of "Eschyle," "Tite Live" and "Jules César." This reminds me of a quaint occurrence when Palmerston was Prime Minister and when some temporary tension existed in Anglo-French relations. The French Ministry made "friendly representations and inquiries" as to some fortifications which were being made in the Isle of Alderney, which figured in their despatch as "Aurigny." Palmerston promptly replied that this was impossible as there was no British possession of that name. Opinion was divided as to whether this was a delicate hint that British Ministers preferred to have British possessions called by their English name, or whether (as is more likely) the British Foreign Office was in blissful ignorance of the misguided French custom of calling Alderney "Aurigny."

It was the habit at Roche's to hold a sort of exchange and mart in postage stamps before the classes began. My own collection was started with the help of Signor Antonio Panizzi, an Italian political refugee, who held a distinguished position at the British Museum and was subsequently knighted. We were keen bargainers, and generally held out to the last moment before effecting a "swap" in the hope of extorting rather better terms. On one occasion when I was thus engaged, my back being towards the door by which Roche entered the classroom, the little girl with whom I was bargaining saw the door open and quickly gathered up her stamps, but I did not see him come in and he confiscated those of mine which were on the table. She was a pretty and intelligent child and a favourite of Roche's, so at the end of the class, as she had done well, he rewarded her with a gift of one of my most valuable duplicates, a triangular Cape Colony. Exhilarated beyond measure, she emphasized her victory by putting out her tongue at me, which was more than boy could endure, so

The Lady Marian Alford

(*horresco referens*) I was so ungallant as to kick her hard on the shin. This produced a good deal of disagreeableness, and her French governess exclaimed, "*Dieu, quel enfant mal élevé!*" with a meaning glance at Mrs Page, who was my escort. "Pagey" did not understand a word of this, but gathering that it was a reference of an uncomplimentary nature to myself, responded by an angry look. She thought it right, however, to enlarge, on our way home, upon my want of gallantry, but viewing the question in a different light, I said: "Yes, perhaps if I had not kicked her *quite* so hard she *might* have given me back my blue Cape Colony."

Dancing was another branch of my education. This was superintended by a stately lady of the name of Miss Birch, whose black silk gown, gold chains, imperial bearing and overpowering elegance surrounded her with an atmosphere of awe. I was in the unfortunate position of being one of the only two boy pupils in her large class, the other being a distant cousin of mine, FitzRoy Stewart, Lord Galloway's son, a little older than myself, dressed more sumptuously and far better behaved. In Miss Birch's eyes we represented the industrious and idle apprentice, and she freely prophesied that FitzRoy would carry all before him in the ballrooms of the future; whilst I— well, the less said about me the better. FitzRoy never really cared for dancing, whilst in later years I was devoted to it, so Miss Birch's prognostications were not fulfilled. All the same, being only one of two boys in a wilderness of girls and being stigmatized as the less hopeful pupil of the two, made one feel a fish out of water. Miss Birch would sweep in in her magnificent manner, and after our bows and curtsies had been rendered and duly criticized, she would ask: "Which young lady will be so *very* kind as to take Master Leveson Gower for a partner?" as though acceptance of this suggestion would be the acme of self-sacrifice. This invitation would be received in stony silence, followed by sundry nudges and whisperings: "Go on, Maude!" "It's your turn." "No, it isn't, I danced with him last Friday." At length some damsel, bolder or more desperate than the rest, would advance towards me with the look of a Caius Curtius about to plunge into the yawning chasm. There was one jolly little girl whom I liked to dance with whenever I had any freedom of choice. She was very small, so our dance generally resembled that which is supposed to be in favour with the apaches, i.e. a violent and somewhat disorderly whirling. I can hear her plaintive and not unreasonable little plea now: "Please, dear George, couldn't you let me have *one* foot on the ground just now and then?"

Miss Birch had two assistants, Miss Elizabeth and Miss Charlotte; the former a sort of Miss Birch in miniature, revolving like a planet round that great luminary. She tried to copy faithfully the deportment of her principal, but not with entire success; being just a trifle too bony and angular for the *"grand air,"* so impressively rendered by Miss Birch's sweeps and curves and billowing rotundities.

Miss Charlotte generally carried on her activities by instructing a section of the pupils in a back room, connected with the big room in front by an arched entrance covered by a portière. She was very pretty and infinitely preferred by most of the girls to the slightly austere Miss Elizabeth. I was told (under the strictest seal of secrecy) that one of the reasons of her popularity was that she occasionally confided to some of the more favoured among her elder pupils personal experiences of a romantic although innocent nature, and indeed I noticed now and then, between the dances, excited whisperings in a small conclave of which she was the centre, which lent some colour to the legend.

And now I pass to a sterner episode in that strange chaotic jumble, so curiously called "Education," which is supposed to prepare an unfortunate child for the duties and trials of life.

CHAPTER II

SHADES OF THE PRISON HOUSE

I WAS eight years old when I was handed over to the tender mercies of a red-headed Hanoverian, a certain Dr Reineke, whom I subsequently nicknamed "Reineke Fuchs." He was a brutal, violent and ill-tempered man, who treated me for a year with great cruelty. Savage blows and kicks were my lot; he would knock me down in a passion, and drag me round the room by my hair, wrenching out a good deal of it in the process. The climax came when he told me (a child of eight) to learn the whole of the chapter of the Epistle to the Corinthians, which deals with Charity (Heaven save the mark!) before breakfast. Time was short and the chapter long, so I had naturally only learnt the first few verses by the time that breakfast came in. He seized me, and in a fury banged my head against the sharp corner of the marble mantelpiece. It is a wonder that he did not do me permanent injury. I thought all this excessively disagreeable but never dreamt of telling my Father, as I supposed that it was the usual thing when you had a German tutor, but it did not make me love the German race nor the German tongue; indeed, whenever I hear that melodious language, my first instinctive sensation has always been that of repulsion. Mrs Page at first tried to soften the Teutonic heart by mending Teutonic shirts, but when this proved inefficacious she made a little bouquet of the hair which he had dragged out of my head and presented this to my Father with a report of sundry untoward happenings. He said that it was all nonsense, and that she exaggerated because she was accustomed to spoil me. In fact his kind heart did not allow him to believe that an educated man could be so cruel to a child. Later on she went to my Uncle Granville with better success, for he questioned me and was convinced of the truth of her story, and ultimately persuaded my Father to dismiss Reineke, whose last gracious remark was: "If you had left him with me for two years I might perhaps have made something of him, now he will never be anything but a fool." This was the end of the experience by which I was initiated into the German doctrine of "Schreckli-chkeit," several decades before the rest of my fellow-countrymen.

Undeterred by this unfortunate episode, a second German was engaged to superintend my education. He was a Prussian of good family, an ex-officer of the Guards, called von Puttkammer, who had wasted his substance in riotous living. After the Hanoverian tragedy came the Prussian comedy; for whereas Reineke Fuchs tried to force too much into my poor little head by curses and violence, the good-natured military wastrel never attempted to teach me anything at all. Mrs Page again remonstrated, although in a different sense, and suggested to my tutor that it might perhaps be as well that I should receive some sort of instruction now and then. The tenor of his answer was: "What is the use of it? Why should I trouble myself? He will not want it. He will always have plenty of money." How-ever, he let me call him "*der armer Bar*,"[1] and carried me about on his back, which, I suppose, he considered an adequate return for his salary.

Exit von Puttkammer and enter the Reverend Henderson, a ritualistic cleric. Why or how my Father came to make such a choice, when he was strongly opposed to ritualism, heaven only knows! He used to take me, when we were in Paris, to Catholic churches without my Father's knowledge, but luckily without any unfortunate results. He was an unctuous little man, who liked to inflict small punishments (which was all right) but also liked to gloat over them (which was all wrong). We were staying with my Uncle Granville at Walmer Castle, he having lately been appointed Lord Warden of the Cinque Ports. Henderson had punished me for some slight offence by depriving me of a boiled egg at breakfast. That I did not mind, but got annoyed when, with a meaning glance at me, he said to my uncle: "What deliciously fresh eggs you have, Lord Granville." My uncle was wondering what was a suitable reply to this compli-ment, when my elbow violently collided with the spoon which was conveying a portion of the commended egg into the Hendersonian mouth, with consequent chokings, gurglings and bespattering of yolk over the table-cloth and clerical waistcoat. Expulsion from the room, disgrace and punishment very properly followed. Only years after-wards my uncle confided to me: "I must admit that, had I been you, I should have done just the same."

[1] The poor bear.

About the same time Lady Lansdowne, wife of the fourth Marquis, came to Walmer on her way from Paris, and being tired had a small and early dinner in her bedroom. My uncle and Father and one or two others joined her. I had come in and was sitting next to her. The conversation seemed to grow more and more purposeless, and then a problem drifted into my mind. I bathed every morning and usually swallowed a certain amount of sea-water which was quite unpleasantly salt; the question was: "Would fresh water, if salt were put into it, taste like sea-water?" An empty tumbler was at Lady Lansdowne's side, a salt-cellar in front of me; spurred by the spirit of scientific research I filled the tumbler with water and, salt-spoon in hand, was just considering what was the proper modicum of salt to be added, when I found my Father's stern gaze fixed upon me. "How dare you try to play such an ungentlemanlike trick upon Lady Lansdowne! Ask her pardon at once and go to your room: I will come to punish you." Vainly did I try to explain that I had never meant the old lady to drink the salt water. It was all useless, and I was only doubly punished for my supposed additional sin of telling a lie. I felt then, as I feel still, that things are awfully hard for children sometimes.

When I was about seven my Father took me to stay with his old friend, Captain Egerton,[1] who commanded Nelson's flagship, the *Victory*, which lay at Portsmouth. He had travelled with my Father in India in 1852. On the way down, my Father thought that I was eating too much luncheon and quoted: "Enough is as good as a feast." "Yes," I said, "but shouldn't it be my 'nuff and not your 'nuff?" At luncheon next day in the *Victory* he also demurred at my having plum-pudding, and I was at first disappointed at the Captain agreeing with him and saying: "Plum-pudding is bad for small boys, at least a little of it is, but it's all right if they eat a lot." This last qualification raised him greatly in my esteem.

A signal had to be fired from a small brass cannon and I begged to be allowed to fire it, but the pull proved too stiff, so the sailor tied the string round my wrist, and laying hold of it gave a good hard tug and the cannon was discharged. The string bit deeply into my wrist, causing my eyes to fill with tears. The Captain thought that I was frightened by the gun going off and said: "Boys should not be

[1] Afterwards Admiral Sir Frank Egerton, who married Lady Louisa Cavendish, the eighth Duke of Devonshire's sister.

frightened by the noise of a gun." I remember my annoyance at being thought cowardly, but could not explain matters, as I fancied that tears might be considered just as contemptible if caused by pain instead of by fear.

A year or so before Lord Palmerston died, my Uncle Granville took me to see him at his house in Piccadilly, now the Naval and Military Club and at one time the French Embassy. I remember him as an upright figure, with bushy white whiskers, a high collar and large blue bow tie. He patted my head and made the conventional inquiry as to what I was going to be when I grew up. I answered that I would tell him then, but he said: "I am afraid that I shall not be here to hear it."

Another recollection is of Garibaldi, when he stayed at Stafford House (now Lancaster House and the London Museum) as the Duchess of Sutherland's guest in 1864 and received an enthusiastic welcome from the London crowds. He had a noble and dignified bearing, a head like a lion and a steady gaze both kindly and serene.

When eleven years old I was taken to Pembroke Lodge, the charming "grace and favour" house (as houses at the free disposal of the Sovereign are called), which lies at the edge of Richmond Park and was then occupied by the veteran statesman, Earl Russell, who good-naturedly played a game of bowls with me and gave me a good beating. Lady Russell had a pony which she drove in her little pony-cart and whose name was Tory. She said that she had given him this name because he was stupid, stubborn and lazy, needed the whip to make him mend his pace and always took the wrong turning if given a chance. For lack of political charity this almost rivals old Lady Holland's answer when a child asked her whether Tories were born bad or became bad: "My dear, they are born bad and they grow worse."

The only other Prime Ministers with whom I ever played a game were Lord Salisbury, his nephew, Lord Balfour, and Mr Gladstone. Lord Salisbury played some sets of the old game of tennis with me in his court at Hatfield when I was staying there in my Oxford days. He allowed me, though rather reluctantly, to give him half fifteen, but would take no greater odds. I thought that I should have an easy game, but had much difficulty in beating him. At lawn tennis I have often played against his nephew, Arthur Balfour, amongst other places at Ashridge and Panshanger. At Castle Ashby I remember a particularly strenuous game which Alfred Lyttelton and I played against Arthur Balfour and my cousin, the late Lord Northampton.

I have also played whist with Mr Gladstone, who played seldom and very badly, partly, no doubt, from want of practice and partly because he did so as a relaxation and did not really give his mind to the cards.

At Ashridge, Lord Brownlow's Hertfordshire home, a huge pile built by Digby Wyatt in 1814 in the faulty Gothic of that period, but surrounded by beautiful gardens and a park of great natural loveliness in which are some of the finest beech trees in the country, there is an immense central hall with statues of Kings, Saints and Bishops set in niches in the walls, conspicuous amongst which is one of Edward VI, above the landing where the great staircase branches off on either side. It was placed there to commemorate the fact that he had lived there, since the old building (later burnt down) had been confiscated by Henry VIII at the Dissolution of the Monasteries, and kept as a royal hunting lodge. Here also Princess Elizabeth had lived during her sister's reign, and here was preserved a wonderful set of baby's garments, beautifully worked by her own hand and destined to be a gift to Queen Mary when she was under the delusion that she was going to bear a child. Brownlow lent these beautiful but minute specimens of needlework to a charity exhibition at Berkhampstead, but the description of them got lost. The secretary, vaguely remembering that they had some connection with Royalty, described the baby's tiny shirt as that which Charles I wore at his execution. When old Mr Edward Cheney saw this in the catalogue, he drily remarked: "I had always thought King Charles was a small minded man, but had no idea that he had so small a body."

My Aunt Florence Compton was kind enough to teach me English history, and in order to make it more vivid, showed me Edward VI's statue and told me that he had lived at Ashridge when he was a little boy. Pressing the analogy too far I asked her whether she had also taught him English history. My comment upon her disclaimer was: "It must have been a *very* long time ago!"

She was a woman of varied and remarkable ability. Her father was the Reverend Robert Anderson, a celebrated preacher of his day, who held a benefice at Brighton. The sixth Duke of Devonshire generally spent some of the winter months there during the latter years of his life and thus made her acquaintance as a young girl. She became a great favourite of his, as she was a most amusing companion and a highly gifted woman. An accomplished musician, a fearless rider, intimate with the language, history and art of France, Italy and Germany, of mordant wit and brilliant repartee, besides being a singularly handsome woman, it is no wonder that he came to value her society very highly. My Father was his favourite nephew and he told him that the one thing that would make him die happy would be if he could see him married to Miss Anderson. He had already told my Father that he meant to leave him everything that he possibly could (that is, all his property that was not entailed, including Bolton Abbey), as his successor to the Dukedom, then Lord Burlington, was his first cousin. My Father, whilst admiring Miss Anderson and her many and varied talents, felt no inclination to become a suitor for her hand, possibly because he was in awe of her very authoritative and somewhat domineering character. When, therefore, he told his uncle that he had no idea of asking her to marry him, the old Duke bitterly reproached him, said that he had denied him his dearest wish and saddened his last days, and my Father attributed to his want of compliance the fact that when the Duke died his will was different from what he had led him to expect and that instead of inheriting all his uncle's unentailed property he only had a legacy of £10,000. My Father never spoke of this with any sense of grievance and told me that he was sure that his uncle, in spite of his disappointment, would have left him more, had he not thought that he would become heir to his elder brother, Lord Granville, who had then no family and whose first wife was still alive.

The sequel is curious; Miss Anderson afterwards married my uncle, Lord Alwyne Compton, and made him a most excellent and capable wife. She thus became my Father's sister-in-law. He said that he never knew whether she was aware of the Duke's wish, and that she certainly never showed any sign of being conscious of this episode.

My Uncle Alwyne, who at Cambridge had taken high mathematical honours, was a man of deep religious feeling. He was Rector of the family living of Castle Ashby. On one occasion he asked his elder brother whether he might have a young pig from the home farm, as he thought that they would be able to fatten it on the kitchen refuse of the Rectory, but finding this supply insufficient he afterwards got leave to supplement it by contributions from the larger resources of the big house. When the pig was ready for killing, he sold it to his brother and afterwards much enjoyed the home-cured ham sent to him by Lord Northampton as a souvenir of the transaction.

He was subsequently Dean of Worcester, and afterwards Bishop of Ely. On the latter occasion two working men were heard discussing the preferment. They apparently had no knowledge of my uncle's personality, but knew of the existence of his nephew, who bore the same name and title and was then in the Army. "'Ere's a pretty go, Bill; wot do yer think this Guv'ment 'as done now? They've gone and taken a Captain of the 10th 'Ussars and made a b—— Bishop of 'im!"

Both the Deanery and the Palace were beautified by my aunt's taste and skill. Her only fault was that she was disposed to be intolerant of what she designated as "nonsense," or, in other words, views and opinions with which she disagreed. She presented the curious contrast of great vigour and originality of mind, combined with a lively dislike of modern ways and inventions. Motor-cars were anathema to her, and when, after her husband resigned the Bishopric, they went to live at St Martin's House at Canterbury (near the very ancient church of that name), she would not allow a motor to drive up to the door. I ventured to compare this aversion to that experienced by Miss Betsy Trotwood to the donkeys who invaded the green in front of her house, but she only said: "Donkeys! It's the donkeys inside the cars that I object to."

When he was Bishop they used to come up for a month or two to Ely House, which is on the western side of Dover Street. It has since become a club, but the Mitre can still be seen carved high up on the outer stone wall. They lived there for such short periods that she did not trouble herself to have it kept clean, so that it presented a marked contrast to the beauty and orderliness of the Palace at Ely; in fact, not to put too fine a point upon it, it was exceptionally dirty. She disliked some of the worldly characteristics of her immediate neighbourhood, and once said that she wished she could get a gigantic scrubbing brush "to make things respectable." Purposely ignoring that she spoke in a metaphorical sense, I suggested that she might do worse than begin with Ely House, a remark which was not received with approbation.

Shortly before our marriage the Bishop asked my future wife whether she was getting her own way: "If you haven't, get it quickly, my dear, because if you don't get it now you never will." Then after a pause: "I never did." And yet although my aunt's rule was auto-cratic he endured it with a certain humorous resignation and seemed quite content to let her have her own way, as well as her own say, in everything. He was very absent minded and also short sighted, which caused him some trouble, as people in his diocese thought that he purposely cut them. Being told this he made this characteristic apology. "I'm sure I'm very sorry, of course I don't mean to cut them, to begin with I'm generally thinking of something else, then I'm too blind to see them, and if I *do* see them, my memory is so bad that I don't remember their faces, and if I happen to remember their faces I usually forget their names."

He was a High Churchman, rather inclined to ritualism. When I was engaged to be married, I went with my Father, my future wife and her sister, to stay at Ely for a Sunday. At that time the two sisters had High Church tendencies, whilst my Father's views were a mixture of his original Evangelical upbringing and of a Broad Church attitude of mind acquired in later years. We went to afternoon service in the Cathedral and sat in the Choir stalls; a procession took place up the Choir, my uncle being robed in the full ecclesiastical vestments of a High Church Bishop, mitre, crozier, etc., all complete. My Father put up his eyeglass and silently contemplated his progress up the Choir. The next day as we were all four of us trundling down in the omnibus to the station my Father suddenly addressed me. "Did you notice how strangely your dear uncle was pranked out in the Cathedral yesterday?" "Well, he had his episcopal vestments on." "Person-ally I think it a great pity that he should make himself ridiculous by dressing himself up like that"—then, after a pause: "especially at his age." This was too much for me, as I noticed the two girls' shocked consternation; the finishing touch particularly implying that whilst a certain amount of ecclesiastical finery might be overlooked in the case of a young and comparatively frivolous prelate, it could hardly be condoned in a bishop of my uncle's advanced years. My Father looked so regretful, and the girls so horrified, that I burst into laughter, and, as neither he nor they could understand the reason of my merri-ment, my appreciation of this fact made me laugh all the more.

On another visit to Ely in mid-winter when it was bitterly cold, the butler announced at about ten o'clock that it was time for evening prayers in the Chapel attached to the Palace. Except my Father, everybody prepared to file out of the drawing-room. He remained reading his book by the fireside. "Aren't you coming to prayers, my dear Freddy?" asked my aunt in a tone in which exhortation predominated over inquiry. "No, my dear Florence." "But why not?" she persisted. "The Chapel is like an ice-house." Which indeed it was—and seeing her still look rather put out he added: "I really don't think I shall be damned for not wanting to catch my death of cold; and if I am it will be all your fault for not having the Chapel properly warmed. So remember, Florence, you would be responsible."

In July 1866 I was going to Ashridge and was driving to Euston in a four-wheeled cab with "Pagey" when at Oxford Street we were blocked by a big procession which was on its way to demonstrate in Hyde Park on behalf of Reform. One of the leaders, who was on horseback, good-naturedly stopped the procession to let us through, saying: "Let the old girl and the kid pass. They want to catch their train." It was on this occasion, when on finding the Park gates closed against them, the crowd pushed the railings down and held their meeting. I believe that, as a matter of fact, they did not do this deliberately, but the railings were weak and old, of the character generally seen in front of areas. The people were pressed up against them and a small section of the railings gave way; the example proved too inviting and the processionists then pushed enough down to give them a clear way inside. The occasion was chiefly memorable not so much because it reduced poor Mr Walpole, the Home Secretary, to tears, as that it paved the way for an effective measure for Reform.

In the spring of 1868, when nearly ten years old, I went to Cheam, the Reverend R. S. Tabor's preparatory school of about a hundred boys, situated between Sutton and Epsom. It was one of the oldest private schools in England, having been started in 1665, when parents removed their sons from London to escape the Great Plague; at least so I have always heard. I cannot pretend that I liked it, but neither was I actually unhappy, except perhaps during the first term, when possibly the fact of being an only child and thus having had fewer playmates than most small boys tended to magnify the roughness and discomforts which fell to the lot of a new boy. It was a good school in essentials; the teaching was thorough, an extraordinarily high standard of morals and of honour prevailed; there was a certain amount of bullying, which, however, never reached an intolerable pitch; the masters were, on the whole, able and cultivated men, and there was the usual healthy love of sports and games. At these I never excelled, partly from shortness of sight and partly from having outgrown my strength. I was 6 ft. 1 inch high before I was fourteen.

But with all these things to the credit of the school, the material standard of living was so low and the general surroundings so rough that they would not be tolerated in a similar school of the present day, and indeed were not creditable even then, considering the high scale of the fees. Tabor was an Evangelical clergyman who preached in a Geneva gown, and was addicted over much to moral exhortations in and (rather noticeably) out of season. He had a system of private interviews with individual boys, in school slang, "pi-jaws," which began by prayer and continued with a series of inquiries which would have aroused the admiration of the German Gestapo, whose methods, I fancy, are much the same. This ingenious course of dialectics was not without its use to the boy who occupied the place of the person described in French legal terminology as "*le prévenu*." I am afraid that the preliminary exercise in prayer was generally regarded by us as a short respite during which we could try to forecast the lines on which our subsequent cross-examination would run and to prepare an adequate and not too transparent scheme of defence which, whilst not incriminating anybody else, would not expose ourselves to the disagreeable accusation of "want of candour," which, being interpreted into our own language, meant refusing "to sneak on the other fellows." Occasionally the fact that Tabor's mind and our own were not moving on the same plane of thought gave rise to somewhat ludicrous misunderstandings, of which I may furnish an instance. Tabor: "And now, my dear child" (the "boy" of classroom or playing field became "child" in the study pi-jaw), "what was it that I told you never to forget?" Myself: "That the perfect of $\tau\acute{v}\pi\tau\omega$ was redoubled, sir." Tabor (momentarily taken aback): "Quite true, my dear child, quite true, but that was not what I was at the moment referring to. I wished you always to remember that I was your best and truest Christian friend."

Tabor supplemented these pi-jaws by other methods of espionage; notably by creeping about the dormitories in felt slippers to satisfy himself that there was no talking or ragging after lights were out. There were no doors to any of the dormitories, but a high wooden screen was fixed to the side of each entrance which Tabor explained to the boys' mothers was to "protect the dear children from draughts," but which we supposed was put there to enable him to listen more conveniently at the doorway. If anyone were caught talking he was dragged out of bed and seized by the arm. He had acquired, through long practice, much skill in inserting thumb and finger between the muscles of your arm so as to cause the maximum of discomfort. Thus one was led downstairs to the entrance hall, which was, in winter, fearfully cold, and there perched in nightshirt and bare feet on a highly polished oak chair. I can feel the chill of that chair to the soles of my feet even now. Two big Liddell and Scott's Lexicons had then to be held balanced one on each hand, our arms fully extended, and there we had to stand in this most uncomfortable position for half an hour before being allowed to go back to bed. I suppose that the Liddell and Scott's were chosen in order to inspire us with a greater love for the Greek language. Tabor would then go into his study and write, leaving his door ajar so that he might keep an eye on his victim to see that he did not try to alter his position. Sometimes if he got up for a moment or two one would try to relieve one's aching arms by tucking one of the heavy books under one arm, but this was not easy and often resulted in a crash which ensured another ten minutes of "penal servitude," as he playfully denominated this form of entertainment. It is a matter of surprise that the health of the boys was not seriously injured by this kind of discipline, but luckily they are, as a rule, hardy little animals.

If, during play-time, we were engaged in any activities which we thought best kept to ourselves, a sentry was posted to "keep *cave*." I was thus once engaged when Tabor whipped round the corner just as I called out "*Cave*." "*Cautum*," he cried as he grabbed my arm. Quite a neat Latin repartee.

He had a large family. Two of the sons, Arthur and Alfred, played cricket for Oxford and Cambridge respectively. Another was in the Navy and was drowned when the *Eurydice* went down in a sudden squall. Mrs Tabor was a motherly woman and very kind to all the boys. Some of us were now and then allowed to go for a walk with her daughters, the younger of whom were disrespectfully known to us as "the kids," whose flaxen pigtails were reminiscent of Dickens' Misses Kenwig. This privilege was chiefly valued as a means of acquiring contraband sweets if funds permitted, in which enterprise we were aided and abetted by Bessie, a dear red-headed girl of about seventeen and a niece, I think, of the Tabors, who lived with them

29

and of whom we were all very fond. On hot days acidulated drops had an inconvenient way of coagulating into a sticky mass in a trouser pocket; if safely smuggled into school their usual hiding-place was the wicker basket under the bed which contained one's clean clothes.

A younger son of Tabor's, Ernie, was one of our schoolfellows, and, I fear, had occasionally to pass through somewhat troublous times, whenever his father had made himself more than usually unpopular. He was a plucky boy, and this entailed his having to engage in frequent fights when he heard his father being abused. We liked him all the better for this, and he was deservedly and generally popular.

Amongst the other masters, mention may be made of Mr Grignon (alias "Little Higgs"), a very fine scholar, who presided with much distinction and urbanity over the Second Class, the highest being taken by Tabor. He wore a single eyeglass and a pointed beard and we loved to imitate his peculiar walk, swaying from side to side, his round little body bent forward and his short arms held in front of him.

The Rev. J. K. Tancock, a Cornishman, was chief Mathematical Master, a good-looking man, a fine cricketer and very popular. He spent several holidays with me both abroad and at Holmbury in order to coach me in mathematics, in which I was weak, before I went up to Eton. His last visit was spent at Holmbury, on the first occasion of our occupying the house in the summer of 1871. His room there was known for thirty years as "Mr Tancock's room" although I do not remember his ever staying with us again.

Then there was a Mr Dickson, a pleasant fellow, who tested our intelligence by shooting out unexpected questions; once he asked the class why in royal proclamations the sovereign always said "we" instead of "I." Nobody knew, in fact I do not think that I know now, so I ventured a joke as the solution: "Because it's the Queen's English, sir." Strange to say, this was almost the only occasion upon which a joke made in class was not followed by punishment. Schoolmasters in my time (I do not know whether it is so now) nearly always regarded a joke as "impertinence," even when no impertinence could obviously have been intended. He afterwards obtained a living in the South of London, where he was deservedly popular. He died at a great age.

Mr Wilson was an athletic, violent and passionate man, inclined to over much boxing of the ears and thus not unnaturally known as

"Baity" Wilson. At the beginning of one summer term in the hope of mitigating his physical violence, the late Lord Annaly, then "Lukey" White, conceived a plan of propitiation. He persuaded all the class to subscribe to a cricket bat to be presented with our best wishes to "Baity," but unluckily the scheme did not work out according to plan. "Why do you boys give me this bat?" was Baity's unpromising exordium. "Not because you are fond of me, because I know you're not; but because you want to make me believe that you are. In other words to make me believe what is not true. And why do you want to make me believe this? Because you hope to bribe me into not punishing you when you misbehave, as you generally do. Well, I am not such a fool as you think, so I won't accept the bat; that is to say, I won't play with it, but I won't give it back to you, just to teach you a lesson in honesty. So just look out, that's all." After class a strained situation arose, as all the subscribers, like a shareholders' meeting when a company's affairs have gone wrong, unanimously clamoured that the unfortunate Lukey should return their subscriptions, which he was naturally unable to do and so incurred considerable unpopularity.

"Baity" called on White soon after during a Greek construe: "Now then, White, what is the English for λευκη?"[1] Resultant roars of laughter when the answer was given.

A pleasant young master of the name of Leach once made a sad slip which must have caused him bitter mortification. When a hamper was sent to us from home some of the contents were placed on a plate every day and the boy to whom they belonged handed them round as dessert after dinner to such of the masters and boys as he chose, keeping some at the end for himself. I was thus handing round some fine peaches, when poor Leach was so ill-advised as to ask me whether he might take one, a request which, of course, I granted. But this incident did not escape the quick eyes of the other boys, and when in the evening dusk we were let out for a few minutes into the playground, the air resounded for several nights with cries of: "Leach, Leach, take a peach!" Small boys are cruel. How that poor man must have suffered for his momentary lapse!

The French master, M. d'Auquier, for some mysterious reason was known as "Bun." He was a large, expansive sort of man. In later life he married a Hungarian Countess who was something of an heiress,

[1] This word is pronounced "leukee," and means "white."

but told me when he called on me in later days, "*que cela a tourné mal.*"
I thought it discreet, however, not to inquire into details.

The German master, Herr Passawer, was, I fancy, as both his name
and appearance seemed to indicate, of Hebraic origin, in spite of, or
perhaps because of, which, he had a pronounced fondness for liver
and bacon. His nickname was "Finck," derived from the real name
of one of his predecessors, which had become the generic name of all
subsequent German masters. He also, long afterwards, came to see
me in London and said that he had become the manager of the Vienna
Tramways Company and was doing very well.

When the Franco-Prussian war broke out, each of these two masters
held rival propaganda meetings in two classrooms on opposite sides
of a lobby, generally ending with impassioned renderings to a piano
accompaniment of the "Marseillaise" and the "Wacht am Rhein,"
in which their respective audiences lustily joined. The two masters
would then stalk off in opposite directions, passing each other with an
air of haughty and studied detachment. The two sets of boys, to
whom such a conclusion seemed an anti-climax, would then join in
deadly fray in the lobby, only to be dispersed by a generous and
impartial distribution of cuffs by Baity Wilson. Tabor finally intervened and vetoed the propaganda meetings as giving rise to what he
was pleased to call "civic tumults," so the French and German masters
were reduced to giving vent to their feelings by dark and distant
scowls.

Mr Rolfe, who came down once a week to teach us drawing, was
an Olympian personality, resplendent with white waistcoats, long
gold chains and bejewelled rings. He had a certain resemblance to
the late Lord Leighton of which I think he was not unconscious.
On Speech Day, the apogee of the Summer Term, an orgy of prize-
giving, recitations, feasting and fireworks, the results of his pupils'
efforts were displayed for the admiration of parents on the classroom
walls. I am afraid that from judicious re-touching and attractive
mounting these youthful masterpieces gave more promise of future
artistic pre-eminence than was justified in later life. However, they
fulfilled their object by pleasing the parents, especially the mothers.
One year rather a *contretemps* occurred from the unfortunate fact that
one of the fathers was a professional artist of some celebrity. He
pounced on the unlucky Rolfe and dragged him up to his son's
production. "Look here, my dear fellow, do you mean to say that

the boy can't do better than that; why, look at this perspective, and that fore-shortening! Whatever *have* you been teaching him?" etc. etc. All this to the disillusionment of by-standing parents, the delight of the boys and the discomfiture of poor Rolfe, and incidentally of Tabor, acutely conscious of the sharp criticism directed at his drawing-master in the regrettable presence of parents.

Sunday was undoubtedly the worst day of the week. We had to work just as hard as on week-days, at less interesting subjects and in an atmosphere of general repression and depression. First of all Collect (and for the older boys, Epistle) to be learnt by heart; morning service; a compulsory letter home; Catechism to be learnt by heart after dinner; a walk in the country in Eton jackets and tall hats with strict prohibition to take the slightest interest in bird, beast or insect, in tree or in flower; evening service; Greek New Testament after tea; and in the short and rare intervals between these activities nothing in the way of literature was allowed but "Sunday books"—and what Sunday books! For dullness and ineptitude I should think unrivalled. No, on the whole, I hardly think that this was the best way to lead boys to look forward to Sunday as a day of happiness and rest.

One punishment in vogue was to place the culprit to stand at a small table in the corner of the dining-room, where he ate his dinner without pudding or dessert. Once thus situated, I communicated with a friend by means of the deaf and dumb alphabet. Tabor detected this and rang the little bell placed at his side. I was marched up to him and asked whether I was not aware that I had no right when "in a state of disgrace" to talk to any of the other boys. I said that I had not opened my lips, which after all was true enough. But the plea was unavailing, stigmatized as "disingenuous" and entailed further punishment.

Billy Hely Hutchinson, Lord Donoughmore's son, was one of the school wags. We had been reading of the defeat of the Romans by the Samnites at the Caudine Forks, so Billy bewildered the footman at dinner by calling out: "Henry, bring the Caudine Forks."

The matron, Mrs Allwright, was fond of talking of Vienna, a city which she had visited in her younger days. She assured me that the language spoken there was French, and when I suggested that it was probably German, she said that could not be so, because the Austrians "couldn't abide the Germans," which settled the question.

The school was good at cricket and we had annual matches with

33

Slough and East Sheen. I cannot recall any notable cricketer of later life among my contemporaries, except Ivo Bligh, the late Lord Darnley, who was Captain of the Test Team which went, in 1882–83, to Australia, where he met the charming lady who afterwards became his wife.

Missions Day was one of the less pleasing recollections of Cheam. Every Summer Term a huge tent was erected in the playing fields and we all had to attend a gathering convened to hear the experiences and to listen to the exhortations of a missionary of the Evangelical type. Hymns and prayers were many, the exposition long, the tents stifling, the benches hard, sixpence was the minimum contribution permitted and its payment vigilantly enforced, and all this took place, of course, on our half holiday. No wonder that we hated it and resented the raid upon our pocket-money, which resembled Charles the First's Ship Money, inasmuch that, whilst nominally "benevolence," it was in reality a "forced loan" out of our slender resources, and with no hope of repayment. Neither were we much impressed, I grieve to say, when the missionary dilated on the blessed privileges which we, as Christian boys, enjoyed, as compared to the sad lot of the benighted heathen. After being shown pictures of merry savages, wreathed in flowers, dancing gaily on the seashore, in the moonlight of the South Seas, I for one wondered whether this might not be a preferable life to struggling with the vagaries of irregular Greek verbs in a stuffy classroom, or learning the interminable Catechism by heart, with interludes of ear-boxing by Baity Wilson.

In 1871, on my last Speech Day when I was thirteen, I had a separate piece of poetry to recite, besides taking part in the French and German plays. It was the custom to give you your choice of three pieces. I forget what the other two pieces were, but I selected Browning's "Ride from Ghent to Aix," partly because it struck me as a jolly stirring thing with lots of swing and go in it, as indeed it is, and partly because I had been for a tour in those parts in the Easter holidays. As it happened, I chanced to be the only boy whose recitation was favourably noticed in the local paper. Years after I met the author of the poem at luncheon at Mrs Percy Wyndham's (the beautiful mother of the gifted George). I told him of my early choice, adding that at that time I did not even know his name, much less that he was the author of the "Ride," which seemed to please him. I persuaded him to read it out to us, which he did with much gusto and emphasis.

He said that it did not refer to any special historical episode, or even to any distinct period or campaign (as to which he had often been questioned), but that he just picked by chance on the line of route which he so vividly depicts. He read it with a vigorous voice, and appropriate gesture, but without that booming, semi-chanting intonation customary with Tennyson when reading his own poems aloud.

It is remarkable what unerring instinct boys have for lighting on appropriate nicknames. I may illustrate this by those given to a few boys (amongst others) at Cheam. One was called "Pike" Beauchamp: he had a dull and fixed eye, a strongly pronounced jaw and a combination of immobility of feature and of rapidity of movement which made the name peculiarly felicitous. Another was "Tiger" Treadwell (the latter the boy's real name). He had a singularly bright eye, a noiseless tread and a feline suppleness and grace. Then as an example of the more obvious there was "Teddy Turntoes," a boy whose Christian name was Edward and who walked with his toes turned in. Another's parents had given him the three Christian names with singular want of foresight of "Arthur Spencer Stanley." He was inevitably doomed to the name of "Donkey."

Some among my contemporaries have since made names for themselves, although no doubt there are others equally deserving of record. Amongst those is the late Sir Lionel Cust, the celebrated art critic, formerly Director of the National Portrait Gallery, and Surveyor of the King's pictures and works of art.

Lord Durham and his twin brother, Freddy Lambton, were also at Cheam. They were so much alike that they were made to wear ties of different colours to distinguish one from the other, a device easily baffled when necessary by a secret and rapid exchange of neckwear. Their brother, Hedworth, afterwards Admiral Sir Hedworth Meux, G.C.B., was also at Cheam in my time.

Among other contemporaries were Eddy Tennant, afterwards created Lord Glenconner, who sat in Parliament and inherited his father's wonderful picture gallery; General Sir Edward Bethune, K.C.B.; Henry and Charles Hardinge, two brothers, of whom the first succeeded his father as Viscount Hardinge, whilst the second had a distinguished diplomatic career, was subsequently Viceroy of India, and is now Lord Hardinge of Penshurst; their cousin, the late Sir Arthur Hardinge, the brilliant diplomatist whose last post was that of Ambassador at Madrid. He was my wife's first cousin and was at the same house with me at Eton and on the same staircase at Balliol. Our Eton tutor said that he had never known a boy of his age with the same accurate and extensive knowledge of history. Then there was W. W. Whitmore, afterwards M.P.; Tom Farrer, the late Lord Farrer, a great authority on railways, and lastly the distinguished General, Sir F. Robb, K.C.B.

I will conclude my account of Cheam by my Father's description of Tabor's speech to the parents after luncheon on Speech Day, an august banquet which, of course, no boy was privileged to attend. The procedure on the four occasions was identical. The most distinguished of the parents would propose Tabor's health in suitable terms, with such compliments as the occasion seemed to require; to which he always made the same reply. "He, Mrs Tabor and his assistants had done what they could; he was very glad that the parents were not dissatisfied with his efforts; but all such efforts would have been quite in vain if it had not been for the excellent home training which the dear children had invariably received."

CHAPTER III

A NEW HOME AND AN OLD SCHOOL

IN 1870 my Father bought Holmbury, an estate on the Surrey hills of some 177 acres on the southern slope of the hill of the same name. He purchased it from Mr Johnson, the proprietor of the *Standard* newspaper. When he asked to what local charities it was customary to subscribe, Mr Johnson answered: "Well, of course, there is the pew rent at Ewhurst Church." Holmbury was beautifully situated, being sheltered on the north and the east. The soil from the top of the hill, some 850 feet above sea level, down to the house, which was 300 feet lower, was sand, whilst immediately below the house the soil was clay. This gave rise to endless trouble and expense as in dry seasons the clay was apt to develop fissures, which displaced the drain pipes and subsequently damaged the foundations of the house itself. A little park lay below the private road beyond which the farm lands stretched away to the south and south-east.

As my Father knew nothing about farming and cared less it is not surprising that the farm was anything but a financial success. Later on it was let to a tenant and the whole property put under an able and experienced agent, but even this change could not effect much improvement. A long range of glass-houses, including one sub-tropical house, was a source of infinite cost, as coal was very dear, having to be carted up the hill four and a half miles from the railway station. Anybody with any experience of glass-houses knows how heavy is the cost of their upkeep and how quickly they get out of repair. It was not always, or even often, possible to find the money necessary for these repairs, so the glass-houses went gradually from bad to worse until at last I was positively ashamed to look at them. My Father was as ignorant of gardening as he was of farming, and as he gave his head gardener a perfectly free hand, as far as his means allowed, the result may easily be imagined. As long as there was a certain amount of flowers in the beds and borders and enough fruit and vegetables for the table he seemed perfectly content to let everything take its course; in the same way he was indifferent to the balance sheet of the farm, provided that there were a plentiful supply of fresh eggs, chickens, milk, cream and butter for the household.

Wadham, the head gardener, had a detestable propensity, unfortunately not uncommon in his profession, of not picking vegetables until they were "fine and large," in other words, stringy, hard and tasteless, and I once ventured on a vain remonstrance to my Father, whom I tried to persuade to order that the peas be picked when young and tender. This he refused to do, so I gathered some myself early one morning and gave them to the cook, a kindly soul of the name of Mrs Coates. My Father thoroughly enjoyed them and said: "I am sure, my dear boy, that you cannot complain of these delicious peas which Wadham has sent in." When told what had happened he was disconcerted but could not reprove me after his warm commendation of the dish. Unluckily my experiment led to no improvement and Wadham continued to supply us with stringy beans, huge filamentous artichokes and hard and wrinkled peas. All this was the more curious as my Father had a really fine knowledge of cookery and a most delicate palate. I can only attribute it to his dislike of any interference on his part with his staff.

I once complimented Wadham on some very beautiful white roses called "Niphetos," from the Greek word for a snow-flake. It should be pronounced "Niphĕtos," with the "e" short, but he corrected me and said: "Yes, sir, it's a very good Niphētos" (rhyming with "defeat us"). When I explained things, he was quite unconvinced and only said: "Indeed, sir; we gardeners always call it 'Niphētos.'" "*Roma locuta est, causa finita est.*"[1]

I was once taking some of our guests, including Lady Downe, round the hot-houses and asked Wadham whether the grapes were promising well. "Yes, sir, all except Lady Downe" (a black grape so named). "Lady Downe is terribly troubled with bugs."

This recalls an incident when I was rook shooting at Panshanger. Lord Cowper picked up a rook which he had shot, but seeing a number of lice upon it, dropped it with disgust. Whereupon the keeper, a great character, reassured him: "You needn't mind them, my lord, the rook's lice would no more come on to your lordship than your lordship's lice would go on to the rook." This keeper had a great

[1] "Rome has spoken, the trial is finished."

38

command of language which he did not always quite understand. When going through a covert, if you asked which way you should go, he used to say: "In rotation, gentlemen, always in rotation," which did not leave one much wiser.

The pheasants came very high at certain beats, and once when the guns were being placed, Lord Cowper sent him down to the bottom of the hill with two guns who were no great performers. When he got there he shouted up to Cowper at the top of the hill: "We want two guns down here, my lord." "But you've got two guns there." "Yes, but they can't SHOO-OO-OOT" (fortissimo, in the hearing of everybody, beaters included, and of the two unfortunate guns themselves).

What my Father really loved was his library. He bought scores of books every year, a large number of which he had sumptuously bound, and thus collected a very interesting and readable library, particularly rich in French and Italian books, which, whilst it contained a good proportion of fine old editions, was not exceptionally valuable from a commercial point of view, as he had nothing of the bibliomaniac's love for specially rare specimens or even for first editions. So that whilst a very large sum was spent on the formation of his library, it could not be disposed of for anything like an equivalent amount.

He entertained a constant succession of guests throughout the year and the visitors' book contained many very famous names. On pointing out to Lady Dorothy Nevill, a witty Conservative, that one page comprised those of Mr Gladstone, the Duke of Argyll and Mr Bright: "Yes, I see," she remarked. "Just 'Gab.'"

To the north of the gardens was a beautiful wood of noble spruce and larch with footpaths winding in every direction; this wood extended up Holmbury Hill and belonged to the estate; all that lay beyond being common land. The wood in spring-time was carpeted with bluebells; Spanish chestnuts grew in an open glade on its western side, and beyond this the paths led still further through masses of rhododendrons and azaleas. The thick shade of the wood made it an ideal retreat in the height of summer. For miles and miles to the north, north-east and north-west of the culminating point of Holmbury Hill, stretched the wooded undulations of Hurtwood Common, blazing with gorse and gorgeous with purple heather, adorned with splendid hollies and junipers and broken here and there by woods of fir and pine. All this wild country furnished an endless choice of walks and rides through beautiful and ever varying scenery. The

D

views were among the finest in the south of England. From the house you saw some forty miles to the south-east and the eye embraced the whole of the Sussex Weald, still largely wooded and formerly known as the Forest of Anderida. Beyond this and far away to the south lay the distant range of the South Downs crowned by the high clump of trees known as Chanctonbury Ring, whilst at Worthing Gap hard by you caught a glimpse of the sea. South-westward lay the Hampshire heights; whilst from the hill-top, but not from the house, you could see the long line of the North Downs, running from Reigate to Guildford, St Martha's Chapel on an isolated hill, and beyond this the Hog's Back further to the west. Far away to the north-west the heights of Berkshire could be discerned. It is indeed a beautiful country, where blackgame were still often seen in the 'seventies. Old Mr Bray, the Lord of the Manor and father of the late Judge, whose family had lived in the neighbourhood of Shere since the time of Edward III, told me that he had shot as many as seven blackcock on the common in a day. They are beautiful birds and it is a great pity that in this neighbourhood they are now extinct.

When we first went to live there in 1871 I decorated my bedroom with spirited sketches of the Franco-Prussian War, the course of which I followed pretty carefully, considering my age.

Mention of this war reminds me that in 1867 my Father and I stayed at the Hotel Bristol in the Place Vendôme.

General Fleury, a favourite of Napoleon III, called on my Father and found me busy arranging tin soldiers representing Austrians and Prussians, it being during the Austro-Prussian War. My Father was rather vexed as the General would not pay the slightest attention to him until he had rearranged my tactical dispositions. *"Nom de Dieu, cet escadron sera foudroyé par cette batterie. Quelle idée d'aligner cette infanterie d'une pareille façon,"* etc. etc.[1] Nothing would satisfy him but a complete reconstruction of the field. I ventured to observe that whilst the Prussians had really won the battle he had arranged the forces so that they must be beaten. *"Ah! Mais non. C'est vraiment trop me demander, de faire mes dispositions pour donner la victoire à ces sacrés Prussiens."*[2]

[1] "Good heavens, that squadron will be annihilated by that battery. What an idea to draw up that infantry in such a way!"

[2] "No, certainly not. It is really too much to ask me to draw up my forces in such a way as to let those infernal Prussians win the battle."

I was taken to see the Comte de Flahaut, at the official residence which he occupied as Chancellor of the Legion of Honour. A fine upstanding old man with a great shock of white hair, he was the son of the beautiful Madame de Flahaut by Talleyrand and was born before the first revolution. He had been a brilliant cavalry officer under Napoleon and saved his servant from dying of cold in the retreat from Moscow by giving him his cloak. This incident is recorded in a painting which I saw at Meikleour, the house which belonged to General de Flahaut's eldest daughter. Her mother was Baroness Nairne in her own right. It is a beautiful place in Perthshire on the banks of the Tay. Mademoiselle de Flahaut married in 1843 the fourth Marquis of Lansdowne, their eldest son holding a number of the highest posts, including that of Viceroy of India and Foreign Secretary.

It is a curious coincidence that in 1790 Gouverneur Morris, who was also one of Madame de Flahaut's favoured lovers, notes in his diary a growing intimacy between his mistress and Lord Wycombe, afterwards second Marquis of Lansdowne.

The fifth Lord Lansdowne, like his brother, the late Lord Fitz-maurice, was an accomplished French scholar. They both must have found this acquirement invaluable at the Foreign Office and in Lord Lansdowne's case when he was Governor-General of Canada. Lady Lansdowne's sister married Monsieur de Lavalette, who was Postmaster-General under Napoleon III. They were both very charming ladies who showed me much kindness in my youth.

In September 1871 I went to Eton, where I took Upper Fourth. I had been expected to take Remove, but was not very well and rather nervous at the examination. However, at the end of the half I took second place in Trials for Remove out of about a hundred and fifty boys.

I went into tails at the end of my first half as I was so tall as to make a jacket look positively ludicrous, and on this occasion at the House Supper had to undergo for the first time the ordeal of making a speech in response to my health being drunk in honour of my success in Trials. To my great disappointment I was forbidden by the doctors to play football after my first half as, from growing so fast, my heart was far too weak and I was subject to fainting fits.

Like, I suppose, nearly everyone who has had the good fortune to be at Eton, I was very happy there, though my career was undistinguished. I was at Marindin's, the big red house opposite the old Fives

Courts, which had only been started a year or so before I went there. It was delightful for a lower boy, as there were so few high enough up in the school to be fag-masters and so fagging was not at all burdensome. During my first half the Captain of the House, F. E. Nugee, a very fine football player who was both in the Field and Wall Elevens, had eighteen mess-fags, of whom I was one, and as the attendance of only three was required at each breakfast or tea, one got off with fagging with only one meal in every third day, and even then one's duties were shared with the two others. A subsequent fag-master of mine was Oliphant, the elder son of the celebrated woman novelist of that name. He was very kind to me and helped me in my initial struggles with the intricacies of Greek iambic verse.

I may perhaps explain that breakfast and tea were taken in the boys' own rooms, two or three messing together. You were allowed to choose your mess-mates at the beginning of each half. Each boy had a ration of three rolls, butter, salt, sugar, milk and either tea or coffee (which you had to prepare yourself either at the fire in your own room or in two miniature kitchens). Any supplementary food had to be bought by yourself up town or was provided by occasional hampers from thoughtful relations. Mess-fags, before attending to their own requirements, had to wait upon their fag-masters. This involved expeditions to the sock shops up town, a good five minutes from my tutor's house, boiling or poaching eggs, preparing buttered eggs or omelettes and also making toast. For the last purpose beautiful long toasting-forks were provided, made of slender twisted metal strands and with four prongs set wide apart, which enabled the toast to be made without scorching the face or hands. If a fag were hasty or careless and the toast either burnt or underdone, his fag-master would tell him to see that it did not happen again. If it did, he was desired to bend over the chair-back, when he received three or four smart strokes from the flat side of the toasting-prongs, the lightly twisted wires of the fork giving it a resilience which added greatly to its efficacy as an instrument of punishment. Eton toast was, in consequence, proverbial for its excellence. Not only was it done to a turn but it was served quite hot and crisp. I have sometimes wondered in after life whether toast of the same quality could not be produced in one's own kitchen, but when I have suggested to the highest domestic authority that the same method of persuasion might

e resorted to, have been informed that its enforcement would be
difficult and would lead to resignations in the lower ranks of the
kitchen staff, not to mention the probability of an action for assault
and battery. Mess-fags, perforce, endured the correction with resignation, but their "resignation" was of a different kind.

On the whole the system of mess-fagging had greater advantages
than drawbacks, as it taught boys to be handy in minor culinary
operations. Its chief disadvantage was that it sometimes left a fag
but little time to get his own breakfast between early school and
chapel. One good thing of the system of mess-mates was that it
enabled boys of congenial tastes to get to know each other better;
another being that it allowed you to offer hospitality to friends who
were in other houses and to new boys who were the sons of friends
of your parents and whom the latter, rather vaguely, asked you "to
look after."

Boys of a certain rank in the school, who had thus acquired the
right to fag, could send any boy below the Fifth Form on any errand.
The method in vogue was for the fag-master to shout "Lower Boy!"
whereupon every lower boy within hearing was supposed to hasten
to the summons, the last to appear having to go on the errand. If
only a suspiciously small number presented themselves, the fag-master
would make a tour of inspection with painful consequences to any
lower boys who might be discovered and might reasonably be held
to have been within ear-shot.

Lower boys were rarely fagged by upper boys belonging to other
houses than their own. I was once hailed in Keate's Lane from a
window in Thackeray's House by my cousin, Alwyne Compton, and
Edwards Moss, the Captain of the Boats. I was told to go down to
the river and to extract a bottle of claret from the recesses of the
Captain's locker. This mission of some difficulty and danger being
successfully accomplished, the bottle being concealed under my coat
and beneath my arm, I was rewarded by a glass. Even then I
realized that it was not of superior quality, but the honour of being
offered a glass by the Captain of the Boats made it more delicious than
any bumper of the most famous vintages.

By a wise provision there was a certain period, I think during the
time that a boy was in Lower Fifth, when he was neither a fag nor
entitled to fag lower boys. This enabled him to exercise his privileges,
when he attained to them, in a reasonable and moderate spirit.

43

On one of my Father's visits I determined to give him an extra good tea and out of my scanty resources provided two special delicacies, tinned lobster and apricot jam. To my disgust he would pertake of neither, and when I remarked, possibly with an eye to a grant in aid, that they had cost a lot of money, was only met with the chilling response that it was a pity that I had wasted my money so foolishly. This I could not help feeling was a rather poor return for hospitality, which was well meant even if mistaken.

From Remove, in a year's time, I passed into Lower Fifth, being ninth in Trials; whilst in the Trials at the end of 1873 I passed into Lower Middle Fifth, thirteenth in order. My Father was dissatisfied at my taking a lower place at each successive Trials (although to take thirteenth out of a hundred and fifty was really not so bad) and removed me from Eton, greatly to my regret, at the end of the first half of 1874. He did not seem able to understand that the reason for my progressive decline was not due to idleness, but to my weakness in mathematics, which got more and more pronounced as they got harder and harder the higher I got up in the school.

Swishing was far more common than it is now, and there were generally six or seven victims in attendance on the Head each day after twelve and about as many awaiting the attentions of the Lower Master, the presiding deity of the Lower School. The said Lower Master was Mr Durnford (alias "Judy"), whose son Walter was afterwards Provost of King's College, Cambridge.

The preliminary procedure was the appearance of the praepostor of the Sixth Form during twelve o'clock school, who opened the door without knocking and asked as a pure matter of form: "Is So-and-so in this Division?" "Yes," would be the Master's answer. "He's to stay," the praepostor replied and forthwith vanished, to continue, like Azrael, his devastating mission. The Division Master would then usually indulge in a few ill-timed pleasantries, which seemed to the boy interested in very poor taste, although they appeared to afford general amusement, and the business of the Division was then resumed.

A. C. Cole, afterwards Governor of the Bank of England, for some unexplained reason nicknamed "Molar," presented himself as praepostor on one of these occasions in Herbert Snow's Division. Snow, who later took the name of Kynaston, published a good edition of Theocritus and eventually became Head Master of (I think) Cheltenham. He had a mordant wit and resented what he regarded as the praepostor's casual manner of entrance. "Is your name Cole?" he asked. "Yes, sir." "Then scuttle."

At the end of the school hour you made your way to the colonnade under Upper School and would there await the Head's appearance from the door of his private room. Thence he issued in cap and gown accompanied by the Sixth Form praepostor and two small and generally nervous Collegers, alias "Tugs." Up the stairs we went, the door of the Sixth Form room was unlocked and one by one in order due we underwent the usual formality: "Mr So-and-so" (one's tutor) "has complained of you. Have you anything to say for yourself?" Naturally one never had. "Kneel down." One knelt down accordingly at what Gilbert described in the *Mikado* as a "big, black block," the two attendant tugs each delicately holding up one corner of one's shirt-tail. The birch resembled a small broom, the twigs composing it being picked, with fiendish ingenuity, in early spring, so that the hard buds should add to its efficiency. Custom allowed one to edge the right arm a little down one's side so as to shield a certain area from the cuts, but this precaution must not be carried too far, and if it were the Head would tap your arm with the handle of the birch and say: "Take that hand away." Seven cuts were the usual ration and blood was generally drawn, but though the operation was disagreeable it was not extremely painful, and I fancy that caning would be much severer, although I must confess that on these occasions I may have wished that I were a more "hardened" offender.

When I was a City member for the London School Board (the abolition of which I regard as a most mistaken policy) from 1897 to 1899, a debate arose on the question of flogging in what had been known as "Reformatories," but which were afterwards, in deference to supposed susceptibilities, called "Industrial Schools." These were special schools under the Board composed of such boys as proved hopelessly refractory under the *régime* of the ordinary schools and, as may be supposed, they were a pretty tough lot. Occasional floggings were considered essential, and in my opinion rightly, for the maintenance of discipline. Mrs Bridges Adams, a Labour member of the Board, was scandalized at the supposed inhumanity of the proceeding, which she denounced in impassioned terms, declaring that flogging "brutalized the manners, dwarfed the intellect and stunted the growth" of the victim. She had procured one of the so-called "instruments of torture," a very insignificant weapon. I then opposed her proposal to abolish birching in these Industrial Schools, and referred to the birch as a fly-flap as compared to that in use at Eton. I narrated my personal experiences and appealed to five fellow Etonians on the Board as to the inexactitude of her forecast of the results of birching. I wound up by saying that although it might be possible, whilst I was not aware of it, that my manners had been brutalized and my intellect dwarfed, I certainly did not think that my growth had been stunted.

Mrs Bridges Adams' proposal was rejected.

To resume my account of the Eton swishing. It was the regrettable custom of certain lewd lower boys of the baser sort to huddle outside the locked door and try to get a peep at the proceedings through chinks therein, an operation generally accompanied by sundry giggles, whisperings and shufflings of the feet. If the noise grew too noticeable the Head would say to the praepostor: "Is there anyone outside the door?" "I will go and see, sir," and the door would be leisurely unlocked whilst hurried scramblings downstairs were audible. "No, sir, there is nobody there." The door would be relocked and the work of penance resumed. When all was over the procession returned down the stairs and the Head would disappear through his doorway, the praepostor walking off in the opposite direction. Then ensued a wild moment; the two small tugs headed rapidly across the School Yard for sanctuary, in the shape of the entrance into College, pursued by the pack of victims illogically bent on seeking redress for their woes on the persons of the involuntary shirt-tail holders. If they got into College before they were caught, well and good, as no small Oppidan would, at such a moment, follow them further; if not, ill and bad for them, poor unlucky scapegoats! But, on the other hand, if carried too far by the ardour of the chase some of the pursuers should venture too near the entrance to College, it now and then happened that a big Colleger would be passing by, who would then pounce upon the adventurous intruder and inflict further chastisement on that portion of his person which recent untoward events had made the least capable of enduring it. On returning to dinner at one's house my tutor would sometimes make ungraceful allusions as to what had taken place by solicitous inquiry as to whether one would like to have a cushion to sit upon and similar jocularities of a doubtful nature.

Flogging was not looked upon as degrading as it was not restricted to serious offences, but was also applied in cases of trivial delinquencies, such as idleness or being persistently late for early school. I was flogged once a year during my three years at Eton, the first two swishings being, if I remember aright, for unpunctuality at early school. The situation of our house was rather a handicap in this respect, as it was a long way from everywhere. Once when I was up to Warre, who took his Division in the pupil room of his own house, he said to me when I came in late one morning: "I saw you running down the lane as I was putting on my braces." It should be explained that this lane ran at first in a straight direction from Marindin's to Warre's house, then took a long sort of hair-pin bend to the right down Judy's lane, past Durnford's house (*inde nomen*), and then round to the left again past Cornish's and Austen Leigh's. Warre was a strict but very fair-minded man and did not resent my answer: "Well, sir, anyhow I was running down the lane before you had left your bedroom." As a remedy for unpunctuality, I, amongst other boys, had to sign a book kept at the Head's house not later than five minutes before early school began. The Head's house was a long way off and this necessitated a still further *détour* from my tutor's to Warre's, so in spite of this precaution I was late again. "You are quite hopeless," said Warre; "it seems no good sending you to sign on at the Head Master's." The only answer I could make was: "If I had not had to sign on, sir, I should have been in time."

The last and most serious trouble arose when I was up to Mr St John Thackeray, a very fine scholar, but a wretched disciplinarian. The boys in his Division used to play him every sort of trick. A stray dog would be brought into the classroom, whence every boy would help Mr Thackeray to eject him, except two who were posted at the door with the express duty of preventing him getting out. At another time, when the sun was shining into the room, every boy's watch-glass would be used to dazzle Mr Thackeray; then again, at a given signal all the heavy books brought into class would simultaneously be pushed over the desk on to the floor. These disorderly scenes culminated at a late afternoon school about the middle of the Football Half. The classroom was on the first floor in the New Schools, outside it was a lobby fitted with hat-pegs and lit by gas. Somebody suggested the desirability of turning out the gas before Mr Thackeray arrived, which I accordingly did, being the tallest boy in the Division. A good deal of hustling took place when Mr Thackeray came and whilst he was trying to unlock the door in the dark. This escapade proved to be the proverbial last straw. The next morning the Sixth Form praepostor delivered a message from the Head that, unless the boy who turned out the gas gave himself up, the whole Division would have to do a Georgic (i.e. write out some 500 lines). Of course there was no alternative to giving oneself up, with the result that I was swished and "turned down," that is, taken out of one's own Division and put into the one next below it. This was Mr Cornish's, and as we were all in the same Remove (that is to say, had all passed out together in the same Trials), we were doing the same school work in both Divisions, although the boys in Thackeray's Division had taken higher in the last Trials than those in Cornish's and therefore were better at their work. At the end of every half each Division had an examination in the work of the half called "Collections," the boy who came out top getting a prize. This I happened to win and Cornish pretended to be put out about it. He addressed me as follows: "Really, Leveson Gower, you give everybody a great deal of trouble. You are guilty of an act of gross insubordination in Mr Thackeray's Division; then you are very properly flogged and turned down into mine. But instead of keeping quiet for the rest of the half, you put me into a position of great difficulty by coming out top at Collections. You really should behave more modestly when in a state of disgrace. It is very hard on the next boy in Collections who would have got the prize if you had not been turned down. It does not seem fair to take the prize from him and give it to you." So I asked him not to trouble himself about it and to give the next boy the prize and he said that he himself thought that this was the right thing to do, but was glad that I had suggested it. The next day he sent for me to his house, shook me cordially by the hand and gave me a much better book than the Collections prize with a pleasant little inscription on the fly-leaf. The next half I was put up again to my old place so no harm was done.

There was, however, an amusing epilogue to this. My aunt, Lady Marian Alford, was highly indignant at the whole business and, at a party she was giving at Ashridge, expressed herself strongly to this effect. My cousin, Charlie Compton, the late Lord Northampton's elder brother, was there, so she appealed to him: "Now, Charlie, you were at Eton. What do you think about it?" Charlie reflected for a moment and then solemnly declared: "Well, Aunt Marian, all I can say is that it served him jolly well right." This so diverted her indignation on to himself that she would not speak to him for a couple of days.

Only a few years ago and shortly before Mr Thackeray's death, when he was a very old man, he spoke to me at the Athenaeum and did me the honour of consulting me about a cameo of the head of Athene. I wondered whether he remembered me as the boy who turned out the gas so long ago.

When Mr Thackeray came up to London for a day or two he used to stay at the Continental Hotel, at the corner of Charles Street and Lower Regent Street, which, he explained to his friends, suited him very well on account of its proximity to the Athenaeum, adding that he found it "a very nice quiet place." As a matter of fact it was anything but this, and the restaurant attached to it was notorious for the noisy and far from respectable revels which took place there during supper time. So much so, indeed, that at the instance of the police, its licence was cancelled and the establishment eventually closed. The old gentleman was totally unconscious of these riotous proceedings as he always went to bed at an early hour.

Some boys had a morbid taste for buying the birch with which they had been swished from the school attendant, to whom such perquisites accrued, although its price had already been charged to their father. They used to adorn it with Eton blue ribbon and preserved it as a queer sort of heirloom. One very unpopular boy, of dirty and untidy appearance, who went by the nickname of "Sus," which my readers will recognize as the Latin for "Sow," had an unpleasant experience when taking his birch home with him for the holidays. Three other boys who were in the railway compartment with him declared that as he was so fond of his birch they must gratify him as far as they could, and promptly swished him there and then. I do not think that it can have been a very painful process, as the confined space of a railway compartment is apt to cramp the style of the executant, or should one say "executioner"?

49

CHAPTER IV

ETON

In the spring of 1872 my Uncle Granville took me up to the Castle to present me to the Queen. Her Majesty received me graciously and asked me how long I had been at Eton. "Two halves, ma'am." "That is a year then." "No, ma'am, there are three halves in a year." When we had left the room my uncle said: "You'll never make a courtier. A nice thing to do, to contradict your Sovereign flat at the very first remark she makes to you." "Well, there *are* three halves in a year, all the same, Uncle," I answered, embarrassed but unconvinced.

It may be explained that the Eton expression of "Half" came down from the days when there were only two terms in the year, before there were any Easter holidays; these broke the scholastic year into three terms instead of two, although each of the three terms continued to be known by the old name of "Half." It was curious, however, that the Queen, who had lived all her life in the immediate neighbourhood of Eton, should not have known the significance of the appellation.

Two other anecdotes occur to me of the Queen's interviews with Eton boys.

Of one she asked whether he ever walked in the Great Park. "Yes, ma'am, I often go on a Sunday as far as the Copper Horse." "Copper Horse, indeed! That is a pretty way to refer to my Grandfather!"[1]

Another Etonian of adventurous spirit smuggled a boar spear from his home, as he heard that there was a small herd of wild pig roaming about in the Great Park. He wrapped it up and accompanied by two friends managed somehow to get it into the Park one Sunday, where, aided by luck, they actually managed to kill a young boar. But murder will out and the deed was eventually traced home to him.

[1] The "Copper Horse" is the name given to the equestrian statue of George III at the end of the Long Walk.

The Head Master wrote to the Queen asking what she wished done; and she had the boy sent up to her. Pretending to be very angry she asked him: "What have you to say for yourself? How dare you go poaching in my Park?" "It wasn't exactly poaching, ma'am, we never meant to sell the boar. We did it more for fun. I am very sorry. I know we should not have done it." The picture of three small boys conveying a dead boar into Windsor for sale to one of the local butchers was too much for the Queen's gravity. "You are very naughty boys," she said; "besides, you might easily have been killed. If you had done this a few hundred years ago you would have been hung or had your heads cut off, I am not sure which. As it is . . ." (an awful pause) "well, don't do it again."

Before leaving the subject of Eton I should like to say something about what seems to me a senseless punishment inflicted in those days in the shape of giving a certain number of lines of Latin or Greek verse to be copied out. It did not matter how badly they were written, which, of course, tended to spoil one's hand-writing, and now and then a device for shortening the term of labour was resorted to, consisting of tying two pens together, the upper one projecting over the lower, thus enabling two lines to be written at the same time. This plan of course had the disadvantage of being liable to detection, but as the Master seldom took the trouble to read the lines but contented himself by counting them to see that you had given full measure, you were not often caught out. It was at the same time prudent only to do this here and there in the course of a "poena" (the technical term for such a punishment). The insensate thing about the whole system was that it made boys loathe Latin verses, although the whole of our education was presumably meant to lead them to appreciate the classics. It was different from learning by heart, which at any rate did something towards implanting verses in your memory, as one never took in their meaning when you were writing them out at express speed, and still less retained any recollection of them.

Towards the end of my time a system was instituted of the Master giving you, on the infliction of a poena, a yellow form with the particulars of your punishment inscribed upon it. This was torn out of a book like a cheque book with a counterfoil. The plan was meant to help the Master to keep track of the various outstanding poenas. This was the subject chosen for one of the sets of Latin verses which we had to compose every week. I can only remember one line of my effort:

"*Nec pueri somnis flava tabella deest.*"[1]

This was, I am bound to admit, a case of poetical licence, for I cannot recall any poena, actual or prospective, disturbing my youthful slumbers.

One Master, Oscar Browning, made a happy and notable departure from this foolish custom of setting lines to be copied out; instead of this, he made the boy come to his pupil room after twelve and would set him some task calculated to arouse his intelligent interest. I remember his once making me copy the well-known bust of Olympian Zeus, which interested me so much that, as I had not finished it by the time when I had to go home to my tutor's, I asked whether I might come back the next day to complete the sketch.

He afterwards became a fellow of King's College, Cambridge. Once when Tennyson was there, Browning, always impulsive and not invariably discreet, rushed up to him and greeted him warmly, although quite unknown to him. When Tennyson looked at him in some surprise he tried to explain matters by saying: "I am Browning." "No," said the bard turning away, "I'm damned if you are."

Although a man of many gifts and of a kindly and generous nature, he was perhaps rather over-addicted to cultivating the society of the great ones of the earth. He once told a friend that he was thinking of writing his Memoirs and asked whether he could suggest some short, distinctive and appropriate title. "Why not 'Kings I have met'?" was the somewhat unkind reply.

In later years he got rather stout, which gave rise to the following epigram:

> "O.B., O.B. if we should see
> Your girth still more increase,
> You then would be, my dear O.B.
> Not one but too obese."

Another thing that strikes me as extraordinarily unintelligent was the way in which the classics were taught. At the beginning of each week a list of lessons was given out, varying of course with the Form in question, each Form consisting of several Divisions of about thirty-five boys in each. There would be the first lesson and the second

[1] "Nor is the yellow ticket absent from the boy's dreams."

lesson of Herodotus, Livy or Euripides, beginning at a certain line and ending at another. Once when put on to construe I came to the end of the part allotted to us to prepare, and announced the fact by saying: "Here endeth the Second Lesson." For which, of course, punishment promptly ensued. These lessons you prepared or were supposed to prepare, beforehand, unaided by any notes, introduction or explanation of any kind, for the only copies of authors allowed to be used were plain texts. Next followed a sort of rehearsal in pupil room, where your tutor (in other words your House Master) took all the boys of the same form in his house through a sort of preliminary canter in the various "lessons," putting them on to construe, parse, etc., so as to see how far they had prepared their work. Then the same operation was gone through in the various Divisions under the Master of each Division.

One ridiculous result of this method of teaching was that a boy could never get any connected or intelligible idea of what he was reading, nor, at any rate until he got into one of the highest Forms in the school (and as to that I cannot speak as I never got higher than Lower Middle Fifth), was he expected to know any more; he was not even much encouraged to use his Classical Dictionary to find out the legends of the gods and heroes of whom he read in the plays, or his Historical Dictionary for the lives of personages mentioned in the histories which he was reading; or to consult his Ancient Atlas so as to form an idea of the position of the various countries or places mentioned. In fact the way in which the classics were read at Eton in my day reminds one of the biblical description of chaos, "the earth was without form and void and darkness was upon the face of the deep."

Again there was no sort of continuity in our reading. I never remember finishing any Greek play which came into one's school lessons, because one moved up into another Form before the play that you were reading was ended. The play, it is true, continued to be read in the Form which you had left, but it was taken up by a different set of boys who had passed up from a lower Division, whilst meanwhile you and the boys in your own Division were beginning some new author, again in the middle of a play or chapter, at the place where your predecessors had left off at the end of the previous half. I vividly remember my introduction to the Greek drama. We were "doing" the Medaea of Euripides. The Division Master said to us at the beginning of the half: "We left off at line 555." ("We" being the boys who were in the Division the half before and who had passed on to the next Division above them.) "The first lesson is from line 555 to line 577. The second from 577 to 600." That was all! No word of explanation as to what a Greek drama was; or of the plot of this particular tragedy; or of the persons therein portrayed; or, in fact, anything about it; and so we were left to sail this uncharted sea without pilot or compass. We had to hack our way through in construing, and occasionally parsing, the lines allotted us; if we did so fairly, then well and good, if not . . . then otherwise. Nothing more was given to us, nothing more expected from us. It was hardly surprising that such a system should leave the mass of boys quite indifferent to classical literature or that they should rapidly make haste to forget whatever shreds of Greek or Latin they had happened to assimilate. Indeed the marvel is, not that so many should forget their classics, but that so many, in spite of such early discouragements, should ripen eventually into capable scholars.

I have sometimes wondered what, if I were a Master, I should do, or at any rate attempt. I should begin by making my pupils understand what were the general conditions of ancient life, how the men and women of those days dressed and were housed. I should bring this home to them with the help of good illustrations, the appearance of the temples and of masterpieces of architecture and sculpture; also the aspect of the country and its physical conditions. Before beginning to read the drama, I should show them what the theatres looked like, and their dispositions for seating the audience and for the performance of the play; also the nature of the chorus and the masks and dresses of the actors; I would explain the general plot of the play, and, above all, by hook or by crook I would somehow contrive that the play which was begun by one set of boys should also be finished by them.

It seems to me that these are not unattainable counsels of perfection, but are really essential to make these studies actual and vivid, such as to arouse a boy's lively and intelligent interest, instead of merely soul-benumbing exercises whose only result is to produce a certain minimum of accurate translation and of grammatical proficiency.

To open a boy's heart and eyes to the marvels and glories of Greek and Roman literature and art, which shall be a life-long possession and refreshment, is to endow him with a priceless heritage: to pretend to do so whilst in reality denying him the needful facilities for entering into this enchanted realm is a cruel and shameful betrayal. I only speak of things as they were at Eton in my day, very likely they have now changed for the better, and I sincerely hope so for they certainly could not have changed for the worse.

A sense of humour at untimely seasons was rigidly discouraged. Herbert Snow, whom I have already mentioned, had a sardonic bent which he exercised, not always justly, at our expense. At times when we had to bring heavy dictionaries to school, he would be on the watch for a late comer and when he heard him pounding along the lobby outside the classroom, would lean against the door. The boy would rush up and finding the door apparently stuck would push against it, when Snow would suddenly step aside. In tumbled the boy, generally dropping all his books and sometimes falling down. "One hundred lines for being late, another hundred for entering in a disorderly fashion," would be the verdict. This was not fair and even less dignified. He would never even listen to, much less allow, any excuse and met any attempt to proffer one in an unpleasantly drastic way.

Snow. "A hundred lines of the Iliad."

Boy. "Please, sir——"

"Two hundred lines."

"But, *sir*——"

"With accents."

"But, SIR——"

"Breathings."

"But, *SIR*——"

"And stops."

It was a case of cumulative penalties with a vengeance!

I got into a scrape over a rather ridiculous occurrence. In summer term I had a window garden of which I was proud. My room overlooked my tutor's garden, and one evening I was watering my plants from my ewer, kneeling on an ottoman in front of the window. A friend, seeing me in so favourable a position, could not resist the temptation to give me a resounding spank. Luckily I held on to the ewer but all the remaining water shot out of the window on to Mrs Marindin who happened to be walking just below. Up came my tutor in a towering passion, asking what I meant by insulting a lady, etc. etc. I had some difficulty in convincing him that it was an accident by saying that even if I was so little of a gentleman as to play

E

a rude and silly trick upon a lady who had always been kind to me, I was not such a fool as to throw water out of my own window, so as to be instantly detected.

Having occasion to reprove me he observed that he was sorry that I was less truthful than when I came to Eton two years before, to which I answered: "But if this be so, to what do you attribute it, sir?" It was easier to give one a punishment of 200 lines for impertinence than to provide an answer.

There was a hexameter and pentameter, or, as we called them, a "long and short," enumerating nine of the masters of my day. It ran:

> "*Nix, Grando, Bellum, Jungit cum Pondere Saxum,*
> *Laniger et Juvenis, tu quoque parva Dies.*"

The said Masters being "Snow, Hale, Warre, Joynes, Waite, Stone, Woolley-Dod, Young, and thou also little Day."

I was spending a long leave early in 1874 with Lady Marian Alford, when Mr Disraeli was announced. He was a great friend of hers and she had in earlier days when he was regarded with a certain amount of suspicion and distaste by the bulk of the Tory Party, undoubtedly helped to overcome this unfavourable feeling, just as Lady Bradford and her sister Lady Chesterfield had even more efficaciously promoted his social and political career. He was very gracious to me and after hearing that I was at Eton asked as to my pursuits. I said that I played cricket and fives and had been for a year in the Volunteers. "Ah!" he said with a certain air of sententiousness and importance. "A force which in the unhappy, and, as we must all hope, improbable event of invasion would indubitably play no inconsiderable part in safeguarding the liberties of our beloved country!" This little speech made me feel like a miniature Marlborough and Wellington rolled into one, and has since struck me as admirably phrased when addressed to a boy of sixteen.

This story recalls one of the time when that force was being formed. My cousin, Earl Brownlow, then a very young man, threw himself heartily into the movement with which he remained closely connected all his life, being President of the National Rifle Association, and shooting for many years in the annual competition between the House of Lords and House of Commons. Lady Marian naturally helped her son when he was raising the first body of recruits from his tenants and neighbours in Hertfordshire. She sent for the head gamekeeper, whose occupation seemed to indicate him as a prospective warrior, but found to her surprise and a little to her indignation that he did not seem very keen on joining the Volunteers. "If the French" (for they were then the supposed potential enemy) "were to land, should we have to fight them, my lady?" "Why, of course, that's what the Volunteers are for!" "Well, I'm afraid I couldn't do it, my lady." "Why, you're not afraid of the French, are you?" "No, no, my lady," with a reassuring and almost patronizing smile as of one seeking to dispel a child's unreasonable alarm. "Not afraid of a Frenchman; one wouldn't be afraid of a Frenchman! But"—scratching his head and looking very serious—"it would be very awkward if they were to come in the egg season!" *Avant tout le métier*. This brings to my mind an anecdote which Lord Derby, the uncle of the present Earl, told me. When he was Foreign Secretary and complications were threatened with Russia, his head gamekeeper asked whether he thought that we should have war. "I hope not, I hope not," said Lord Derby. "But things are looking rather serious." "Oh, I don't suppose it would matter much, my lord, if we *did* go to war, not with the Roosians." "Why do you say that?" "Well, not if they don't shoot better than that Ambassador!" The Russian Ambassador had recently been a guest at Knowsley and had not acquitted himself at all well with a gun.

On March 16, 1873, I got leave to spend the day at Lord Westminster's (who was created a Duke the following year) at Cliveden, which he later sold to the late Lord Astor. There I found my Father, Mr, Mrs and Miss Gladstone and Willy Gladstone, the Duke and Duchess of Argyll, Lord and Lady Frederick Cavendish and Dr Radcliffe. The conversation turned upon church architecture and it was stated that though there were some cathedrals on the Continent more magnificent than any in England, the beauty of the average of English churches exceeded that of those abroad. The Duke of Argyll admired Norman architecture, but Mr Gladstone disliked their windows whilst liking their porches.

Dr Radcliffe cited the case of a young Frenchwoman, who could talk no other language but French, married an American and going to America forgot all her French and talked English only. Subsequently she received a severe shock which deprived her of all memory of her later life. She forgot all her English and when asked her name and where she lived would give her maiden name and the street in Paris in which her early home was situated.

Mr Gladstone made the following joke at dinner: "Why cannot a Bishop eat his apron?" "Because it goes against his stomach!"

I observe that I noted with gratification that my host tipped me a pound.

There is a record in my diary of our House Sports. "We then had the Jockey Race. I had to carry Gage" (the late Viscount Gage), "who is about as heavy as myself; first of all he made two muff shots at mounting, and then when once on rolled over one side of me, after I had with great difficulty staggered on about three yards, and clutching me by the neck, naturally brought me a whacking smash right over him. Altogether our performance was not quite first rate." My jockey on this unsuccessful occasion was a quiet and retiring boy, generally known as "Charcoal Jim" on account of his swarthy complexion. An ancestor of Gage's several centuries ago introduced into England from abroad two kinds of plum, one red and one green. They were originally called a "red gage" and a "green gage," but only the latter appellation has survived.

Many stories are current of the witty Bishop Wilberforce. He had more than one brush with Lord Chancellor Westbury and when the latter had to resign his high office in painful circumstances, he met Wilberforce and rather unadvisedly remarked: "Hast thou found me, O, mine enemy?" The Bishop could not resist completing the quotation: "Yea, I have found thee, because thou hast sold thyself to work iniquity." At Ashridge, where Wilberforce and Lord Houghton were guests, the latter had a seat in an open carriage which was taking some of the party to church and overtook Wilberforce who was going there on foot; leaning out of the carriage Houghton quoted:

"How blest is he who n'eer consents
By ill advice to walk."

Again the Bishop completed the quotation:

"Nor stands in sinners' ways nor sits
Where men profanely talk."

Arthur Purey Cust, Dean of York, was a great admirer of his, and after the Bishop's death, finding himself in the neighbourhood of a parish where Wilberforce had held a living in his younger days, sought out an aged parishioner whom he tried to pump for reminiscences. Not being very successful and finding the old gentleman not particularly enthusiastic, he asked him whether he did not greatly admire the Bishop's character. He was surprised and shocked at the old farmer answering that he did not, and asked him why. "Well, you see, sir, 'e was a tarrible selfish gentleman!" "Selfish!" cried the indignant Cust. "Why, he was one of the most saintly, the most unselfish of men I ever knew!" "Ah, yes, 'e was selfish, sir. Why, no sooner 'ad 'e got his own hay in than he'd be whipping out the prayer for rain!"

The Bishop's grandson, who was inclined to be a little wild, did not come home one night as early as his father (a canon of Westminster) thought he should have done, and when the youth at length arrived at an unduly late, or rather early, hour, his father thus greeted him: "Good morning, son of the Devil!" "Good morning, Papa!" was the unabashed reply.

I remember in July 1873, being much shocked by reading in the newspaper the account of Bishop Wilberforce's death near Abinger, by a fall from his horse when he was riding with Lord Granville on his way to stay with my Father at Holmbury. My uncle was riding in front of him and so did not see the accident, but the groom, who was following them, said that the Bishop was riding carelessly and with a loose rein, that his horse stumbled, pitching his rider over his neck. Wilberforce was a heavy man; he broke his neck and death was instantaneous.

In the summer of 1873 the Shah of Persia came on a visit to England. He was a swarthy, thick-set man of unprepossessing appearance. A review was held in his honour in Windsor Great Park. A ridiculous *contretemps* occurred as the horse of one of his suite bolted past the line of troops and finally threw his rider ignominiously. The unfortunate Persian made straight for the railway station and took the first train to London, where he disappeared for good, knowing that his royal master would never forgive him and that if he remained in his service his days would not be long in the land.

The Shah was bored at having to go to the Ascot Races, saying, not altogether unreasonably, that he was aware that one horse could run faster than another and as he knew none of their owners he did not care a pin which won. He yielded on being told that it was a royal function, but this was not the end of complications. On the first day when the time came near for the procession to start, word was brought that the Shah was fast asleep and that none of his suite dared to rouse him. The difficulty was ingeniously solved by the Guards Band playing the Persian National Anthem *fortissimo* under his windows. When he got to the races his interest was aroused, and on his return to Persia he instituted an imitation of Royal Ascot. This, however, was not a success, as the horses of several of his noblemen had the want of tact to beat those belonging to the Shah, which resulted in disagreeable consequences to their owners, including the transference of the winners to the royal stables without compensation.

The Shah paid visits to certain great country houses; but owing to his disregard of European moral conventions and to the uncleanly habits of his suite, these were not a success. Amongst other places he went to Ashridge, and at the end of his visit presented Brownlow with a huge and appallingly bad marble bust of himself, which was relegated to a dark and remote corridor. He also went to Dunrobin, where the Duke of Sutherland entertained him with a torchlight procession and various Highland sports and martial exercises. On the Shah's return to London the Prince of Wales said that he hoped that he had enjoyed his visit. The Shah drew him aside and declared that whilst he had had an interesting time in the north he thought it his duty to warn the Prince that the Duke might be getting too powerful in that remote region of the kingdom, as he seemed to have a number of armed men in his service, and that it might be prudent to keep an eye on him. The Prince gravely thanked him and when he next saw the Duke told him that from reliable information he feared that he might soon be under the painful necessity of committing him to the Tower as a rebel.

The General Election of 1874 took place during my last half at Eton. On polling day Windsor was put out of bounds, which we looked upon as a direct challenge to get there. Two or three Masters held the bridge, like Horatius and his comrades, between Eton and Windsor to prevent anyone getting across, so with sound strategic instinct we turned the enemy's flank by crossing Datchet Bridge lower down the river. I found myself in the midst of a crowd in front of the White Hart Hotel, from a window of which one of the candidates was delivering a harangue; suddenly I was aware of a Master to whom, luckily, I was personally unknown, edging his way towards me through the throng. He made a dive for my tall hat, but I ducked and just prevented him getting it. It should be explained that in such contingencies it was a rule of the game for the Master to try to secure one's topper, as if one lost it all was up, for one's initials were inside the crown, and apart from the clue which these afforded, a hatless return to one's tutor's furnished evidence enough for conviction. With the crowd's connivance, which a boy could always rely upon in such emergencies, I wormed my way into the open and ran for it, the Master following. I am still grateful to that crowd for hampering him as much as was possible short of physical violence. I dodged past the Town Hall, but a half tipsy loafer tripped me up and I fell headlong in the mud. Getting up, I spurted round the corner into a little street leading towards the Castle. Seeing the open door of a humble house I dashed through it into the presence of a startled but kindly old dame who at once set to work to tidy me up, as what with my flight and my fall I was not very presentable. I then asked her to look down the street and to tell me whether she could see any Eton Master. "Shall I call him, sir, if I do?" "Oh, no; anything but that;" and whilst she was looking out, would she mind shutting the front door? No Master in sight, thank heaven! Her son next put in an appearance, a free and independent elector of stalwart build and rather the better for beer. He somewhat truculently inquired what the —— I was doing in his —— house. His mother reassured him as to my intentions, and explained that she had just been tidying me up a bit, and that I was running away from a Master who was trying to catch me. Hereupon, with a sudden change of view as surprising as it was gratifying, he announced his intention of punching any —— Master's —— head who showed his —— nose within his —— door. The coast now being reported clear, I ventured out again but had hardly taken three steps before the recently apostrophized Master reappeared and the chase was resumed. I headed for Henry VIII's Gateway in the Castle and it was lucky that I did so for, quite unknown to me, the officer on guard was an old Etonian who, hearing of Windsor being put out of bounds and guessing what was likely to happen, had given strict, though probably quite irregular, orders to the sentry at the gate to stop any Master if he should see him pursuing an Eton boy through the gateway. These orders were carried out with eminently satisfactory discipline, the Master was pulled up on the threshold in mid-career and the sentry directed me to go up some stairs to the room of the officer on guard. He received me kindly, and warmly congratulating me on my escape, offered me cake and sherry. I accepted the former, but declined the wine, as I was afraid that it might go to my head after this succession of emotions and thus hinder my escape; eventually I got home to my tutor's, undetected but rather weary.

My Father made it a point of continually taking me abroad during the holidays whilst I was at school, and in this way I saw a good deal of France, Belgium, Holland and Germany. I enjoyed travelling and sight-seeing, and probably picked up a good deal of knowledge half-unconsciously during these early peregrinations. These journeys also incidentally prevented one's French and German getting too rusty.

When my two cousins, Brownlow and his brother, were at Eton, in the later 'fifties, there was no heating apparatus of any sort in Chapel and the cold was intense. Their mother started an agitation which led to its being properly warmed, for which all subsequent generations of Etonians should be grateful to her memory.

Chapel was not without its occasional humours. There is a Psalm, each verse of which ends with the words, "For His mercy endureth for ever." This was set to a good swinging tune which we all joined in lustily; so lustily indeed that the authorities regarded the noise we made as something of a scandal, to avoid which the tune was changed. We were not to be defeated so easily, and when the time next came round for the Psalm to be sung, we all shouted the old tune whilst the new tune was being played on the organ, making confusion worse confounded. The Master "in desk" who was specially charged with the duty of seeing that order was kept during service, selected one or two of the more vigorous vocalists and had them up for punishment for the rather curiously phrased offence of "indecent singing."

Provost Goodford, alias "Goody," read the lessons and prayers with much emotion and emphasis, rather as though he had just composed them himself. This, combined with a tendency to make slips, had a ludicrous effect. Once he earnestly prayed for "the maintenance of wickedness and vice and the suppression of *all* true religion and virtue." Another time he proclaimed in the Confession that "we have done that which we ought to have done, and we have *not* done that which we ought not to have done." These variants remind one of the young clergyman who also read the lessons with rather too much emphasis. Reading the account of the sacrifice of Isaac, he rendered one passage as follows: "And he said unto the young men, 'Saddle me the ass,' and they saddled *him*."

It must not be thought, because I have allowed myself certain criticisms upon various methods and practices, that I do not very dearly love my old school. Very likely many of these blemishes have by now either disappeared or been greatly diminished. The memory of my Eton days remains with me, as with most old Etonians, as that of one of the happiest and most cherished periods of my life.

CHAPTER V

A NORTHAMPTONSHIRE RECTORY

On leaving Eton at the end of the Easter half in 1874, I went to read, as his only pupil, with an old friend of my mother's family, the Rev William Lucas Collins, Rector of Lowick, near Thrapston in Northamptonshire, a pretty stone-built village, some seventeen miles from my uncle's home, Castle Ashby. He belonged to the old "High and Dry," "Church and Queen" school, but was by no means a ritualist. At village suppers at Harvest Home, or some such festivity, he used to give the toast of "Church and Queen" and once was slightly put out by my transposing the order and drinking to "Queen and Church," which seemed to me only reasonable, seeing that the Sovereign is the head of the Church as well as of the State. Later on Mr Gladstone criticized ideas which I had had the boldness to advance in some similar connection, and said half regretfully and half banteringly: "But I suppose it is hopeless. You are an Erastian, as all you Whigs always have been and always will be." Mr Collins was an elegant and accurate scholar and taught me with care and enthusiasm. I shall always feel deeply grateful to him as having, more than anybody else, inspired me with a love and a certain measure of understanding of the glories of the Classics. He had edited two series of little volumes, which were published by Blackwood and were rightly popular in their day. One was *Ancient Classics for English Readers*, the other, *Foreign Classics for English Readers*. Some of these he wrote himself and for others obtained the services of distinguished collaborators. He also contributed to the *Quarterly Review* and to *Blackwood's Magazine*; the owner of the latter, Mr Blackwood, was a shrewd old Scotch gentleman. His son, who had been at my House at Eton with me, also spent a week at Lowick, and we made a very rough and ready golf course in the neighbouring Park at Drayton, which I should think was one of the very first inland links in England. It was a very unambitious affair, just nine holes with no artificial bunkers and nothing but natural obstacles, but we got a good deal of fun out of it. Mr Collins, who was a Jesus man (Oxford), was of a spare habit of body, he was a great gentleman and (in the best sense) a man of the world, gifted with a ready wit and a kindly sense of humour. His wife was very kind to me, her only fault was that she was apt to be a little over anxious. They had two sons; the elder, Clifton, had been a Demy at Magdalen, where he had taken high honours. He was short sighted, of a studious and retiring disposition, but very pleasant and friendly. He died unmarried and comparatively young. The other son, Willie, who had also been at Jesus, was a fine cricketer and played for the Free Foresters. He afterwards married Margaret Stopford-Sackville, one of the many attractive daughters of the neighbouring great house of Drayton, and took a private school near Slough. Drayton House was the home of Mrs Stopford-Sackville, who would have been Duke of Dorset had she been a boy, a fact which she was not disposed to forget. She had married Mr Stopford, who was no longer living when I came to Lowick, and in view of the property being hers had retained her maiden name. Although very small in stature, she was pre-eminently a "grande dame" and, beneath her retiring and unobtrusive manner, possessed a character of much determination and strength of will. She and all her family showed me the greatest kindness during the two and a half years that I spent at Lowick and sensibly contributed to making it a delightful place of residence. I much missed their companionship when they went to London for the season.

Drayton was the home, in the 18th century, of that remarkable woman, Lady Betty Germaine. In the Hall, there was a life-sized portrait of Henry VIII, in his usual posture, legs astraddle and hands on hips. When Mrs Sackville's infant grand-daughter was shown this and asked who it was, she answered "Dum-dum," her name for her grandmother. A greater contrast could scarcely be conceived. At this time Mrs Sackville's eldest son, Sackville George Stopford Sackville, was M.P. for the Northern Division of the county. He was turned out in 1880 by Bobby Spencer, the late Lord Spencer, afterwards a fellow-whip of mine. Bobby, during this election, was addressing an open-air meeting, when his opponents led a donkey past decked out in the Liberal colours, amidst roars of laughter, which Bobby adroitly turned by saying that he was glad that he had converted at least one of the other side.

I played cricket in Drayton Park, but for want of practice did not acquire any great proficiency. One of Mrs Sackville's daughters, Beatrice (who had married a diplomat, Mr Clarke Jervoise), promised me as a reward at a match, that if I made twenty runs I might hold her baby daughter, who grew up into a beautiful girl, but it was a "pleasure" which was denied to me as I only made eighteen. When the said baby was born at Lisbon, her husband cut off a bit from his astrakhan waistcoat and sent it to his mother-in-law as a specimen of her grand-daughter's hair, a fraud which, when discovered later on, excited considerable indignation. We used to play Uppingham and Oundle Schools and other elevens, but as we were rather a scratch team we generally got beaten, but enjoyed ourselves all the same.

In the summer of 1874 I brought down a set of lawn tennis things and laid out a court on the Rectory lawn. I believe that it was the first to be started in the county, and anyhow, from its novelty, became very popular and made Lowick quite a fashionable centre. I also brought down two targets and some bows and arrows and instituted a series of miniature archery meetings. In these ways I tried to make some little return for all the kindness and hospitality of our neighbours. I further had a clay pigeon machine at which I practised, for I was often asked to join shooting parties in the neighbourhood. At the bottom of the little valley, on one slope of which was the Rectory, ran a small brook, in the marshy meadows on either side of which snipe were to be found. I used to go after them, but generally with little success owing to the fact that in my inexperience I did not realize that I ought to use No. 7 shot instead of No. 5. I was further hampered by the persistence with which Jock, my fox terrier, followed me. In vain I locked him up in the stable, he displayed perfectly diabolical ingenuity in getting out and rejoining me. Once there it was impossible to get rid of him, short of shooting him, and if by any lucky chance I bagged a snipe, we had a desperate race as to who should retrieve it first, for if I failed there was no hope of snipe for dinner, as Jock was anything but a sporting dog and looked upon whatever fell to my gun as his legitimate perquisite.

I got some coarse fishing in the River Nene, which flowed past Thrapston some two miles from Lowick, and caught a fine bream in the mill pond at Addington, which I brought home in triumph, assuring Mrs Collins, quite conjecturally, that it was excellent eating. The good lady used some port wine and a lot of stuffing to prepare it and was correspondingly disappointed when it tasted of very little else than mud. I often fished for pike in the company of a neighbouring clergyman, Mr Roberts, who held the living of Aldwinckle All Saints. He was a tall, massive, sallow, silent and rather saturnine man, with a vivacious little black-haired wife, with a complexion like a lemon, who looked exactly like a parrot and was a martyr to indigestion. At the other end of what was practically the same village was another benefice, Aldwinckle St Peters, the incumbent of which, Mr Ward, was a cheery old bachelor, a rubicund, bearded, rather portly and talkative man. His two hobbies were roses, which he grew to perfection, and collecting rubbings of old brass memorials in neighbouring churches; I helped him prune his roses and also to take rubbings of these brasses, thus incidentally acquiring a little knowledge of rose-growing, and also of the history and architecture of the churches within a radius of a good many miles.

These two old friends of mine, although such near neighbours, would never meet or speak, on account of some ancient and secret feud, the nature of which they refused to impart to me. When I tried to question them they assumed a deeply pained and mysterious air, intended to convey the impression that it was of so serious a character that it would not bear speaking of. My own belief was that it was some trifling quarrel, of so petty a kind that they were ashamed to acknowledge it. Anyhow, by alternate coaxing and bullying, I at last got them to make it up and before leaving Lowick had the satisfaction of seeing them good friends again. When I was at Oxford I was much pleased to get a letter from each of them thanking me warmly for having effected their reconciliation.

Mr Ward was looking round a church when in Italy; he had a good-looking niece with him. The *parroco* (i.e. the priest of the parish) courteously offered to show them some things of interest, and thinking that he was talking to a layman, entered into certain superfluous explanations. "*Anch' io son prete*" ("I also am a priest") said Ward; whereupon the *parroco* touched his arm with a sort of "You sly dog" sort of look, followed by a glance towards his niece. Ward thereupon explained her relationship to him, which only increased the ecclesiastic's politely restrained amusement.

This reminds me of a story of a hotel-keeper at Sorrento, who was careful to tell his English visitors that the Bishop of Gibraltar often stayed there during the summer heats. He would show them a summer-house in a retired corner of the garden where the Bishop read morning prayers to his family, and would announce in awed undertones: "*Ecco il tempietto, dove il Vescovo, colla sua Vescova e i suoi Vescovini, facevano i loro sacrifici.*" ("Here is the little temple where the Bishop, with his Bishopess and his Bishoplings performed their sacrifices"). He was evidently persuaded that a Bishop who openly indulged in such uncanonical luxuries would perform dark and unholy rites, the nature of which it were better not to divulge in polite society.

Lowick Rectory was a handsome and substantial stone building. Curiously enough the imaginary sketch of Mr Casaubon's Rectory, drawn, I think, by Birket Foster, as frontispiece for an edition of George Eliot's *Middlemarch*, was very like it, although he had never seen Lowick, and this so struck her publisher that he reproduced a view of Lowick Church as a gilt vignette on the outside binding of an edition of that novel, a copy of which, a gift of Mr Collins, is in my possession.

I met George Eliot once when I was an undergraduate at a dinner given by the Master of Balliol. I did not have any conversation with her but was much struck by her appearance, which was not, on the whole, prepossessing; her features were harsh and very pronounced and she looked partly like a horse and partly like Savonarola, but her expression was earnest and rather melancholy and she had fine, dark and thoughtful eyes. In later life I was intimate with her second husband, Mr J. W. Cross, a banker, who wrote her biography. We first became acquainted through his writing a financial article for me when I was European Editor of the *North American Review*. He was excellent company, and we played many a game of piquet at the Athenaeum, where he was known as "George Eliot's widow."

But to return to Lowick Church. It was a beautiful structure in the perpendicular style with a particularly lovely tower crowned by an octagonal lantern, and containing several fine monuments, one being a tomb of alabaster with recumbent effigies of Sir Ralph Greene, of Drayton, and of his wife Catherine, erected by her in 1419; another also of alabaster, of Edward Stafford, second Earl of Wiltshire who died in 1499. There was some good stained glass of the 14th century in four windows of the North Aisle. Mr Collins having no curate, I offered to read the lessons, and he gladly accepted, as he found it rather a strain to do the whole of the service. This proved capital practice for the exercise and control of the voice, and is useful for anyone who may have to speak in public. The first lesson one Sunday was that of the fiery furnace in which Shadrach, Meshach and Abednego play a part. It may be remembered that there is more than one repetition of a longish list of various court officials and also of the musical instruments which were employed. Several of the young Sackvilles suggested to me before church that I might as well shorten the lesson by saying, when I came to the said repetitions, "the above-mentioned gentlemen," and "brass band as before," instead of reading out the whole of the two lists *de novo*. The lectern unluckily stood just in front of the Sackville pew, and I was conscious of the steady gaze of five pairs of eyes, which seemed to concentrate themselves upon my face, especially as I neared the fateful passages. How I managed to get through without breaking down or laughing I really do not know.

I had two horses, a roan cob called Murad after the unlucky and short-lived Sultan, and another of whom I ceased to be the owner in the following circumstances.

At the beginning of the Summer Term of 1878, when I was at Oxford, my Father wrote to me that he thought that my horse had better be sold, as I was not riding him that term, and it seemed a useless expense to keep him till hunting began. I answered that I did not want to sell him, to which he replied that he had decided to do so. Presently he wrote to say that the horse had fetched £150. I replied that I was delighted that he had sold so well and intimated that a cheque for the amount would be welcome. To this he answered that I had quite misunderstood the position, that the horse was his and not mine, and that he was only mine in the sense that he had allowed me to ride him; therefore there was no question of any remittance. A day or two later my hopes revived on getting a letter from him saying, "I have been thinking about the question of the horse"—and I expected that he was going to add that he would send me some *solatium* for my disappointment. Judge of my disgust when the letter continued, "and as you are now relieved of the cost of keeping him, I am going to reduce your allowance by £50." A shrewd and cruel blow! Murad had been sold before, so I was now horseless. I suspect that he thought that I should read more if my hunting was stopped, and I daresay that he was right.

My two first hunting seasons at Oxford I generally went out with the South Oxfordshire and Old Berkshire and occasionally with the Bicester. My horse stood with Charlie Simmonds, in Holywell, where he was well looked after. Many Oxford men will recall old Charlie's stout little figure, red face, high stock and big blue tie, as well as the nervous affection which caused him to shake his head from side to side, investing his utterances with an air of almost preternatural wisdom.

From Lowick I hunted with the Woodland Pytchley and occasionally with the Fitzwilliam. Anthony Trollope, the novelist, used to spend four or five weeks every year at the Rectory to hunt, and we always went out and often came home together. He brought down a string of seven hunters, which excited my envy. He was a big, bearded, red-faced, jovial man with a loud voice and hearty manner. He told me that, when as a young man he was employed in the Post Office, he once had to take the mails from Paris to London in the depth of winter. It was in the days when the diligence carried the mails and it stuck fast in a deep snow drift a few miles from Calais. There was nothing for it but to unharness the best of the horses and to make his way to Calais through the driving snow with the mail bags slung before and behind him. He was fearful of losing his way and of missing the boat, but caught it just in time. This recalls an experience of my own as a boy when I was returning to England with my Father. We reached Calais in bitterly cold weather, and a fellow traveller assured us that the omnibus always took two trips from the railway station to the boat (it was before the railway had been brought down to the quay side), and that there was no need to hurry off by the first omnibus, so my Father sent on his valet, the faithful Musson, with the luggage, whilst we had some refreshment at the buffet. On going down in the second omnibus, we saw the boat steaming out of the harbour, and Musson vainly expostulating with the captain. The worst of it was that we had not even kept my Father's handbag which contained his money, and we had nothing with us but a few stray francs. So we made our way to the British Consul to ask for a loan. At first he received us rather coolly, but his manner underwent a complete and rapid change when he found that my Father was the Foreign Secretary's brother, whereupon he offered to lend us money on a positively lavish scale.

Matthew Arnold was entrusted, when a School Inspector, by the Foreign Office at the Education Department's request, with a mission to report upon certain particulars of school management in France and Switzerland. Although he was really acting for the Education Department, he was thus temporarily employed by the Foreign Office, who provided his travelling expenses. This he considered was on too meagre a scale, but his request for an increase was refused. Towards the end of his stay at Paris, where he had lived very frugally, he determined to treat himself to one really good dinner, which he ordered at a first-class restaurant. Whilst he was enjoying this, my Father came in. At that time, before he grew a beard, he was strikingly like his brother, who was then Foreign Secretary. He knew Arnold slightly and looked at him closely in order to satisfy himself whether it was he. This threw poor Mat. into an agony of embarrassment, as he took him for Lord Granville. He confessed that he thought: "No wonder Lord G. will think that I consider my pay insufficient if this is the way in which I habitually live!" and when my Father, who of course knew nothing of the whole matter, came up to shake hands, he very nearly embarked on an explanatory self-justification. The incident is related in the late George Russell's *Life and Letters of Matthew Arnold*, but as I also heard it from my Father, with the addition of certain details not included therein, I hope that I may be pardoned for repeating it.

The only other packs with which I hunted were the West Street Harriers, which were kept at Walmer by my uncle, when Lord Warden of the Cinque Ports, and occasionally with Lord Guilford's foxhounds in the same neighbourhood. I was mounted, and very well too, by my uncle, and had many enjoyable days on those wonderful Downs. Lord Granville was a fine horseman and at one time Master of the Royal Buckhounds. A Conservative peer saying in the course of a debate that the Liberals were not a sporting lot, my uncle promptly challenged any four Tory peers to ride a cross-country steeplechase against himself, Lord Spencer, Lord Cork and Lord Ribblesdale, but the challenge was not taken up, which was a pity, as it would have been an interesting sporting event.

At Lowick I had a pet jackdaw, who became a general favourite as he was most amusing, having learnt to talk a little and being an accomplished mimic. He and the horses became great friends and he generally perched on the back of one or the other of them. Alas! he met with an ignominious end, as he overbalanced on the edge of the hog-tub which he was trying to explore.

Castle Ashby was some seventeen miles from Lowick and I occasionally rode over there for a Saturday to Monday visit, my groom taking my luggage by train. One summer when either seventeen or eighteen, I accompanied my aunt, Lady Alwyne, and Mademoiselle de Peyronnet (afterwards Lady Sligo) on a day's expedition to Cambridge. My uncle, Lord Northampton, jokingly said that he hoped I should not fall into the Cam, which was exactly what I did, as I took the two ladies for a row, and the rope at the bow being too short I slipped as I was making it fast to a tree. They took me to the Provost of King's, Dr Okes, upon whom they were going to call, and he kindly lent me some of his clothes whilst mine were being dried, and a pretty ridiculous figure I cut as he was very short and stout and I very tall and, at that time, slim. I swore them to secrecy, and was correspondingly indignant when at dinner that night my uncle drew a bow at a venture and asked: "Well, George, did you fall in?" I, of course, thought that they had betrayed me, which, as a matter of fact, they had not done.

One Sunday Mr Collins preached on the subject of the First Lesson, which was the murder of Sisera by Jaël. He sharply criticized her action and incidentally let it be known that he had no higher opinion of Deborah, the eulogist of this treacherous deed. At luncheon the critic was criticized by his wife, who expressed her unbounded astonishment and regret that a clergyman should "distress and bewilder" his flock by disparagement of what Scripture had set forth as a great and laudable action. Whereto he rejoined that he thought it his duty to denounce baseness and treachery wherever he met or heard of it and should certainly continue to do so, whilst he did not believe that his flock were either distressed or bewildered "with perhaps one notable and regrettable exception." At this stage of the argument I thought it politic to slip out into the garden, so as to leave the polemists free to continue the discussion unembarrassed by an audience.

In the spring of 1875 I was confirmed by Dr Magee, the Bishop of Peterborough. This ceremony should have taken place at Eton a year before, but the moral turpitude evidenced by the sad gas-extinguishing incident previously recounted had placed me temporarily beyond the spiritual pale. Mr Collins was preparing a class of village youths and maidens for confirmation, who were nearly all a year or two younger than myself. He thought that my presence among them would be incongruous and possibly embarrassing to them, and therefore contented himself with asking me whether I had any religious doubts or difficulties, and when I said "None of any importance," passed me as fit for confirmation. Magee was an active and able prelate, best known, perhaps, for his manly declaration that he would rather see "England free than England sober," which occasioned much melancholy head-shaking among the stricter advocates of total abstinence. He was also celebrated for a sermon during the passage of the Act disestablishing the Church of Ireland, preached whilst he was a Bishop of that body, for which he took as his text: "Come over into Macedonia and help us." This sermon, which caused considerable sensation, is believed by many to have influenced his translation from an Irish to an English see. He was a great smoker, and used to hide his short black pipe behind some ponderous volumes of Church Fathers in his library. When he wanted a quiet smoke in the garden he would say to one of his children: "My dear, I want to consult a passage in Tertullian" (or Origen, as the case might be), and the pipe would presently appear. I heard the following account of the consecration of an addition to the graveyard at a neighbouring church, to which the clergy came from some miles round. They were a motley crew, some in full canonicals, others in black Geneva gowns, some in college mortar-boards, others in tall hats, in soft black felt hats, even one or two in straw hats, some in cassocks, others without. Nor was their procession more orderly than their attire. Instead of walking two and two, they strolled along in groups of three or four, with intervening gaps and without that general observance of silence which the occasion seemed to demand. The Bishop was rather vexed by this, and during the luncheon which followed the ceremony, somewhat perturbed the company by remarking, *à propos de bottes*: "What a striking passage that is in the Psalms: 'They reeled and staggered like drunken men and were at their wits' end.'"

I was taken to one or two Diocesan Conferences, which I am afraid I rather regarded as occasions for meeting friends and neighbours than for following involved and occasionally heated controversies upon matters of faith and observance. Indeed, what chiefly impressed me was the apparent extraordinary triviality of some of the topics which were capable of arousing so much anger and animosity. I suppose that I was too young to estimate the effects of the "odium theologicum" upon the minds of a certain type of cleric. Many years afterwards, when I was a Whip in the Government which was engaged in passing the Welsh Disestablishment Act, I received an invitation to stay with Dr Legge, Bishop of Lichfield, in which diocese my constituency of Stoke-on-Trent was situated and to address a Diocesan Conference, in which that Bill was one of the subjects for discussion. In spite of Mrs Legge having been one of the Miss Stopford Sackvilles of Drayton, I thought it prudent to decline. As I told the Bishop, there was only one recorded instance of a Daniel coming unscathed out of the den of lions, and so adopted the ignominious policy of "Safety First."

In our neighbourhood at Lowick during the summer there was a pleasant institution called "The Shakespeare Club." It chiefly consisted of the clergy and their families, who met monthly at each other's houses to read a play of Shakespeare, with intervals for tea and supper. In order to avoid jealousy the parts were assigned by lot, and I once had the rôle of Richard II, which greatly interested me. The disadvantage of this plan was an occasional inappropriate distribution of the characters. Once we were reading *Julius Cæsar* the title rôle having fallen to a rather nervous girl of eighteen. One fussy clergyman had taken upon himself to act as prompter, and she and I were giggling together in a corner over some silly joke, so that for the moment she was not following the text and failed to take up her cue. "Julius Cæsar!" cried the prompter. "Where's Julius Cæsar? Now then, Miss So-and-so! Enter Julius Cæsar in his night-gown!" I could not say whether she blushed or giggled the more. A large brake was often hired for these meetings. One evening as we were returning, forming a largish party, the horses were fresh and the turnings sharp. Mr Collins was sitting at the end of the brake, there was no rail to it, and he was a little apprehensive of being shot out on to the road. One girl, a member of a large family of pretty daughters of a neighbouring Rector sat next to him, so for greater safety he put his arm round her waist. "My dear William!" cried his scandalized wife. "Do you see what you're doing?" "What, my dear?" "Why, you've got your arm round E——'s waist. Not, of course, that *I* mind; but it would look very strange if one of your parishioners were to see you!" "Well, I'll chance meeting a parishioner, and even if we do you'll be able to tell him that it's all right and that you are chaperoning me—not that he'll understand what that means. But as *you* don't mind, and as I'm sure E—— don't mind, and as it is a good solid waist, I'd rather, on the whole, have my arm round it than have my head bumped on this hard road!" Encouraged by this example of my "pastor and master," I slipped my arm round the waist of one of her sisters, but not without escaping Mrs Collins' eagle eye, who addressed me: "Anyhow, you need not do the same, George!" "But I haven't got any parishioners, Mrs Collins." "Never mind; let go of F—— at once. Besides, you've not got the same excuse, you are not sitting at the end of the brake." To which I could only answer: "I only wish I were!" as I reluctantly abandoned my agreeable position.

The clergy with whom I made friends were, with hardly an exception, pleasant companions; practically all University men and many of good family. They entered largely into the social life of the neighbourhood, entertaining on a moderate scale and taking part in the sports and recreations as well as in the more serious occupations of country life. Many played cricket, shot or fished. A few hunted in a modest way. One was devoted to coursing and was active in putting down anything like unfairness in this pursuit. Most of them were skilful gardeners and knew something of farming. Some remained fine scholars and nearly all were interested in archæology, history and architecture. With all this they were anything but remiss in the discharge of their duties, whether in their churches, parishes or schools, and had gained, on the whole, the affection and respect of their parishoners whether these belonged to the Church of England or to some other denomination.

Mr Collins told me that when he was a young clergyman and held a living in Wales, he was a member of a local cricket club. One day his Bishop sent for him and said that he had been distressed by a rumour which had come to him orally and the author of which he could not disclose. He himself did not believe it, but at the same time thought it only right to mention it and to give Mr Collins an opportunity of disculpating himself from the charge. "Yes, my lord," said the bewildered Collins, "but what is it?" "Well, my informant told me that you were in the habit of gambling in the mountains." For the moment Collins was utterly perplexed, but suddenly a light broke in upon him. Remembering the strictness of view of the average Welsh Nonconformist (for such he had ascertained the Bishop's informant to be), and his frequent difficulties with the finer points of the English language, he realized that the "gambling in the mountains" referred to the cricket club, which was somewhere up in the hills, and that it was not the "gambling" as practised at Monte Carlo which was alleged, but the "gambolling" of cricketers, whose performances were thus compared to the friskings of innocent lambs. "*Solvuntur risu tabulæ, tu missus abibis.*"[1]

The incumbent of Sudborough, Mr W. Duthy, was strikingly like the great Duke of Wellington and told me that in former days he had often been either cheered or hooted, according to the vicissitudes of popularity which his illustrious double experienced.

At the back of Apsley House is a large triangular garden, reserved for subscribers. Here I used to play as a little boy. At the apex of the triangle near Stanhope Gate, there is a summer-house still standing. This featured in a game which we children invented. Dividing into two sides, one party tried to prevent the other from reaching the summer-house, which the opponents alternately attacked and defended for periods of ten minutes. Whichever side succeeded in getting the larger number within the summer-house won the game. All sorts of *ruses* were adopted, the favourite being to worm your way on your stomach through the thickest bushes like a Red Indian to the nearest point from whence you could make a sudden dash for the goal. It was not a popular game with nurses and governesses as at its conclusion we looked more like chimney sweeps than anything else, but it was capital fun.

When, as a small boy, I lived in South Audley Street, Chesterfield House was occupied by Mr Charles Magniac, M.P. There was then a large garden at the back, on the site of the present row of houses known as Chesterfield Gardens, in which grew a fine mulberry tree, the leaves of which I was allowed to pick to feed my silk-worms. From these I managed to get quite a lot of silk.

[1] The case ends in laughter and you leave the court acquitted.

CHAPTER VI

SOCIAL LIFE

It must, I think, have been in September 1875 that my Father took me to Castle Howard, Lord Carlisle's magnificent home in Yorkshire. It was then in the occupation of Lord Lanerton, Lord Carlisle's brother. They were my Father's first cousins, Lady Carlisle being my grand-mother's elder sister, and the recipient of those very witty and enter-taining letters written to her by Lady Granville, subsequently published by my Father. He said that he was struck by the marked difference between the appetite of the Howards and that of my Mother's family, the Comptons. The Howards were all hearty eaters who rallied my Father on his small appetite, whilst when he was with the Comptons, he was served with such small helpings that he often had to ask for more, whereupon his plate would return piled high with an enormous help as though it were determined that the insatiable ogre should at any rate have enough this time. There is a story of one of the ladies of an older generation of the Howards, who, in the days of posting, heard that a boiled chicken was a capital thing to eat before a journey, whereupon she made it her practice to eat the whole of a boiled chicken, as well as the very hearty dinner which she ordinarily con-sumed. She observed that she thought that her informant must have been mistaken as she invariably suffered from a disagreeable sense of repletion. Lord Carlisle's younger brother, Mr Charles Howard, for many years Liberal M.P. for Cumberland, died before his elder brother, so the Earldom passed to his son, George Howard, whose tastes were artistic. He was of a gentle and rather meditative dis-position. He married Rosalind, daughter of Lord Stanley of Alderley, an impetuous and warm-hearted woman, full of all sorts of theories, which she vigorously and rigorously put into practice. As an un-compromising teetotaller, when her husband succeeded, she had the contents of the magnificent cellar emptied into the lake, imitating the regrettable example of the late Sir Wilfrid Lawson. I once dined with the latter in Grosvenor Crescent. He warned me that I should get nothing to drink, "at least not what *you* would call drink," he added. It was a large party in the middle of the London season, and at first all went swimmingly, despite the absence of alcohol, until about the entrée stage, when conversation began to flag woefully and things got worse and worse until dinner ended. As I was leaving, he asked me whether I was going on anywhere and on hearing that I was due at a ball given by Mr Bass (afterwards Lord Burton) at Chesterfield House, exhorted me not to drink too much beer. I said that other liquid refreshment would probably be provided, that I was not in the habit of getting drunk, but that if I did exceed that evening and were run in by the police I should say that it was all Sir Wilfrid's fault. He did not mind being chaffed and answered that he would bear witness that at any rate I was sober when I left his house. To return to Lady Carlisle; her husband, always a very moderate man, contenting himself with a glass or two of claret, conformed to her teetotal views, as he set a high price on domestic concord. At a big luncheon, she called to him from the further end of the table: "George, do not take the jelly! There's maraschino in it. It might renew the craving!" Whereon he turned to the startled lady sitting next to him and said in his slow, soft voice: "I'm not really a brand snatched from the burning, though you might think so." Lady Carlisle was also a strong democrat and at one time insisted on the servants having their meals with the family, a practice abandoned not only on account of domestic difficulties, but of the extreme embarrassment in which it involved the household staff. She heard that one great Tory lady had dismissed her nursemaid for saying that it had served Charles I quite right to have his head cut off, whereupon Lady Carlisle hunted the girl up and took her into her service. She was not, however, always quite consistent in her democratic principles, and impressed on a friend the absurdity of addressing letters to one man as "Esquire" and to another as "Mr," and when he agreed, said: "Very well then, when I write to you in future I shall put 'Mr'"; but when he addressed his answer to "Mrs Carlisle," she was annoyed and pointed out that that was quite a different thing. She was very direct and outspoken, but was not the only one who sometimes found it hard to allow the same freedom to others. I was staying at their beautiful old home, Naworth Castle, on the Cumberland border, in 1882, during Arabi Pasha's rebellion in Egypt. She remarked that the Egyptians would never be quiet until they were contented, in itself a perfectly sound proposition. I had been rather nettled by some disparaging remarks which she had made about Mr Gladstone, to whom I was then private secretary, and about my uncle, then Secretary for Foreign Affairs, and so answered that I did not care so much about the Egyptians being contented as long as they were quiet, which so displeased her that she would not speak to me for two days. During the same visit we went to Lanercost Abbey, the fine ruin which the family has since surrendered to the nation. The children had got up to the clerestory round which they were chasing each other. Lady Carlisle did not mind a bit but my Father got anxious for their safety and at last insisted on my going up there "to look after them." How I could look after them I did not know, as I had a bad head for heights, but up I went and found myself in the position of the hen whose ducklings have taken to the water, for it was as much as I could do to look after myself.

This recalls an incident when I was a youth and when the first Lord Farrer (then Sir Thomas) was building his new house at Abinger Hall. My Father sent me over on my cob with a letter. Hearing that Sir Thomas was superintending the building operations, I saw him on the scaffolding about the height of the second floor. He called to me to come up, and before reaching him I had to cross a single plank some ten feet long and without any handrail, which swayed up and down as I crossed it. My mind was so much occupied with the prospect of having to recross that plank at that great height, that I quite forgot to deliver the letter and returned home with it in my pocket.

When I was treasurer of the Home Counties Liberal Federation I spent a day at Gravesend during a bye-election in 1898, visiting committees and canvassing. On the station platform when I was going home I met Lady Carlisle, then an old lady, with a son and a daughter who had been similarly engaged; she asked what in the world I was doing at Gravesend, and when I told her, said: "Well, that's splendid of you!" adding, as I thought superfluously: "I should never have thought that you were so public spirited or so unselfish!" Soon after the Home Rule split Lady Carlisle was calling on her mother, Lady Stanley of Alderley. Miss Maud Stanley, Rosalind's sister, said: "I am afraid that we must say good-bye now, as we have presently got a meeting here of the Liberal Unionist Women's Committee." "But why should I go? I should love to hear them. I can't conceive what they can have to say. It would interest me very much." "I'm afraid that wouldn't do. Knowing your strong adverse views, they would not be able to talk freely." "Why shouldn't they? I shouldn't mind, and if I don't why should they? However, if they are so ashamed of their views, as well they may be, I could hide behind a screen, like Lady Teazle." This last suggestion being negatived and Lady Carlisle positively refusing to withdraw, "unless you call a policeman to turn me out," the L.U. Ladies began to arrive; in vain they whispered together, hoping that Lady C. would retire, but she stuck to her guns, and her seat, like a man. So finally the meeting was adjourned and it was the L.U. Ladies who retired, *re infecta*, leaving Lady C. in triumphant possession of the field.

In 1874 she and her husband built what I always considered a very gloomy and inconvenient house on a Crown site in Kensington Palace Gardens. When the lease recently expired the Crown found it impossible to dispose of it; but a great clamour arose when it was proposed to devote the site to some other purpose, as it was maintained that the house was a unique specimen of the domestic architecture of that period. "Unique" it certainly was, but whether therefore worth preserving is quite another question.

Whatever Lady Carlisle's superficial peculiarities may have been, she was a large-hearted, generous-minded woman, always ready to fling herself into the support of any cause, however unpopular, which she thought right, and deservedly adored by her large family, who in their turn have grown up imbued with her lofty ideals and endowed with her great gifts of feeling and of intellect.

The Stanleys were all a remarkable family; the eldest brother, Lord Stanley of Alderley, embraced the faith of Islam. He was speaking in the House of Lords, when Lord Shaftesbury, who was very indignant at his change of faith, found him difficult to hear, and accordingly kept up a running commentary on his speech: "I can't hear a word the fellow's saying! The fellow's a Mohammedan! I can't hear a word the fellow's saying! The fellow's a Mohammedan!" *ad. lib.*, which at last reduced the Peers to such a state of uncontrollable laughter that the poor orator had to resume his seat.

One of the Stanley sisters married Lord Airlie. She was a beautiful and gracious woman. I stayed at Cortachy at the age of seven. When I was at Oxford she most kindly offered to lend me the romantic and lovely Airlie Castle for a reading party in the Long Vacation, an offer which I regretfully had to decline through difficulties of getting servants. This was the historic "bonnie house of Airlie" as to the burning of which "Gleyd Argyll" had played so notorious a part that no Campbell has since been admitted over the threshold.

Lord Airlie was a great talker, as was his brother-in-law, Lyulph Stanley, who afterwards became Lord Sheffield. These two, together with my Father and Henry Cowper (Lord Cowper's brother) once went into Hyde Park to watch some big demonstration. My Father and Henry getting separated from the others, the former said: "I wonder where they are." There was a prodigious noise, orators speaking simultaneously from many platforms, cheering multitudes, bands playing, etc. "Stop!" said Henry, "listen where there is most noise. We'll soon find them!" Lyulph and his beautiful young bride were at Naworth when I was there as quite a lad; returning from a picnic I was entrusted with her safety on the way home, having to drive a spirited chestnut in a high dog-cart. We came to a rapid stream with steep banks on either side. "Do you think you can manage it?" asked Mrs. Lyulph with not unnatural nervousness. "Of course I can," I answered, though with secret doubts. We scrambled through somehow, and I was amused when she reminded me of the incident some fifty years later at Longleat at my cousin Northampton's wedding to Lord Bath's charming daughter.

Another of the Stanleys turned Catholic and became Bishop of Emmaus. In short, they were a family with strongly marked and widely differing individualities. One of them observed that they all disagreed upon every subject except one: they were all strong free traders, which shows what a sensible family they are.

From Naworth we had a beautiful drive to Langholm, where we stayed for a day or two with the Duke of Buccleuch, stopping to lunch at Netherby, the home of the Grahams and the scene of the exploit of "Young Lochinvar."

At a cricket match at Langholm on a very hot day, the Duchess noticed that a young under-gardener was batting very vigorously in his coat. She suggested to the head gardener that he might like to take it off. "'Tis kind of Your Grace, but 'deed he's no vara great confidence in his shir-r-rt."

From Langholm we went on to Strathconon, then Mr Arthur Balfour's shooting lodge in Ross-shire. Here I had my first stalk.

A grim stalker, mistrusting my youth, took me for preliminary target practice, with the encouraging remark: "If ye'll no hit her" (i.e. the target) "it'll a' be but just labour in vain!" Coming home I drove a "machine" with one "wee laddie" who had "but little English." I had never been that way before, the steeds were rough, and there were precipitous places to pass. As long as the light held we got on fairly well, but when we reached a river, more or less in spate, it had got pitch dark, and I could not see the further bank. We struck the ford all right, but when I asked the laddie which way to keep the horses' heads he could only ejaculate "Wast" ("West"), which was not of much use as the locality was quite unknown to me, and in the murky night it was impossible to guess the points of the compass. However, the horses knew the way if I didn't. I think that a special providence must watch over me in the matter of fords.

One night the minister came to dinner. Our host asked him to say grace, and, expecting this to be expedited in a few words or a sentence or two, remained in a bent posture, ready to resume his seat. He should have known his Scotch minister better, for he went on and on, leaving our poor host suspended, like Mohammed's coffin, between earth and heaven, and uncertain whether he ought to "straighten up" or not. I am inclined to suspect that the minister gave us an extra dose, as a little rebuke to A.J.B. for not "straightening up" from the beginning. He may even perhaps have had a sense of humour.

On September 9, 1874, the Prince and Princess of Roumania came to Holmbury for one night. It was before he had been made King. They had come to England as the Prince foresaw the probability of a war between Russia and Turkey and was desirous of consolidating his position before hostilities were declared. His object was to secure such support from England and France as would enable him to maintain the neutrality of his country, which he knew would be impossible without vigorous backing from the Western Powers. I believe that he wished England and France to put such pressure on the Porte that Turkey would be forced to grant reforms and guarantees of such a substantial nature as would make life and property secure for her Christian subjects. This would not only safeguard their liberties and render their existence tolerable but would have almost certainly averted war between Russia and Turkey, which the Prince dreaded as, whatever its issue, he considered that it would be disastrous for Roumania. His country could obviously not be an ally of Turkey;

and without Western support could not keep neutral under the penalty of becoming the cockpit of the two antagonists. The Prince anticipated that, if he were forced into war as an ally of Russia, Roumania would bear the brunt of hostilities. If Turkey won, Roumania would be exposed to the vengeance of the Turks, whilst if the Russians were victors it was probable that they would become masters of Constantinople and so shut off Roumania from sea communications with the outer world, whilst any advantages which Roumania was likely to reap would be of an unsubstantial and illusory character. The consequences of the Russo-Turkish War a few years later proved how correctly he had anticipated future developments, as Roumania was deprived by her ally of the fertile province of Bessarabia and received the swamps of the Dobrudscha as fictitious compensation. Disraeli turned a deaf ear to the Prince's arguments, so his mission proved completely futile.

In manner Prince Charles was courteous, if a little formal and stiff, but the Princess, who will be remembered as a writer under the name of Carmen Sylva, was quite charming; bright and unaffected and full of interest for all that she saw or heard. She won the hearts of all at Holmbury.

The visit was a landmark at Holmbury in one respect; the Prince was allowed to smoke in the dining-room, which my Father, although a great smoker, had never before permitted. After this precedent had been established it was never revoked but it was some years before he allowed smoking in the drawing-room. Similarly for the first few years lawn tennis and cards were forbidden on Sunday, but were allowed later on.

CHAPTER VII

ITALY

On October 14, 1875, my Father took me to Italy for three or four months. On the Master of Balliol's recommendation he engaged as my travelling tutor the late Mr E. L. Vaughan ("Toddy"), who had just gone through his final schools at Oxford, subsequently became a Master at Eton (where he had been before going to Balliol), and was for years secretary of the Old Etonian Association. We returned at the end of the following January after visits of various duration at Turin, Genoa, Pisa, Florence, Perugia, Assisi, Castellamare, Amalfi, Naples, Rome, Orvieto and Siena; our tour concluded by a drive along the eastern and western Rivieras, starting at Spezia and ending at Cannes. At the impressionable age of between seventeen and eighteen, it was an incalculable advantage to have seen the great master-pieces of architecture, painting and sculpture of Italy. I also had the advantage of meeting interesting people at the Embassies at Paris and at Rome, as well as at numerous private houses. We occasionally went to the play or the opera, and were so assiduous in sight-seeing that I do not think that we missed anything of importance; at the same time I was kept hard at work all the morning and between dusk and dinner at my Greek and Latin, and also had French lessons from tutors at Rome and Florence. So although it was most enjoyable, it was pretty strenuous.

We started from Walmer Castle, being accompanied as far as Calais by Henry Calcraft, an old friend of our family, a well-known wit and not over-scrupulous as to how he raised a laugh. A member of the Travellers, whose son was coming up for election, was extremely anxious as to the result. He joined a knot of acquaintances, amongst whom was Calcraft, whilst the voting was going on and asked them whether they thought that it would be better taste if he did not stop in the room. Unfortunately he was afflicted · with offensive breath, which prompted Calcraft's brutal reply: "I don't know about better taste, but there would be a better smell."

Another anecdote may be given to illustrate his indifference to the feelings of others. Conversation turning upon the inconveniences of Spanish travel, an ill-favoured and unpopular man remarked that he had been for a long time in Spain but had never been bitten by a bug: "Come, come, my dear fellow," was Calcraft's comment, "even a Spanish bug must draw the line somewhere!"

He ended his Civil Service career as Secretary of the Board of Trade. The hangman of the day had the same name, with the natural result that he got the nickname of "The Hangman," which he hoped to get rid of when his namesake retired from his gruesome occupation. The next public executioner was called Marwood, whereupon all Henry's acquaintances nicknamed him "Marwood." By a really remarkable coincidence Henry Calcraft was succeded in his secretary-ship of the Board of Trade by a gentleman also named Marwood. So that alike at the Board of Trade and at the service of the gallows, a Calcraft and a Marwood, both uncommon names, succeeded each other.

This reminds me of a singular experience of my Father, when M.P. for Bodmin. The railway stopped at Bodmin Road some three or four miles from the town, an omnibus carrying passengers over the intervening distance. One day my Father, on getting into the omnibus, was surprised to see that although it was raining only one other person got inside, everybody else either getting outside or starting to walk. His fellow passenger was a middle-aged man of quiet and respectable appearance; my Father conversed with him and found him agreeable and intelligent; he afterwards learnt that he was the hangman who was coming to Bodmin in his official capacity and my Father's political opponents made a great joke of it at the time.

On board the boat to Calais was Serjeant Ballantyne, a well-known Q.C. of the day, considered the best Counsel for Election Petitions. When a petition was lodged against my Father's return, he secured the Serjeant's services. My Father's supporters were indignant at Ballantyne's very perfunctory cross-examination and mild handling of hostile witnesses, and were disappointed at the failure of the great gun to rub it in to their opponents, a treat to which they had been much looking forward. My Father won his case hands down, the Judge declaring the petition to be frivolous and unfounded and the election one of the purest that he had ever known. When the case was concluded my Father told Ballantyne that his friends thought that he had let the other side off very easily, to which he answered: "You, as a former barrister, my dear Mr Leveson, will readily realize that with such an extraordinary strong case as ours, it is good policy to stick to the facts and not to seem to the Judge to be raising side issues." Charles Bowen, afterwards the Judge so celebrated for his wit, was Ballantyne's Junior Counsel, and told my Father years later that this was not his leader's reason at all, but that he had so acted as he had not read a single word of his brief. An easy if not a creditable way of earning a very high fee! This petition was less successful than a previous one brought against my Father, on his return for Derby in 1847. He was unseated in consequence of his agent's having inadvertently included a few voters amongst his canvassers and having given them sandwiches and beer for luncheon.

Ballantyne was accompanied by a young and pretty girl, whom he introduced to Calcraft as his niece. Curiously enough he was also on the same boat in which we returned from Calais some three months later, when he had another good-looking young woman as his companion, whom he likewise presented as his niece to my Father. When I observed later that it was a different niece from the lady whom we had met on our way out, my Father said: "Yes, he is rather careless. He changes them too often."

The boat we crossed in was of a new design, being what was called a "twin-ship"; she had two hulls, bound together by girders, with an intermediate space of only four feet, and with a single deck. She had four anchors, two at each end, whilst her paddles were on the inner side of each hull. She was named *The Castalia*, after my aunt, Lady Granville, and when launched my uncle said that he hoped that she would have two merits not often combined in those of her sex and that she would prove both fast and steady. She was certainly not very fast as the crossing to Calais took two hours and ten minutes.

At Calais we were joined by Sir Wilfrid Lawson, the witty M.P. to whom I have already referred. I recollect two examples of his parliamentary wit. A motion being made to enact that all whisky should be kept in bond for ten years, so as to improve its quality, he expressed his cordial approval, in fact he even wished to strengthen the measure by moving the omission of the word "ten" and the substitution of the words "one hundred."

On another occasion a Local Option motion was violently opposed after dinner by a Member who seemed to have a good deal of liquor on board; Sir Wilfrid, who followed him, referred to "The Honourable Member, who is evidently very full of his subject." But the reputation of a wit has one drawback in the House, i.e. that nobody will ever take him seriously. As M.P. for West Cumberland he once had to speak on a Private Bill which interested his constituents; his voice had a curious sort of crack in it which seemed to add to the point of his jokes and every time he mentioned the word "Cockermouth," a town in his constituency, the House roared with laughter, as they were accustomed to regard every utterance of his as a witticism. The poor man was seriously annoyed and said: "Upon my word, I'll never be funny again . . . if I can help it." I met him at a party given by Lord Scarsdale (father of the late Lord Curzon), at Kedleston, in 1882. He and Lord Scarsdale were brothers-in-law, each having married a Miss Senhouse. One of the young men of the party was rather merry after dinner, although he could not have been said to be tipsy. Sir Wilfrid noticed this when we were in the billiard room, and drew my attention to him. "Now," said he, "I am going to give that young fellow a lesson," and forthwith bet him £1 that he would beat him at billiards. "Certainly," was the answer, "but why not make it £5?" Sir Wilfrid accepted, but was handsomely beaten, his opponent having had enough to give him confidence, but not enough to impair his aim. "I'd have beaten him all right," Sir Wilfrid confided to me in a melancholy tone, "if only he'd been a little less drunk or a little more."

On our way through Paris we met Lady Dorothy Nevill, a very old friend of my Father's and a delightful and witty old lady, whose book of Reminiscences was well-known. As a child I had stayed at her home at Dangstein near Petersfield, and her daughter and two sons were amongst my earliest playmates. Later she was often kind enough to invite me to lunch with her in Charles Street, and at these pleasant gatherings one met all sorts of celebrities, political, social, artistic, literary and theatrical. She dearly loved controversial sparring in which she herself took an active part and to promote this enjoyed getting people of the most contrary opinions to meet at her table. She was a strong Tory and used to attack me vigorously on political subjects, exhorting me meanwhile to "stand to my guns," which I did to the best of my ability. Her playful nickname for me was "Advocatus Diaboli," which I originally earned by a strenuous defence of my chief, Mr Gladstone.

During this Italian tour, when changing trains at Alessandria, in Lombardy, I ran across Miss Hatty Hosmer, a witty American and talented sculptress, and a great friend of Lady Marian Alford, who met her originally when she was studying at Rome under Milner Gibson. My aunt acquired his beautiful life-sized statue of Pandora, which she placed in the drawing-room at Ashridge. This statue was slightly tinted, in imitation of what is now known to have been the practice of the Ancient World. To my mind the experiment was an undoubted success and I wonder that it has not been more often repeated. Miss Hosmer also executed a large fountain adorned with cupids and dolphins which was erected in a spacious marble-paved conservatory at Alford House. This house was bought later on by Lord Ashton. Miss Hosmer invented a process for making imitation marble; the material thus produced was very successful as far as its appearance went but did not, I fancy, prove a commercial success. Towards the close of her life she was absorbed in futile attempts to produce a machine to create perpetual motion, an idea which proved a source of much anxiety and distress to her many friends as well as to herself.

At Voltri, to the west of Genoa, we were the guests of the Duke and Duchess of Galliera. She was a relation of Lady Acton, the first wife of my uncle, Lord Granville. The Duke had amassed an enormous fortune, but his son, the late Philippe Ferrari, for some reason best known to himself, refusing to inherit it, he left it after his widow's decease to the City of Genoa. The sum amounted to £800,000 and was employed in improving the harbour. My Father, on hearing from him of his intention, said that this was indeed a gift of princely magnificence; to which the Duke replied: "*Mais, mon cher, si je pouvais emporter ma fortune avec moi, certainement je le ferais, mais puisque je ne le peux pas et puisque Philippe n'en veut pas, que voulez-vous que j'en fasse?*" Delicacy, I suppose, prevented my Father's suggesting an alternative. The Duchess, in her turn, as her son would only consent to receive a certain proportion of her own large fortune, left a great part of it to the Empress Frederick, which was thought remarkable, seeing that the Duchess was a very devout Catholic. The son Philippe was a queer creature; in early youth he showed inclination towards Socialism, but later in life he developed strong Catholic tendencies. He had one of the finest collections of postage stamps in existence. During the siege of Paris, he lunched with my uncle at Bruton Street, and was asked by him what were his favourite studies; he answered: "Persian History." My uncle, being rather deaf, thought he said "personal," and warmly assented, saying that he quite agreed that that was far the most interesting kind of history. I could not help laughing as I knew that Persian history would be the last subject to which my uncle was likely to apply himself.

Genoa experienced the bounty of the Duchess as well as that of her husband, for she gave the city, during her lifetime, the magnificent Palazzo Brignole Salé, with its splendid picture gallery.

On passing Lake Trasimene on the railway between Florence and Perugia, I was struck by the facility with which one could follow Livy's account of the battle, all the different features of the ground being quite easy to identify.

The porter of our hotel at Naples amused us by his eccentric English, which he had learnt from an Irishman. He grew eloquent as to the respective merits of two rival cabmen, the hiring of one of whom he strongly deprecated. "No, no, him very bad man; him big humbug man; him big humbuggest man I know!" Then turning to the other candidate with an ineffable air of benediction: "The man in the orange trousers, he is the honest man!" This was uttered with deep solemnity and with the air of a Delphic oracle. I wonder how much this testimonial had cost the orange-trousered paragon.

At Rome I heard of a curious experience which had befallen the Austrian Ambassador two or three years before. He arrived at the Quirinal in a particularly smart brougham for an audience with the King, but was stopped at the gate by the porter, who had strict orders only to admit carriages and pairs. "Do you know who I am?" he cried in indignant tones. "Signore, I have not that honour." "I am Ambassador of the Emperor of Austria-Hungary to the King of Italy, and I demand admittance." "It grieves me much, Eccellenza, but I am forbidden to admit one-horse carriages; the Eccellenza must return with a carriage and pair." "I will return with a jackass!" shouted the Ambassador in a towering passion. "In that case," replied the porter with a low bow, "there will not be the slightest difficulty to Your Excellency's admission."

At Rome we dined with Minghetti and his wife; he either was at that time, or had previously been, Prime Minister and she had been a beauty in her day and was an old friend of my uncle's. Roast chicken being served, it was accompanied by a weird compound in which lumps of bread floated about in melted butter and thin white sauce. Madame Minghetti explained to us that she knew that English people always liked bread sauce with their chicken and that she had shown her cook how to make it, so we perforce had to help ourselves to the unappetizing mixture. "How you can like it," she added, "is a wonder, but English tastes, I know, are peculiar. You will find nobody else here will appreciate the sauce." And in effect everybody refused it after a brief glance of mingled wonder and dismay. Among the guests was a Signor Bonghi, then Minister of Finance, a very short man of ridiculous appearance who, in imitation of his King, wore a perfectly enormous pair of moustaches turned up at the end. I remember his cutting a queer figure when he entered the room, as he carried a huge tall hat, half as high as himself, under the crook of his arm. Just at the moment of madame's remark I saw Bonghi helping himself to the sauce, and drew her attention to the fact that at any rate one of her guests seemed to like it! "*Ah! ce Bonghi, il ne sait pas ce qu'il fait.*" An observation immediately confirmed by his spitting out the first mouthful on to his plate. Madame was not the least disconcerted and said: "*Vous voyez bien que j'ai raison! Mais*"—(as a happy after thought)—"*il en reste assez pour que vous en repreniez.*" So my Father and I had to dispose of a second help of this nauseous concoction. Verily the battlefield is not the only scene of deeds of heroism!

We dined one night at the English club where we met a Mr Tighe, who talked interestingly on archæology. He then told us of a murder which had been committed in his presence. He was standing in a café one afternoon, when a man touched his shoulder. Tighe made way for him and saw him draw a dagger and strike a man dead. The assassin then walked calmly away. Mr Tighe was so near that the blood spurted over his boots, whilst nobody took any notice. The murderer was eventually acquitted.

M. de Candia, better known as the great singer Mario, dined with us one night. He was a kindly looking old gentleman with a flowing white beard. His daughter was married to a brother of my tutor, Vaughan. When he and Grisi were singing together in London they were Lord Dudley's guests. He received Madame Grisi with the inquiry, "*Come sta?*" ("How goes it?" or "How are you?"), but on greeting Mario thought that he should change his form of salutation into what he supposed was the masculine gender, and startled him by saying, "*Come sto?*" which of course meant "How am I?" Mario squandered the greater part of the huge sums which he had received, in building a fantastically costly villa on the shores of one of the Italian lakes, with marble terraces and every sort of luxury, but had to abandon his scheme long before completion.

At Florence we saw a good deal of Sir James Lacaita, an old friend of my Father's, who was as delightful as he was distinguished. He was a Neapolitan and as a young man was a barrister of pronounced Liberal opinions. The Bourbon Government (stigmatized by Mr Gladstone as "the negation of God") threw him into prison in circumstances of peculiar injustice and severity, which being brought to Gladstone's notice started him on his campaign in 1851 against the Government of the Kingdom of Naples, which had much to do in unveiling its numerous iniquities and largely contributed to its eventual downfall. Lacaita made his way to England, having married a Scotch lady, Miss Carmichael. His fine scholarship and charming conversation, as well as the notoriety which he obtained through his persecution at Naples made him a general favourite. He himself has recorded how, when Garibaldi, after carrying everything before him in Sicily in his expedition of the "Thousand," was threatened by the possibility of the English fleet prohibiting his crossing the Straits of Messina into Italy, he (Sir James) was able to render signal service to the cause of Italian unity and freedom. Although very ill, on receipt of this news one night, he left his bed and hastened to Lord John Russell's house but was unable to see him. Lady John, however, received him, and his supplications so affected that generous-hearted lady that she promised to do her utmost to persuade her husband to order our fleet to give free passage to Garibaldi's forces. In this she succeeded and to this circumstance must be attributed the rapid succession of great and stirring events which overthrew the rule of the Bourbons in Naples and thus brought the cause of Italian unity a long way nearer realization. He received an English Knighthood and acted for some time as Librarian to the Duke of Devonshire; nobody could have been better qualified to care for the treasures contained in the Chatsworth Library. When we saw him at Florence he was a Senator of the Kingdom of Italy. To deep and extensive learning he added the zest and high spirits which made him so popular with young people.

When a young man he had been dining at a house in the hills above
Naples and was coming home down a steep path between high walls
which had a bad reputation as a resort of footpads. Suddenly he
saw a man lower down the slope slink into a dark opening in the wall.
Pulling out an enormous front door key, he advanced to the spot
where the man had disappeared and turned sharply round the corner,
where he saw the supposed malefactor ready, as he imagined, to spring
on him. Pointing his key at his breast, and hoping that the gleam of
the moonlight might give it the appearance of a pistol, he summoned
the miscreant to surrender. The man fell on his knees imploring
him to take all that he had but to spare his life. Closer inspection
proved him to be an intimate friend, who described how he had tried
to conceal himself from a cut-throat of repulsive aspect whom he had
seen descending the path, and who he felt convinced had marked him
down as his prey.

He also told me a story of a young acquaintance of his who occasionally visited a house in Naples which did not bear the best of reputations.
Although his friend was not easily shocked he was scandalized at
seeing a statuette of the Virgin in a niche above the front door with
a light burning before it; on remonstrating with the proprietress of
the house, she flung up her hands and exclaimed: *"Ma, senti, signorino,
senza l'aiuto della Santissima Madonna, qui si farebbe niente da niente."*
("But, listen, young gentleman, without the help of the most holy
Madonna we should do no business here at all.") Had she some dim
ancestral recollection of a goddess of a more ancient religion?

When out driving with a German acquaintance in the neighbourhood of Naples, his friend being in a hurry to get home, they were
stopped at the *Octroi*. The impatient German put his head out of
the window and shouted to the coachman to go on; intending to say
"Badate" he mispronounced it, as Teutons often do, as *"Patate."*
"Patate," exclaimed the *octroi* official, *"non si pagano. Passa."*
("Potatoes, there is no duty on them. You can pass!") Taine, the
French writer, was similarly misunderstood when, staying in Oxford,
he asked for potatoes which he pronounced "Pŏ-tă-toes," and was
served with—buttered toast!

Lacaita gave an instance of another misapprehension. He was
dining in a restaurant at Naples, when a young Englishman asked for
curaçao, pronouncing it "curasson," which he fancied was the correct
Italian. This, in Neapolitan dialect, resembles the way in which

"*Che ore sono?*" ("What o'clock is it?") is pronounced. The waiter therefore answered: "*Sono le sette, Signor*" ("It is seven o'clock, sir"), which the Englishman did not understand, thinking it the equivalent for "Anon, sir." The question and answer were repeated more than once with growing irritation on either side, until Lacaita thought it time to intervene with an explanation.

I met him at luncheon at my uncle's at 18 Carlton House Terrace when I was a young man, and we got talking about the Neapolitan dance called the "Tarantella," so named from the frenzied motions of the dancers giving them the appearance of having been bitten by the tarantula, a venomous spider. "Come up into the ball-room," cried the energetic old gentleman, "and I will show you how it is danced." A little later Lady Granville, coming into that big empty room, was much surprised to see me on one knee with Sir James hopping vigorously in a circle round me, both snapping our fingers and singing at the top of our voices.

He had two homes in Italy, a charming apartment in Florence and a country house in the south, near Taranto, called, from time immemorial, Leocaspide, which translated from the Greek is "White Shields." To show the tenacity of tenure in those out of the way parts he told me that a neighbour of his, a country gentleman, had the same name as that borne by a previous owner, who was a correspondent of Cicero's. The name of the property was also identical. Even if his genealogy could not be proved, this evidenced the long persistence of tradition. This instance quite eclipses one related to me by the late Lord Harcourt, when I was visiting his father, Sir William, at Malwood in the New Forest. Loulou Harcourt told me that a charcoal burner of the same name as the man who plied that trade and who brought William Rufus' body on his cart to Winchester Cathedral, was living in the same place as his remote predecessor.

Near Florence is the Villa Belvedere di Careggi, which once belonged to a Mr Sloane, who died in 1873. His history is curious. He had been tutor to a Russian family. He invested some £300 or £400 in some boracic mines, and in time amassed a fortune of £80,000 to £100,000 a year, a great part of which, with his wife's encouragement and assent, he left to his pupils' children, who, sad to say, treated his widow with base ingratitude.

At Pisa we saw George Howard (afterwards Lord Carlisle) with his family. He objected to the restoration by the Municipality of the lovely little Chapel of Santa Maria della Spina on the Arno, on the ground that the architects could not imagine nor the workmen execute the designs of the original builders.

When passing through Paris on our way home we dined at the Embassy with Lord Lyons and went on to see an excellent play, wonderfully well acted, called "Les Danicheff." The house was keenly interested and certain sentiments fairly brought it down, e.g. a serf on entering a monastery remarks: "*Le Czar est le maître de son peuple, mais Dieu est le maître du Czar*"; also, when describing an incident in a bear hunt, a French attaché, grasping a young Russian by the hand, exclaims: "*La bête fauve s'est ruée sur moi, mais il y avait tout près un Russe qui a tué cette bête fauve, Chaque fois qu'une bête fauve tombera sur un Français pour le déchirer, il y aura près de lui un Russe qui sauvera son ami!*" The spiciness of the allusion to Germany was vastly relished by the audience, who rose in a body and cheered continuously. How little did I anticipate that some forty years later this prediction would be verified, still less that we should share in the grim task of laying the wild beast low.

Before the curtain, Vaughan hurried away in search of an architect whom he was employing. He was trustee of some property, including a house, which on inspection was found to have a mighty crack running down all one side of it. This defect he determined should be repaired. In vain we told him that his architect would either be in bed or away from home, but nothing could keep him, and off he rushed on his quest. He had previously consulted my cousin, Willie Compton (the late Lord Northampton), then a Secretary at our Embassy, as to the choice of an architect, and Willie maliciously suggested Viollet le Duc.

On our return from the theatre to the Hôtel Westminster an amusing incident happened. A very grand gentleman was waiting for my Father, saluted him and said that he had heard that he wished to see him on business. My Father asked him to sit down saying that he would be back in a few minutes. Wishing to make myself agreeable, and jumping to the conclusion that he was Vaughan's architect, I stood bowing at the door and insisting on his going in first, which he at length did after many protestations. I then remarked: "*Vous avez déjà vu le petit Monsieur?*" (alluding to Vaughan). He looked surprised but answered: "*Certainement, Monsieur.*" I then said that he must take great pride in his profession, to which he assented with the greatest effusion. My Father then came in and said: "*Le chef de Monsieur le Duc de Galliera m'a dit que vous avez été cuisinier chez. . . .*"

Not long before, Willie was returning by a night train from Cannes. He shared an apartment with three young Frenchmen who objected to the slightest crack of window being open. He was a very good French scholar, but in order to obtain a little air feigned complete ignorance of the language and continued, in spite of all remonstrances, to open the window as often as they shut it. They discussed his manners and appearance with great freedom, lavishing a number of the most uncomplimentary epithets upon him, all of which he received with simulated incomprehension and the blandest of smiles. In the morning the Frenchmen engaged in an animated political discussion which greatly interested him, so, entirely forgetting his pretended ignorance of French, he joined in the conversation, speaking with the utmost fluency and correctness of idiom, in addition to which he knew far more about the subjects under discussion than his companions. "*Mais comment donc. Monsieur qui ne comprenait pas un mot de français! Ah! mon Dieu! qu'avons nous dit hier soir.*" It all ended as a capital joke and they parted the best of friends.

Our delightful tour ended at the same place as that whence it had begun, as my uncle met us at Dover and drove us to Walmer Castle.

CHAPTER VIII

OXFORD

On December 27, 1876, I paid a visit to Lord Ailesbury at Savernake for a shooting party, where I made friends with the son and daughter of General Jim Macdonald, she being a clever and pretty girl of about fifteen and he a year or two younger. He was at my tutor's at Eton and I won his goodwill by helping him with some Latin verses which he had to do for his holiday task, whilst she and I were husband and wife in some theatricals. She saucily made herself up as an imitation of Maria, Lady Ailesbury, with a big, curly auburn wig, and took her off to the life, imitating her deep voice and her habit of frequently introducing "My dear" into her conversation. Luckily the old lady was not at all offended and congratulated my "wife" on the success of her impersonation, with which she declared herself, and I believe quite sincerely, greatly amused.

I often took part in theatricals, which were the fashion in those days. At Ashridge in particular, they were frequent. A charming little theatre was situated quite at the end of the house in a place called the Orangery, fully equipped with all dramatic accessories, including machines for imitating thunder and lightning, hail and rain. Those talented artists, the Vokes family, from time to time helped our amateur efforts by their professional abilities, but this was before my day. After the signature of the Berlin Treaty a great charade was produced, the words of the acrostic being "Peace" and "Honor"— the latter having to be spelt in the American way so as to reduce it to the required five letters. My Father and Henry Cowper were among the few Liberals in the audience, and when the former remarked on the curious way in which the word "Honor" was spelt, without the "u," Henry answered: "My dear Freddy, that's all right, it is not at all the sort of honour that you and I are accustomed to; this is quite a different thing!" Just about this time Schliemann had discovered the tomb of Agamemnon at Mycenæ and for the third word of the acrostic my aunt and other ladies prepared, with the help of much gilt tinsel, a magnificent *simulacrum* of the corpse of the "King of men." I was entrusted with the rôle of the Professor, which I rendered with a pronounced German accent. Lymington (afterwards Lord Portsmouth) good-naturedly undertook to represent a Greek labourer at work on the excavations, although I suspect that he was not altogether pleased at being given so subordinate a part. I had to exhort him, under the highly improbable name of Pericles-Agesilaos, to moderate the energy with which he wielded his pick, the noise of which rendered everything else quite inaudible.

At the end of the acrostic Maisie Baring, Louisa Lady Ashburton's daughter, who afterwards married Willie Compton, looking, in the character of Fame, beautiful in classical white robes, placed laurel wreaths on the busts of Disraeli and Lord Salisbury, which were erected on tall gilt pedestals.

A propos of this, Lady Gwendolen Cecil, who has written such a masterly biography of her father, told me some little time afterwards that she was looking into a shop window where a poster was displayed with portraits of Disraeli and her father, above which the words "Peace with Honour" were inscribed. An old lady at her side gazed earnestly at them and inquired: "Could you kindly tell me, Miss, which is the criminal?" It should be explained that just then the trial of Charles Peace, the well-known murderer, was making a great sensation, and that the old lady imagined that one of the two portraits represented the assassin. I could not help saying to Lady Gwendolen: "I suppose you did not answer 'Both'?"

Had the statesmen of that day been gifted with foresight they would have refrained from minimizing the effect of Russia's hard-won victory and would have allowed the original treaty of San Stefano between Russia and Turkey to stand. Had they done so the Great War, even if not wholly averted, would have been much shorter and Germany would have probably been beaten within a year. The resultant gain to civilization and humanity would have been incalculable and the trials and sufferings of the world in general and more especially of this country proportionately diminished. This shortsighted policy of the Tory Government, although hailed at the time by their supporters as an evidence of transcendent sagacity, has since been proved by events to have been the fatal seed of persistent impoverishment, innumerable evils and widespread misery.

But to return to Ashridge theatricals. Another very successful production was *The Babes in the Wood*, the title parts being performed by Brownlow, who was 6 feet 4 inches high, and Miss Mary Boyle, an excessively clever and amusing elderly lady of diminutive stature and a great favourite at Ashridge. They were in the dress of the beginning of the last century, she with frilled pantalettes, he in buckled shoes, tight white trousers fitting closely to the leg and coming well above the waist, a light blue jacket with cut steel buttons, open at the throat and with ruffles at the neck and wrists, the whole surmounted by a blue cap with a huge yellow tassel. They entered at a run holding hands, she trundling a hoop and he with a toy tin trumpet, and were greeted with loud applause. Archie Stuart Wortley (the late Lord Stuart of Wortley's younger brother) and I were the villains, dressed in traditional costume and had a terrific fight according to the approved style of Adelphi melodrama, varied by bits of by-play. The Robin was performed by Captain Walter Carpenter (Lady Brownlow's brother), whose family nickname was Robin, and who played the part with a pantomime robin's head, a bright red waistcoat and light brown tights. When he had to cover the dead Babes with enormous leaves manufactured for the purpose, something went wrong with the string which worked his beak and his resultant awkwardness added much to the entertainment.

Miss Boyle knew Heine well in Paris during the last years of his life. When I questioned her about him, I could never get anything out of her, she only looked sad and said: "Poor Heine! Poor Heine!" She wrote excellent descriptive catalogues of the portraits in the picture galleries of Wrest, Longleat and Marston, for Lord Cowper, Lord Bath and her kinsman Lord Cork respectively. She used to say that when all trades failed she would set up as a professional interpreter of Lady Marian Alford's hand-writing, which was indeed hard to decipher. Her features were very plain, and in consequence, as a child, I disliked being kissed by her. On one occasion I told my scandalized nurse: "Miss Boyle did give me a kiss to-day but I spitted it out!" Again on being reproached for my reluctance in returning her embraces, I tried to excuse myself in what seemed to me the most delicate way: "Different people has different tastes—my taste not for kissing Miss Boyle."

Lady Cowper gave a series of historical tableaux at Wrest, their place in Bedfordshire. Lord Houghton, who was one of the guests, pleaded to be allowed to represent Milton dictating his poetry to his wo daughters, and when the objection was raised that there was no costume for him, solved it naïvely enough by saying: "Oh! I have brought it down with me." Lady Cowper and, I think, Lady De Vesci, took the daughters' parts, and very charming they both looked, but the dramatic effect of the tableau was rather marred, as when Houghton (after posing in an attitude of fitting solemnity) opened his lips to dictate his immortal verse, his false teeth fell with a clatter on the stage, necessitating a hasty curtain.

In September 1876 I went for a few weeks for a final polish up before going in for my Matriculation Examination for Balliol, to Mr Alexander Bell. I was his first pupil and was joined by Leonard Shoobridge, with whom I here laid the foundation of a life-long friendship. Very soon after I went up he prepared pupils for the University at Limpsfield, near my distant cousin, Granville Leveson Gower, at Titsey Place.

On one or two occasions Shoobridge and I, when we were at Oxford, spent a week or two with Bell at Limpsfield during vacation to put in a bit of reading. I quote from a letter to Shoobridge written from Hawarden Castle on December 30, 1877, where, with my Father, I was staying with Mr Gladstone and when I was apparently prevented from participating in one of those studious visits.

"It is certainly a great disappointment not to be able to be at Bell's, but still I shall have a melancholy satisfaction on cold and wintry mornings (or rather nights), when I awake and think of a friend having to get up by candle-light for a bath tempered with but a small modicum of tepid water, followed by a plain and wholesome breakfast and chilling grind ($K\rho\nu\epsilon\rho o\acute{\iota}o$ $\gamma o o\acute{\iota}o$)[1]; and then I shall turn over and think, 'I shan't have to get up for another two hours, and when I *do* get up, I shall have a *warm* bath, and then sausages and omelette for breakfast, then a big shoot, then Macaulay" (I was reading Trevelyan's delightful *Life and Letters* of his Uncle), "dressing-gown and slippers and hot tub for feet; then scrumptious dinner with pretty girl to take in; then gamble at cards, then smoke cigar and B. and S. and then bed! Yoicks!"

I may add that I did not contemplate carrying out this disgracefully luxurious programme at Hawarden but at some less austere country house to which I was going later on.

[1] Of chilling woe.

My letter continues: "The re-assembling of Parliament has made my Father excessively sore at having his holidays cut short, which is amusing when you consider his righteous indignation at the 'undue length of Oxford vacations!'"

Bell's exaggerated scrupulousness got him into difficulties and injured his prospects; for instance, he refused to continue to coach the son of Dr Warre, then Head Master of Eton, as he had caught him smoking a cigarette, which was against his rules, a case in which some much milder penalty would clearly have been appropriate. But he was a kindly man who inspired one with a real affection and his wife, although no beauty, was one of the merriest of little souls. Before I went to Bell's my Father kindly offered to present me with a dressing-gown. The salesman displayed a most gorgeous robe of purple with a scarlet lining, saying: "This is the colour which His Grace the Archbishop of Canterbury always chooses for his dressing-gowns!" This decided me and I subsequently felt a thrill of pride and joy when sitting garbed in this archiepiscopal raiment. Bell put me through my paces, including the first two books of Euclid, my weakest spot, but I had been so assiduously drilled in it that for the moment I was letter perfect, so he gave me no further work on that and I was only too glad to be rid of it to think of rubbing up that subject just before the examination. The result was that in a month's time I had forgotten most of it and very nearly got ploughed in consequence, in spite of which I somehow managed to come out first out of the twelve who passed into the College. Whilst I was with Bell I amused myself by sailing a centre-board on the Upper River up to Godstow, playing racquets with him and, chiefly, by learning the noble game of real tennis under the tuition of old Tompkins, the professional. It was a capital opportunity, as being still vacation I practically had the court to myself. Tompkins was a marvel. In spite of his figure resembling a round table he got about the court with the greatest ease, and after delivering a stroke would waddle across to the spot to which he seemed to know that his adversary must infallibly return the ball. I have known him beat quite a fair player, when using a soda-water bottle instead of a racquet. I played tennis assiduously all the time that I was at Oxford, giving up racquets after my first term, as I found that it was bad for my tennis stroke. Tennis is a splendid game, as it can be played in all weathers, and is particularly suitable for reading men, as it gives an hour and a half's hard exercise without any subsequent lassitude. When I was in Paris in 1867, I saw Barre play; he was in those days the greatest professional exponent of the game. There is a portrait of him in the "dedans" of the Tennis Court at Lords.

My rooms at Balliol were on the ground floor of a new building called "The Cottage," which only consisted of four sets of rooms, and was situated in the north-east corner of the Garden Quad, close to Trinity. They had only just been finished, and were built at the same time as the ugly new Hall, which adjoined them. This was an advantage in one way as I was their first occupant and they were consequently quite fresh and clean, whilst I could choose my own furniture, which I did with a good deal of care, instead of having to take over whatever had been left by a predecessor. A drawback, on the other hand, was that the rooms had not been allowed time to get properly dry, so that the damp injured some good books and prints which I had brought with me. However, these, with some china, helped to make my quarters look comfortable, whilst in the summer term I always had window boxes full of good flowers. One other disadvantage to my rooms, being, as I said, on the ground floor, was that one's friends used to engage one in conversation through the open window, especially in the summer term, which interrupted one's reading so much that I did most of this in my friend Shoobridge's room, which was at the top of the staircase just west of the Master's Lodge and looked into the Broad. When furnishing my sitting-room one of the walls presented some difficulty, as it was built in a curve. I solved this problem by having a top of corresponding shape and covered with green velvet fitted above my bookcase on that side of the room; this not only looked well but prevented things slipping off and getting irretrievably lost at the back of the bookcase. On revisiting my rooms more than forty years after leaving them, I was pleased to see the top of the bookcase still in existence, although naturally rather the worse for wear.

As I have said, the new Hall was only approaching completion at the beginning of the Michaelmas Term of 1876. A long ladder was left standing reaching right up to the roof. Malcolm Macmillan accepted a challenge to climb it. He was of stout build, and, to our delight, in his descent a projecting nail tore his trousers from Dan even to Beersheba, so that one trouser leg flapped to and fro like a sail torn from the yard arm. The exposure of so large a surface of his portly figure in such a conspicuous position was naturally a source of general jubilation. In later years he was lost on Mount Olympus in the Troad, during an ascent made with his old friend, Arthur Hardinge from whom he got momentarily separated. His body was never found, and the secret of this tragic mystery was never solved.

I may here give extracts from letters written by me to my aunt the late Lady Alwyne Compton.

"Balliol,
"January 31, 1877.

"At Longleat we had a pleasant and very learned party, including Mr Gladstone, Canon Liddon and Professor Freeman.

"Now I have got an interesting bit of news for you! About a week ago the following placard was posted about Oxford:

"Mr Charles Bradlaugh
Will deliver a Lecture at the Town Hall
on Wednesday evening, January 24
on
Taxation. Its Origin
Who ought to bear it and who do bear it.

"To the Town Hall I went accordingly, with a chosen band of friends; ten of us took up a stand near the door; ten more on a certain elevated gallery, and about seventeen in front and on the sides of the platform.

"He delivered a most violent address, but we were quite quiet until he attacked pensions granted for public services to the nation. Here we protested, and when he cried, 'Ought these names to remain on the pension list,' alluding to the descendants of the Duke of Marlborough, the audience shouted 'No,' and we, by way of a little variety, cried 'Yes.' A townsman here struck one of our people, who knocked him down and general uproar and the prospect of a free fight prevailed. Order, however, was restored, and, with the exception of Bradlaugh's calling one of us a liar and another a blackguard, the lecture ended quietly enough."

A liberal dispensation at Balliol allowed those who chose to attend Roll Call in the porter's lodge instead of attending early Chapel. A girl who was staying at the Master's when the weather was unusually hot saw a number of men hurrying across the Quad early in the morning, muffled up to the chin in thick ulsters. At breakfast she asked the Master why they wore such unseasonable costume: "Pressure of time and not of climate," he chirruped out.

The anecdotes of Jowett are so many and have appeared so often that one feels that to record any is something of a risk. But in spite of this I cannot help relating a few, in the hope that they may be new to my readers, or, if not, that they will skip them and forgive me. Some may have already been published, but if so, I am not conscious of the fact. No doubt his appearance, manner and voice added much to the point of his observations. He has been not inaptly described as a "discontented elderly cherub," and his smooth, round features, his snow-white hair, and his expression in which amusement and criticism, benevolence and thoughtfulness were strangely blended, together with his plump figure and squeaky voice, gave some justification for the epigram.

When Jowett was made Regius Professor of Greek, some of his theological opponents in the University hoped that he would be unable to accept the post, as it was necessary for him to sign the Thirty-Nine Articles. He was accordingly asked, before his induction, whether he had any difficulty in doing so, and to his adversaries' secret delight he confessed that he had. On being pressed to particularize the nature of his difficulties he blinked and, looking round, said: "I don't see any pen." At least such is the story which I have often heard though I cannot vouch for its exactitude.

The Master's butler, Knight, occasionally showed visitors round the College. There is a legend that sometimes he would point out the Master's Lodge: "That's the Master's Lodge and"—throwing a pebble against his library window—"that's him!" when he looked out to see what was the matter. I must admit that I never saw Knight do this or heard of anybody who actually did so, but his manner with Jowett was so free and easy that the story is not altogether improbable, although it is more likely that it occasioned its invention. Jowett paid for the education of his son, whom he afterwards employed as a Private Secretary.

The following lines might have been added to The Masque of Balliol:

> "I am Dr Jowett's butler,
> Where could you find any subtler.
> Want to see the Master's phiz?
> Chuck a pebble. There he is!"

He was taking one of his formidable walks with an undergraduate, on which occasions the necessity of breaking through the defences of the Master's stubborn silence and the fear of thereby incurring a withering rebuke strove for mastery in the victim's breast, and his companion said, as they passed Trinity gateway: "It is curious, Master, that there should be four statues and not three over the gateway of Trinity." "Not at all," snapped Jowett, "three persons and one God."

Two Siamese princes, undergoing a course of tuition at Balliol, were unlucky enough to be proctorized when taking the air in the Parks arm in arm with two young women on a summer's night. The proctor, in view of their rank and nationality, thought it better to report the matter to the Master and to leave it in his hands. He asked what they had to say for themselves; they said that being newly arrived at Oxford they had lost their way in the Parks and had been fortunate enough to meet these ladies who had very kindly offered to put them on their way home. As to their being found walking arm in arm, this was due to the night being so dark that their companions were afraid that unless carefully guided they might lose their way again. Jowett blinked at them and then exclaimed: "Don't let it happen again: go away, disingenuous and lascivious Orientals!"

He always wore evening dress; although there is a legend that before one Long Vacation a friend represented to him that this was scarcely the costume for the hills and moors of the Highlands, as he was going on a round of visits in Scotland. He accordingly asked his tailor to show him some suitable patterns and chose a quiet grey tweed. On being asked how he wished it cut, he answered: "The same as usual." This suit of grey tweed cut like evening clothes would indeed be a rarity deserving a place in a sartorial museum, for it must surely be unique.

Sir Robert Morier, when Ambassador at St Petersburg, came to see his son at Balliol. He himself had been there and was an old friend of the Master, with whom he was staying. After dinner when the ladies had withdrawn, Morier embarked on a series of stories each more highly spiced than the last. The Master grew uneasy as several undergraduates were his guests. At last after some particularly purple specimen from Sir Robert's répertoire, he squeaked out "Shall we continue this conversation in the drawing-room, Morier?"

and gave the signal for a move. Morier was once my fellow guest at the Brownlows', who had taken Lord Kenmare's beautiful house above the Lake of Killarney, together with the adjoining shooting of Herbert of Muckross, where incidentally I was so lucky as to get a fine stag. Some of us went out fishing one day, and met the older members of the house-party for a tea picnic at a summer-house in the woods. Bertram Talbot slipped when crossing some stepping-stones over a stream and dropped a string of fine trout which he was carrying on a hazel crook. From Morier's despair you would have thought that he had lost the whole of his fortune. "What! *all* gone! Every one of them! What a catastrophe!"

Morier's son fell in love with a married Russian lady of high degree and told her that he would shoot himself if she did not favour his suit. Her answer was, in effect: "Shoot away!" He did so, but so clumsily that he wounded himself in that part that he sat upon. He left St Petersburg.

Miss Jex Blake, sister of the Head Master of Rugby, a very voluble lady, was dining at Balliol and monopolized the conversation, much to Jowett's displeasure. When the ladies had retired he said: "I know that *lex* is the Latin for 'law,' can anyone tell me what is the English for 'jex'?"

Turgénieff, a big man rather like Anthony Trollope, whom I have already described, was asked by the Master at his own table what he thought of Dostoieffsky: "He is no good; all schlimm-schlamm and vish-vash, what you call Brod Church." The Master said nothing but, blinking a good deal, slowly surveyed his guests in turn. I think he wished to test our power of self-control.

A man of the name of Vassall, who afterwards became a Catholic, set up a private oratory in his rooms. This came to Jowett's ears, who sent for him and told him that he must do away with it. "But surely, sir," Vassall remonstrated, "you cannot wish to prevent me from praying in my own rooms?" "You can pray there as much as you like, Mr Vassall, but I am not going to have one of the rooms in the College made the subject of ridicule!" Vassall was an excitable little man, and speaking once at the Union waved his arms about so vigorously that the streamers of his gown flapped about him. He was followed by A. A. Baumann, also a Balliol man and later Conservative Member for a South London constituency. With a single eyeglass in his eye, he gazed at Vassall for a moment and thus began his reply:

> "Birdie, wait a little longer
> Till your little wings are stronger."

This so amused the house that further confutation seemed almost superfluous.

Another undergraduate of a different type thought to give himself importance and perhaps to arouse Jowett's interest by calling on him to submit certain religious doubts with which he was troubled. The Master only said: "Mr ——, you will find God within two days or go down for the rest of the term." This may seem to some, to use a favourite phrase of his own, "frivolous and flippant," but it was not so; he knew his man and knew how to talk to him.

Like the other Dons, the Master used to hear some of us read our weekly essay. He usually had three of us up for that purpose, and hospitably asked us in to dessert before indulging in the "feast of reason." First walnuts and wine and then the essays. He disliked "purple patches" and generally criticized what we thought were our happiest efforts. I remember one Scotsman declaiming: "And what a magneeficent poseetion was this that was occupied by the gr-r-rand old Greek philosophers, swinging for ever on a pendulum between the opposite poles of Being and Not-Being!" The Master sniffed: "Not at all a magnificent position, Mr. ——: very uncomfortable, I should think."

He sometimes dozed off during our essays, especially in winter when sitting before the dining-room fire. This happened during one of my performances, but he woke up with a start when I ended. "Your essay did not begin so badly, Mr Leveson Gower, but towards the end it got very vague, very vague indeed!" I wondered whether this may not have been a humorous way of excusing his little lapse. The same thing happened to Jules Clarétie, to whom a young aspirant was reading his five-act tragedy. The young man noticed this with annoyance but read bravely on. At the end Clarétie made certain criticisms and generally, although courteously, indicated that his opinion of the tragedy was not high. *"Mais, cher maître, vous vous êtes endormi pendant ma lecture, comment juger de ma pièce, quand vous n'en avez entendu qu'une partie?"* *"Eh! mon cher, le sommeil est aussi une opinion!"*[1]

[1] "But, cher Maître, you fell asleep whilst I was reading, how can you judge my play when you only heard a part of it?" "Well, my dear fellow, sleep is also a criticism."

The Master had a curious trick, when bored or displeased with an essay. He would look out of the window, stand with his hands behind his back and rub one calf with the heel of the boot on the other leg. This was an infallible storm signal.

One glorious summer night Matthew Arnold, a frequent guest of the Master, was looking out on to the moonlit quad and descanting in impassioned style on the beauties of the scene to a bevy of admiring ladies. The Master, getting more and more impatient, sank ever deeper into his arm-chair, and at last protested: "My dear Mat, you get more and more like Macaulay every year—without his memory."

When the Master preached Chapel was always crowded. On one of these occasions Matthew Arnold and my Father came in late and could only find accommodation on the steps in front of the communion table, which were low. My Father was rather weak in the knees, and remained seated when it was customary for the congregation to rise. Mat treated him afterwards to a taste of his irony. "I admired you so much, Mr Leveson. I thought it showed such independence and strength of character. In fact I should have liked to have imitated you myself, but, perhaps because I am a clergyman's son, I thought that I ought to pay a certain observance to the decencies of public worship."

I took it as a compliment that the Master introduced into one of his sermons a quotation from Wordsworth's "Happy Warrior," which I had inserted into an essay read to him a few days before. The words were:

> "Who in the heat of conflict keeps the law
> In calmness made and sees what he foresaw."

Matthew Arnold's son, Dick, was at Balliol with me. He was very good at football but this was his chief distinction; indeed it is rumoured that his getting into the College at all was due to his being his father's son. Once he was away for a night without leave, one of the mortal sins in the College code, and gave as his excuse that he had been to his great-aunt's (or some such fictitious relative's) funeral. "That won't do, Mr Arnold," snapped the Master. "It's no good trying to deceive me; I know all your family much better than you do!"

I myself experienced the difficulty of getting leave for a night out, which I cannot illustrate better than by quoting from a letter of my own, dated Friday, November 23, 1877:

"On Wednesday night a very pressing telegram arrived from Lady Brownlow, urging me to come down last Thursday for a ball at Ashridge, with shooting afterwards to-day, with two friends.

"What could be more tempting, more delightful! I hesitated a moment. There were Mr Gladstone's 'three courses' open to me:

"(1) To pretend to get drunk, smash some lamps in the Quad and so get sent down.

"(2) To square the porter and my scout, send in an 'aeger' to Dons whose lectures I attended, and make a clean bolt for a couple of nights.

"(3) To appeal to the Master's sense of justice and mercy and crave leave for a couple of days, for change of air and relaxation.

The first course was rejected at once as undignified; the second as dangerous; the third remained. I spoke to my tutor, who approved. I went to the Master who said *he* disapproved, saying that it was against College rules, etc. etc.; and when I urged my tutor's views he cut up rough and wished me 'A very good morning!' I wished that I'd had the nerve to adopt course No. (2)."

CHAPTER IX

WITH JOWETT AT WEST MALVERN

ALTHOUGH not wealthy, Jowett was most generous in helping poor undergraduates and his benefactions were far more numerous than was supposed as, out of delicacy for the recipent's feelings, they were given in such a way as precluded their being generally known. He took a little villa, called Ashfield House, at West Malvern, on the western slopes of those beautiful hills, where during the vacations he frequently entertained reading-parties. He twice did me the honour of including me, and when my Father wished to make some pecuniary acknowledgment, refused on the ground that to some of the undergraduates it was a material advantage to receive board and tuition *gratis* for six or seven weeks, and that it would be invidious to accept money from some and not from others; he added that he valued these parties as furnishing an opportunity of wider mutual acquaintance among men of different sets. To each he gave tuition for one hour daily, no slight sacrifice when it is remembered that at the time he was engaged upon important and exacting literary work of his own. I may perhaps be allowed to give extracts from letters written during the Long Vacation of 1878, the first being written to Shoobridge and the others to a lady.

> "Ashfield House,
> "('Maison Jowl')
> "West Malvern,
> "August 11, 1878.

"DEAR ⟨shoe sketch⟩

"I have got whole cartloads of anecdotes only if I once began I know I should never stop. Jowl himself is in high health and spirits and makes himself extremely agreeable. I am now getting accustomed to the pauses. I am getting beastly bored though, because there is nothing at all to do, except go for walks. I came here on the 1st, and stay till the 5th of next month ($\check{o}\iota\mu o\iota\ \delta\nu\sigma\tau a\lambda a\varsigma$!)[1]

[1] Alas! Unhappy me!

We breakfast at 9, after very little warm water provided for morning ablutions, then Jowl if he wants the Unkempt (another under-graduate not at all a friend of mine) and myself both to come, says, 'Let's go for a walk!' If he wants a solitary confab with the Unkempt he chirps out, 'Let's go and talk shop!' in which case I gracefully retire. Grind from 10.15 to 1.45 at Aristotle's Ethics; they're the very devil and give one awful headaches. I have to translate about ten pages a day for Jowl and read the translation to him in the evening, when I have to ask him questions, and then he asks me questions which generally stump me awfully. Next I have to read him some piffle I have to write every day; as for instance, 'The Origin of our Moral Ideas,' and such-like stuff; upon which he makes caustic remarks. We lunch in a little back room at 1.45, minus Jowl; then smoke, read the paper and grind again till 5, when we dine (5 if you please!!) at 6.30 take a walk which varies in length from an hour to two and a half; tea at about 9; grind till 11 and so to bed. It is the very devil. And the Unkempt won't utter at meals, whilst Forbes prefaces all his remarks with 'O, I s—s—say, Master, what do you think about . . . etc.?' So dull!"

> "Ashfield House,
> "West Malvern, August 4, 1878.

. . . "The Master is good-humoured and comes out with very good stories about one per hour; but oh! such terrible pauses and silences between! I too am becoming quite taciturn and sit for ten minutes without uttering. You would scarcely know me, but it really is impossible to maintain a conversation against three silent people single handed."

I may break in upon this letter to illustrate to what hard conver-sational shifts we were put owing to the silent character of three of our party and to the uneventfulness of our existence. The Master offered a prize of half a crown to anybody who would tell a perfectly new and amusing story. Whilst out for a walk, without thinking of this "prize," I told him a Spanish story. The tale runs that a cheeky young cockerel going off to "see the world," disregarded his mother's advice to be kind and considerate to all whom he met. He accord-ingly spurned requests of assistance made to him by the wind, the fire, the water and the sun, and finally insulted St Peter by crowing loudly as he passed him outside his church. Each element then takes its revenge upon him, and he is finally caught by St Peter in a woe-begone condition and stuck at the top of the weather-vane, where he is for evermore blown about by the wind, broiled by the sun and drenched with rain. At dinner the Master reproduced this tale and, to my astonishment, asked us whether he had not earned his own half-crown. The others agreed, whereupon he handed it to me.

"I took 'little Benjamin, our ruler,' to church this morning, I think he felt bound to go to keep up his character in the neighbour-hood. He appeared in his old swallow tail, with a greyish waistcoat and a tie like a German waiter's. I am sorry to say that he only scoffed and jibed at services and sermons in general and this service and sermon in particular, so I fear it did not do the old gentleman much good. A really fair sermon was preached, nothing out of the way, but still useful and instructive enough. 'I do dislike hearing those platitudes,' he said, 'I have heard those arguments so often before that when one of those men begins on those lines I know what he is going to say to a syllable. I know every argument he is going to dwell upon, and I groan inwardly and calculate the exact time it will take the individual to lead his fine arguments up to—as he thinks—a satisfactory and convincing conclusion.' Afterwards he thought a little and said, 'Oh! he does look so pleased with himself and so convinced that he is quite right! How I should like to get up and prove to him how far he is all wrong!' It would no doubt be an interesting experience."

This again from another letter from the same place and dated August 21, 1878.

"I was amused at your letter; so cross and dissatisfied and wanting me to go away. You talk as if it were merely a question of telling the Master that I have had enough of it, packing up and going off to the station. I should like to do nothing better, but it is out of the question. I am just like a bull with a ring in his nose and have to let the Master pull me about precisely as he likes. The other day I told him I was going away on the 29th, to assist at the coming of age of an Oxford friend, Tom Legh" (now Lord Newton). "His only remark was, 'No, I am not going till the 5th and you must stay till then.' Again, I told him I was going to spend next Saturday to Monday at Stanway, Lord Elcho's, about 16 miles from here. 'No,' he said, 'it will interfere with your work. You must not go. You must go with me the Saturday after.' What are you to do with such a man! I am not a free agent, and the only remedy for this blackest of despotisms would be a revolution which scarcely '*vaudrait la chandelle*' one would have to pay during the next two years under him at Ball. Coll. After all one gets through a lot of reading, more than one would at home, and, if I were not so indescribably bored with my two other companions, I should like it very much. However, Swinburne, the great poet, is coming to-day, an event I look forward to with much relief, as he cannot fail to be amusing. He will also probably get drunk, which will be another source of excitement; possibly he may attack the Master, which would be prime!"

(Alas, he never came!)

"It is instructive to see him saying grace at dinner; he scrambles over it in a most unceremonious way.

"Joking apart though, you don't know what a help he is to one in reading hard bits of Aristotle; he is most awfully good at explaining difficult questions and passages.

"The other day he remarked that 'the popular paganism stood in the same relation to the great philosophers of Greece, as popular Christianity does to the superior minds of the present day.'

"There are two very nice-looking girls living near, looking really jolly besides being pretty, whom I should like to know; but we don't know anybody here although there are heaps of pleasant people in the neighbourhood: quite a case of 'Water, water everywhere, and not a drop to drink.' The tiresome old gentleman won't know anybody. The other day he asked me if 'I did not think it much pleasanter to be all alone like this, than continually having a lot of people you had to go to see and who were always coming to see you?' I suppose that I ought to have acquiesced, but I said, 'No, I didn't think it was,' which took him rather aback.

"These girls look as if they would play lawn tennis and talk and all that sort of thing. The other day I was coming out of church immediately behind them with the Master. In the porch one said to the other, 'Did you see the old gentleman in the pew to our right, Alice? That was Dr Jowett, you know. I wonder what—'

suddenly she turned round and caught sight of me; neither of us could help smiling."

A passage here follows describing an incident at a masked ball at Frances Lady Waldegrave's at Strawberry Hill, the fantastic building erected at Twickenham by Horace Walpole. This ball was given before I had gone to West Malvern. I stopped at the Star and Garter at Richmond for the night, together with my cousin, FitzRoy Stewart, who was at University College. He once told us at Oxford that his branch of the family was the elder branch of the Stuarts, and added quite gravely, "But we lay no claim to the Crown," an utterance which earned him the nickname of "H.R.H." My great-grandmother, the first Lady Stafford, was a Stewart.

It was a most successful affair, and the large gardens were beautifully illuminated. I will let my own letter describe my personal experiences.

"The 'masker,' as we call it in our Balliol slang, was great fun. I was bullied by three masks and bullied two, whilst with two others I was on terms of friendly neutrality. One girl let me in tremendously. I made certain it was Miss Charteris, whom I knew pretty well." (She was the late Lord Wemyss' sister, and was the present Lord Midleton's first wife.) "I went and talked to her as such, she saw whom I was taking her for and put on her voice. I believe I said most fearful things. My suspicions were aroused by a mistake which she made. I said that I could not use a pencil she (Miss Charteris) had given me. 'Oh!' she said, 'that's all very well, a nice way of concealing that you have either lost it or cut it all away!' Now the pencil given me by Miss Charteris was a little silver one, so I could not have 'cut it all away.' I afterwards got a peep when she was drinking at supper, saw under her mask and discovered not only that it was not Miss C., but somebody I did not even know, although I knew who she was. For the moment I felt horribly out of it, but pretending not to have recognised her and that I was still under the delusion, mimicked all her relations, until she could stand it no longer, began to laugh and confessed her deception."

Lady Waldegrave was a daughter of Braham, the well-known singer, and was a charming hostess and the best natured of women.

She was married three times, her last husband being Mr Chichester Fortescue, afterwards created Lord Carlingford. When he was Chief Secretary to the Lord Lieutenant of Ireland, they went to a Dublin theatre, and an impudent gallery boy called out to her by name and asked which of her three husbands she liked the best. Not a whit abashed and with admirable *aplomb* she answered: "Why, the Irish one, of course!" an answer which was naturally greeted with rapturous applause.

Two rival wits, Abraham Hayward and Bernal Osborne, were guests together at Strawberry Hill. Hayward had prepared notes of some amusing impromptus, with which he proposed to enliven the dinner, but unluckily left them in the gallery where they were found by Osborne, who learnt them by heart and at dinner fired them off in rapid succession, to Hayward's unspeakable disgust. Hayward was unkindly described by Disraeli as "that louse of literature," as he was only celebrated as a critic without having any original work to his credit. He was at Holmbury at the same time as Count de Bylandt, the Dutch Minister, and his wife, a Russian by birth. Of this fact Hayward was ignorant, as he showed by quoting with an execrable French accent, the proverb "*Si vous grattez le Rousse vous trouvez le Tartare.*" Madame de Bylandt, a hot-tempered woman, who like many of her compatriots had no love for the Jewish race, to which, by his features as well as by his first name, Hayward evidently belonged, at once retorted: "*Oui, et si vous grattez le malappris vous trouvez le Juif.*" It took some little diplomacy to restore a semblance of harmony. Bernal Osborne, like some other wits, was an overbearing fellow. At a party of Lord and Lady Amherst's at Linton, near Maidstone, I had picked a beautiful rose and was going to offer it to a lady. Osborne blustered up and said: "Here! give me that rose; I will give it to Mrs ——" I was quite a young fellow, but was determined not to hand it over. The situation was ended by the lady herself, who had watched the scene from a little way off. She came up to me and said: "Thank you very much, as the kind thought to give it me was yours, I had rather have it from you."

A ludicrous incident happened at Linton during a party in the middle of August. The Amhersts wanted to let the place, and old Baroness Burdett Coutts and her young husband came down to see whether it would suit them. Lady Amherst took the Baroness upstairs, and he was left for a short time with the house-party. He was not exactly a general favourite and none of us knew him personally although of course we knew all about him. He tried to break an awkward pause, not perhaps in quite the happiest manner. "I don't know whether any of you have yet had the opportunity of tasting grouse this year; the Baroness and I find them deficient in flavour."

At one of the Strawberry Hill Saturday to Monday parties, I stole off into a retired part of the garden during a quiet interval to get on with my Aristotle. My Father, discovering me, told me to put it away at once, as if I were found reading it people would call me a prig. I readily obeyed, and presently started a game of hide and seek with Candida, Lady William Hay, a pretty young bride of about my age whose husband (afterwards Lord Tweeddale) was much older than herself. This occupation was also discountenanced by my Father, whom I asked in despair what I was to do if I were neither allowed to work nor to play. The fact was that he never could understand that it was impossible to take fairly high honours (which he expected me to do) without putting in a certain amount of hard work. Another instance of this took place at Holmbury. Mr Gladstone was staying there and said that he was going to write in the library. I was reading for Greats and asked whether it would disturb him if I remained, which he readily permitted. I had been working for about three hours when my Father peeped in and challenged me to a game of billiards, a challenge which I willingly accepted. Mr G. afterwards gave him a tremendous dressing down for interrupting me in my work. "But he had been reading quite a long time, I thought it time for him to have a rest." "A long time!" retorted Mr G., himself a prodigious worker. "Three hours! You call that a long time! Why! he was just getting into his stride! If he don't get a First it will be your fault and not his!" I am afraid that I did not soothe my Father's feelings by telling him later on that I did not think that he was to blame, as of course a Christ Church passman could not fairly be expected to realize what hard reading meant.

To return to West Malvern.

During a walk, when several miles from home, I was badly bitten in the leg by a large chow. He came up behind me and smelt my leg, which I had hitherto found in my commerce with strange dog, a proceeding which established my respectability. When he bit me in the calf I caught him a heavy blow with my stick and got three successive shots home with flints from a heap hard by. He fled yelping, and two maids, in whose charge he was supposed to be, asked indignantly how I could be "so crool to a pore dumb animal." I answered: "He may be dumb but he knows how to open his mouth." It was some time before I could apply caustic, and my friends pretended to be afraid that I should develop hydrophobia.

After this visit I went on to Lord Somers', at Eastnor Castle, near Ledbury, which was in the neighbourhood. There we shot and skated and were all charmed by the singing of Lord Somers' niece, Miss Agnes Somers Cocks, now Mrs Arkwright, whose voice was as beautiful as herself, and more it would be impossible to say. She had a great success with a French comic song called "*Les Godillots*," the name for the ugly and uncomfortable shoes then in use in the French Army. She sang it very well, but it was greeted with such shouts of laughter and applause that she rightly surmised that this was not only due to her own admirable rendering, and out of the corner of her eye she saw Albert Grey (afterwards Lord Grey) and myself beating time with two pairs of slippers behind her back. Grey was well-known for having received an equal number of votes with Edward Ridley, who was afterwards made a Judge, in a hard fought contest in Northumberland, the seat falling to Ridley by the Sheriff's casting vote. Grey was also the founder of the Committee called by his name which was originated to promote the Liberal cause in the General Election of 1880, and which afterwards developed into the Eighty Club, which still flourishes, and of which I was one of the early members. His Liberalism was not, however, robust, and together with some thirty other Whigs, he fell away from the party at the vote of want of confidence which turned the Conservative Government out at the beginning of the Session of 1886, after the General Election of 1885 had returned a Liberal majority. This vote of want of confidence took the shape of a motion in favour of Mr Jesse Collings' policy of agricultural reform, popularly known as that of "Three Acres and a Cow." This was before their Home Rule Bill brought the short-lived Liberal Government to an end, and Grey and Jesse Collings found themselves united in opposition. I remember Grey canvassing me in the lobby to vote against my party on the Collings motion and my answering that it was hardly likely that I should stultify myself by turning my coat on the very first vote that I recorded. I also recall Sir William Harcourt humorously complaining that he thought it very hard that Savile Crossley (afterwards Lord

Somerleyton) should vote against his party on this occasion, "after I went down to speak for him, was driven about on the top of a four-in-hand in a blizzard, and was pelted by a Tory mob with snowballs—and with stones in them too!" "I suppose, however," he added with mournful resignation, "it's all in the day's work!" Grey afterwards became prominent in the Chartered Company's affairs, and actively promoted Cecil Rhodes's South African policy. A few weeks before the outbreak of the Boer War my Father was his guest at Howick. He told me that during his visit he thought it courteous to avoid politics, as he differed so widely from his host, but that just as he was leaving he could not resist expressing his earnest hope that there would not be war. "War! my dear Mr Leveson. War! Pray put your mind quite at rest as to that. The idea of old Krüger fighting! Of course he's bluffing. There may still be difficulties before a settlement is reached, but of war there is no danger whatever." Less than three weeks after this emphatic reassurance war was declared! Personally Grey was one of the most delightful of men and a universal favourite.

In the early autumn of 1878, I went to France with my Father. I greatly enjoyed the Exhibition, as I did a visit to the Castles of Touraine. At Tours I had a slight attack of diphtheria. The clever doctor who put me right sent in a bill for 25 francs, and on my Father's saying that this must be a mistake and that he was sure that he must owe him more, he said that it was his usual charge, 5 francs a visit! He was, however, persuaded to accept a box of good cigars as a very slight additional acknowledgment of his valuable services.

CHAPTER X

A DUEL, A DEBATE AND PROCTORS

Two great friends of mine at Balliol had a difference based on misunderstanding early in 1878, and resolved to fight a duel. The both asked me to act as second, but I said that I would have nothing to do with what seemed to me a ridiculous affair. Indeed, had I not been assured by their two eventual seconds, each of whom afterwards attained to positions of very high distinction, that they would take care that there were no bullets in the pistols, I should have denounced the whole business. The principals were quite unaware of this precaution. A harmless exchange of shots took place very early in the morning at a remote and secluded spot, honour was declared satisfied and they again became the very greatest of friends.

I received the compliment of being invited to propose a motion at the Oxford Union at the first meeting of the Michaelmas Term, on October 18, 1877. I wanted to speak on another subject, but the President and Committee thought that the first debate should be on the Eastern question, which was then engrossing everybody's thoughts, and as they had done me, a more or less unknown member of the Society, the honour of giving me the invitation and as all my friends advised me to comply with their wishes, I had practically no choice. I should explain that I was not at that time in sympathy with the Bulgarian agitation and was rather under the influence of the anti-Russian movement which was its counterpart. I have subsequently realized that my views were mistaken and that, as the late Lord Salisbury said of himself, I had "put my money on the wrong horse." But I never took an extreme line on the question, and I fancy that the sentiment which chiefly influenced me was an intense horror of war, which I have always entertained from my earliest years. My motion ran as follows: "That this House condemns the action of Russia in entering upon the present war, and would deprecate any agitation in this country which might encourage her to prolong the conflict."

Although I fear that it is couched in somewhat egotistical terms, I must again have recourse to one of my letters, written only three days after the debate, as it reproduces the impression which it made upon me whilst it was still fresh in my mind.

"Etonian Club,
"Oxford,
"October 21, 1877.

"There were about 300 people present, including a good many ladies in the gallery, but after the three first speeches about an hour and a half of fearful drivel quite emptied the House; otherwise my majority would have been overwhelming. The opponents of the Motion all stayed on till the end. My speech lasted rather under half an hour and was very well received. I got through my chain of arguments unbroken and was cheered very frequently and heartily. There were no interruptions. Once, indeed, when I hesitated, they applauded at some length, to allow me time to collect my ideas. I was much cheered when I sat down. The speech was moderate in tone and I tried to keep it free from declamation. I think it was forcible. Only one man opposed me with any bitterness and I cut him up as much as I could in my answer. Two amendments were put by the Secretary and Treasurer but were defeated and my Motion carried by 32 to 25; a small division considering the number of people present at the opening of the debate. A short notice of it appeared in yesterday's *Morning Post*."

I see that I have the grace to add: "You must think all this fearfully egotistical about this wretched speech, but you said you wanted to hear all about it, so I have told you." Whether my readers will be animated by the same friendly sentiment is, however, doubtful.

The Etonian Club, whence this letter was dated and which I hope still exists, was an agreeable resort of a couple of good rooms on the first floor of a house on the south side of the High. It had two admirable institutions. All letters were posted free and notes within the town were taken round, equally gratis, by a messenger. A College messenger, who naturally went by the name of "The Angel," performed the same service for Balliol men. I may perhaps be allowed to recall an incident in this connection. A great friend, the late Mr William Radcliffe, gained later a well-earned celebrity by what is universally allowed to be a standard work on the History of Fishing from pre-historic times, and as admirable for its style as for its learning and research. In our curious Balliol slang he was known to his friends as "The Radder," and as such I addressed a note to be taken to his lodgings by "The Angel." He thereupon intimated his disapproval, saying that whilst he did not mind our calling him anything we liked, he thought it derogatory to have his nickname proclaimed to a College servant. I apologized and asked how he would like to have his letters addressed, "Just plain William Radcliffe." My next note to him which was entrusted to "The Angel" was accordingly directed to "Plain William Radcliffe."

I occasionally attended the debates at the Union, but did not often take part in them, as I did not care to speak without careful preparation. I was more active in the debates of our College Debating Society, the Dervorguilla, so called after John Balliol's wife and joint foundress with him of the College. We did not have bad debates, although an option was left to the opener, in my opinion mistakenly, to read a paper instead of confining himself to speech. Election was by ballot, and candidates were elected if a majority of votes were in their favour. This regulation once led to a curious situation. I happened to be in the chair when a candidate came up for ballot whose success was by no means assured. He was a scholar of the College, and whilst greatly liked by his immediate friends was not generally well known, being of a studious and retiring disposition. He had quite unconsciously given some offence to the young bloods of the College by neglecting to change his surplice at the Chapel services quite as often as they thought necessary. The Chairman did not vote unless his casting vote were required in the case of a tie, which was what happened at this ballot. I am afraid that if I had not been in the chair I should have voted against him, but, being in this position, it seemed to me proper to support his candidature, as there was no serious reason for rejecting him. He afterwards not only had a most brilliant career, but subsequently occupied a distinguished position in the University and holds a very high place in contemporary British literature.

The annual Town and Gown rows in November were not quite obsolete, although much milder affairs than in the past. In my first term I find in a letter of mine, dated November 7, 1876, the following:

"Yesterday evening there was no row at all; I was out and prepared to take part in one but there was none to take part in. I accordingly went to a charming concert of Hallé's and Madame Norman Néruda. I hobbled past three successive parties of Proctors and Bull-dogs, brushing close past them, not one of whom addressed me. Great luck! I have rather a game leg from football, but that is a trifle."

And so it seemed that "music had charms to soothe the savage breast." One would hardly think that "a game leg from football" was the best equipment for deadly fray with townsmen; however, at eighteen . . .!

A year or two later these traditional hostilities broke out with renewed vigour. My recollection of them is more a subject for the Comic than the Tragic Muse. Baron de Monbrison, a young Frenchman of an old Huguenot family in Languedoc, came up to Balliol, where he delighted us all by his unfailing cheeriness and his adventurous incursions into the English idiom. He was over six feet high, thin in person, with a pale complexion and a short black beard; altogether a striking personality. I believe that in later days he became well-known in French racing circles. One Town and Gown night, it happened to be a wet one, he sallied forth with us, garbed in an immensely long, shiny white mackintosh, of the kind affected by coachmen. In our first brush with the Town, he naturally attracted the enemy's attention and when his nationality was disclosed by sundry strange oaths and exclamations he at once became the centre of interest. A boy got behind him and seizing the two ends of his mackintosh ripped it right up to the collar, with the result that as the fray surged ἐνθὰ καὶ ἐνθὰ, as Homer had it, or, as we should now say, backward and forward, the two sundered portions of his mackintosh flapped vigorously on either side. He was just boxing the ears of the youth who had damaged his raincoat, when the Proctor, McGrath of Queens, came round the corner and took his name and College. The next day we all escorted him to Queen's, ostensibly to show the solidarity of our sympathy, but really, I am afraid, hoping for fun. Nor were we disappointed. "Monsieur de Monbrison," began the Proctor in his severest tones, "your case is a peculiarly serious one. You are admitted, as a foreigner, to partake of the hospitality of this University and to share in the privileges and advantages which it confers upon its members. You reward this hospitality by mixing in disgraceful and vulgar brawls. What have you to say for yourself?"

"*Pardon, Monsieur le Procteur . . .*" "Speak English, sir!" "It was to vindicate the ancient honour of the University against the *canaille* that I rushed into the fray!" "The less said about that the better. Do you think that you vindicated this honour by cuffing a lad not much more than two-thirds of your size and of your age?" "But he had bisected my impermeable most cowardly, coming from behind! Also he was the first to assail: he struck me on the loin!" This was too much for McGrath as indeed it was for everybody, and amid roars of laughter the champion of the University was dismissed on payment of a ten-shilling fine.

"The Breezer," as we called him, had prepared himself for free and easy converse with academic youth by a course of Fielding and of Smollett, and delighted us by freely incorporating eighteenth-century expressions into his conversation. Once when he had much amused us and we were all laughing, he put in: "Zounds! I did but say it to make delight for you roaring blades!" Again at a Commem. luncheon a girl asked him whether he liked champagne. "Champagne, yes," he said, "but not this, this is but the infernal gooseberry!" He was a dear, good fellow; we were all very fond of him and were heartily sorry when he left us.

In 1877 my uncle, Lord Northampton, after many years' suffering, died at Castle Ashby and I went to his funeral. The train reached Oxford too late for dinner in Hall, so I had some at the Mitre. The Proctor arrived in the course of my meal, and next day I had to wait on him. After he had ascertained that Lord N. *was* my uncle, that the Master had given me leave to go, and, after consulting Bradshaw, that I could not have returned earlier, I had the unusual satisfaction of escaping a fine. Nor did he repeat Dean Gaisford's observation, when in earlier days an undergraduate had asked leave for a similar purpose: "Well, Mr ——, I suppose I must let you go to your uncle's funeral, although I could have wished that it had been a somewhat nearer relation." It was also under Gaisford's rule that the last but one Lord Wemyss, then Frank Charteris, my Father's great friend at Christ Church, being commanded to a State Ball at Buckingham Palace, asked for leave for the night. When the Dean naturally asked the reason of his request, he said that, having strained the muscles of his leg he had been advised to consult a celebrated London surgeon. Subsequently he was somewhat disconcerted, a sensation he seldom experienced, by being confronted at the Ball by the Dean in person. On returning to Christ Church he was summoned to the Deanery, and Gaisford thus addressed him: "I assume, Mr Charteris, that your medical adviser recommended saltatory exercise!"

I and some Balliol friends for a term or two used to dine at the King's Arms, at the corner of Holywell Street, instead of in Hall. This was against University regulations, and one night just before nine we were caught by the Proctor as we were leaving the inn. Dick Farrer, one of our number, was a celebrated sprinter, who had won the Quarter of a Mile at Eton, whilst he also played tennis (the real game) for the University. He thought that he could get into College before the Gate closed at nine o'clock and made a dash for it. He easily outstripped the pursuing bull-dogs but only reached the Gate just after the last stroke of Great Tom had sounded and found it shut in his face. He was caught before he could gain admittance, so whilst we were let off for a five-shilling fine he had to pay ten. "The race is not always to the swift." He was an excellent scholar, being Newcastle medallist at Eton, a distinction seldom won by an Oppidan, and gained a Balliol scholarship, being afterwards elected Fellow of All Souls. During my first term in lodgings, in Michaelmas 1879, Shoobridge and I shared with him a house in the Turl, No. 4, kept by an excellent man of the name of Davies. Dick went down at the end of that term. He afterwards read for the law and was Private Secretary to Lord Iddesleigh, better known as Sir Stafford Northcote, whom a French journalist once described as "*Lord Strafford, mieux connu sous le nom de Sir Northcote*." To the lasting regret of his many friends he died of consumption whilst quite young, but, had he lived, his great talents, combined with his social charm and marked versatility, would undoubtedly have assured him a brilliant career.

The late Lord Curzon, whilst still at Eton, had an amusing encounter with a Proctor. He was staying at Oxford and was out one night with some friends when that official came on the scene. George Nathaniel took to his heels and, after a hot pursuit, was captured; when asked his name and College, he gave the former and added "Eton College." "But why," asked the Proctor, "if you are not a member of the University did you run away?" "It is a pleasant evening and I thought a little gentle exercise would be agreeable. And now, sir," continued George with a change of tone, "may I in my turn ask why you had the audacity to order your minions to pursue me? A gross violation of the liberties of a British subject!"

Ignoring this inquiry the Proctor answered: "Although, Mr Curzon, you are not yet a member of this University, I believe that you are likely to become one before long; after which happy event," he added significantly, "I shall look forward to the pleasure of meeting you again." Little did he think that his prospective victim would eventually become Chancellor of the University!

CHAPTER XI

DONS, UNDERGRADUATES AND FRIENDS

EVELYN ABBOTT was my tutor, a very charming and able man. In his youth an athlete, he was, as I have heard, struck down by paralysis during his examination for Greats, which he was consequently unable to complete. His papers were, however, so exceptionally good and his reputation as a scholar so firmly established that the Examiners had no hesitation in giving him his First. In spite of his crippled state he was singularly handsome. He used to be wheeled about College in a chair, which when he went further abroad was converted into a pony-carriage. Myself, Hugo Charteris (afterwards Lord Wemyss) and Leonard Shoobridge made up a reading-party under his auspices during the first seven weeks of the Long in 1877. We took a little house called Rose Cottage, at Applethwaite on the southern slopes of Skiddaw, commanding a magnificent view of Lake Derwentwater and the surrounding mountains, but the weather was atrocious; out of forty-nine days we only had two fine ones. One pleasant feature of our stay, although it would have been pleasanter had it been finer, was our custom of making excursions every Saturday to Monday; Abbott in his pony-carriage, led by his servant the faithful Tom, and we on foot with knapsacks on our backs. The pony and ourselves gradually and simultaneously got into training, and at last we always did the level ground running, thus covering some seven miles an hour. In consequence we explored the whole of the Lake District before we left and got an agreeable weekly interval in our hard reading.

Abbott published a fascinating collection of Essays entitled *Hellenica*, as well as an edition of Sophocles in collaboration with R. C. Jebb, and also, together with Lewis Campbell, a Life of Jowett, to whom he was greatly attached. He was very hospitable, and not only frequently had his pupils to luncheon but also entertained their friends and relations. In later years he took a small house near Oxford.

He did not live to an advanced age and died greatly mourned by a large number of pupils and friends.

Strachan Davidson was Dean in my days. Later he became Master, although not elected, as many thought was his due, as Jowett's immediate successor. He was a tall, thin man with a slight stoop and a rather straggling beard; he had a keen sense of humour and a pretty turn of irony. In the earlier years of his Fellowship he was supposed to be threatened with consumption, and after the end of Michaelmas Term always spent his winters in Egypt. There he acquired a fine collection of coins of the Ptolemaic and Roman periods, of which he was not a little, and quite justly, proud. We read our weekly Essays to different Dons each term, and it was a legend amongst us that when we had to read one to him, if it were not of reasonable length or composed with sufficient care, the best way to avoid unpleasantness was to ask him to show one his collection of coins. This he always did with pleasure and alacrity and in the discussion of their respective beauties over tea and cigarettes, the shortcomings of one's Essay were often overlooked. I had put up a Scotsman to this manœuvre, but he did not bring it off very well, as he was tactless enough to inquire: "And noo, Mr Dean, what propor-r-tion o' these do ye suppose will be genuine?" "I think I am too old a connoisseur to be easily taken in," was Strachan's frigid rejoinder. "And now about your Essay. I was sorry to see, etc. etc." As Abbott's *forte* was Greek, so Strachan Davidson's was Latin; he was especially good at Roman History and points of the Roman constitution and law. He was lecturing on Tacitus, and in order to illustrate a comparison which he was making between Augustus and Tiberius brought down to the lecture-room two large photographs of the well-known statues of those Emperors. When he had finished, an Unattached Student not very happily inquired if he would mind pointing out which was which. "Dear me, Mr Davenport, I had hoped that I had made myself sufficiently clear!" The same man was put on to construe a passage from Tacitus in which it was stated that the Germans were equally expert in wielding a lance or a shield; this he unfortunately rendered: "The Germans were experts in wielding a weapon which they used either as a lance or a shield." "Really, Mr Davenport, that must have been a very remarkable weapon!"

An undergraduate of the name of Trevor, a general favourite for his high spirits, had rooms looking out on the *enclave* belonging to St

John's in front of the Gate of that College in which was a row of high elm trees. When the young rooks were out he amused himself by potting them with an air-gun, a form of sport which did not commend itself to the St John's authorities, who complained to Strachan David-son, as our Dean. Sending for Trevor he asked whether he could account for the recent remarkable mortality amongst the young rooks in the elms in front of St John's. Trevor replied that he understood that the rooks were that year afflicted by a mysterious disease which claimed a number of victims. "Is that so, Mr Trevor? Well, unless a remedy for this unfortunate disease is immediately discovered, I fear that you may find yourself attacked by an illness known as 'Goingdownitis,' which necessitates the temporary withdrawal of the patient to healthier air than we are favoured with at Oxford." The rooks at once recovered from their disease!

Another exploit of Trevor's was a hoax which he played on Billy Grenfell (now Lord Desborough). One night he dressed up a dummy figure in some of Billy's clothes, which he hung by a rope to a branch of a tree in the Quad. Rushing in to Billy's rooms he announced that a man had hung himself. Out dashed Billy with a table knife and cut down the supposed suicide. On discovering the truth—or rather the fraud—he proceeded to slash the clothes, till Trevor told him they were his own. Thereupon he returned to his rooms, whence he reappeared with a large supply of soda-water bottles. Pursuing the really alarmed Trevor he discharged a succession of these at his head; they burst like bombs against the walls but luckily all wide of the mark, although Trevor, after a wild chase of five minutes, only felt safe behind the sported oak of his own rooms.

"Bay" Middleton, who used to pilot the beautiful Empress of Austria in the hunting field, played a similar trick on Lord William Beresford, who objected at a country house party to his coming down to the smoking-room without changing his evening coat; finally threatening to rip his coat up if he did it again; which he accordingly did on a repetition of the offence. Middleton took it quite calmly and Beresford, thinking that he had gone too far, apologized and remarked on the wonderful equanimity with which Middleton had borne this act of violence. "That's all right, old chap," was Bay's reply, "why should I mind? It's your coat."

Lewis Nettleship, another Don, was much beloved. His tragic death during an Alpine ascent will be recollected by many. He and his guide were caught by a thick fog at a very high altitude in bitterly cold weather, and had to spend the night where they were. He insisted on putting his own coat round the guide, who was a married man with a family, thus saving the guide's life at the cost of his own. His memory is still venerated among the population of the neighbouring valleys.

A. L. Smith, who succeeded Strachan Davidson as Master, was a History tutor in my day. He was a man of boundless energy and besides his tutorial and other work, was greatly interested in the College rowing.

I did not see much of him as we had no official relations, but did not feel greatly in sympathy with him, not for any definite reason but possibly because our interests and outlook on life were rather different. Years afterwards I met him in Pall Mall and we had a pleasant and cordial little chat. I mentioned this to my Father and said how much more easy I found him to get on with than when I was at Oxford. A day or two later he met my Father at luncheon, spoke of our meeting, and was kind enough to say that he thought me much improved. "Really," answered my Father, "it is very kind of you to say that; and, do you know, my son said just the same thing of you." When he was elected Master I wrote him a letter of congratulation, but begged him not to trouble himself to answer as I knew how busy he must be at such a time. To this he sent a most charming reply, saying that I must indeed think ill of him if I fancied that he could be capable of not answering the congratulations of so old a friend. And now, he too is gone!

Altogether the Dons and undergraduates were, I suppose, on happier and easier terms at Balliol than in any other College, which of course is in itself a tremendous asset.

I used to ride with several of the Dons, amongst whom were Strachan Davidson, R. W. Raper, Dean of Trinity (himself an old Balliol man) and Tommy Shepherd, the Bursar of Exeter. My undergraduate companions on these excursions were Shoobridge, Lymington (afterwards Lord Portsmouth), St John Brodrick (now Lord Midleton) and others. Raper was very reserved but a delightful companion. He gave many pleasant luncheons. He lived near West Malvern in the vacations and once in that neighbourhood was a guest at a luncheon given by a widow lady. He was not a clergyman, but his hostess, under the impression that he was, unexpectedly called upon him to say grace. Taken quite aback the best that he could produce was "For what we are about to receive, may the Lord in His mercy preserve us." This recalls a story of a Scotch minister who nicely graded his benedictions according to the quality of the fare which he anticipated. If he did not expect much of the meal he would begin: "For these the least of all Thy mercies . . ." but when he saw champagne glasses his rapturous exordium would be: "O! bountiful Jehovah! . . ."

The late Lord Abingdon very kindly gave me a pass, which enabled me and my friends to enjoy many pleasant rides in his beautiful park at Wytham. Specially present to my mind is one long stretch of turf which runs along the top of the hill at the edge of the woods, commanding a wide view over the valley of the river above Oxford. He occasionally asked me to dine and now and then gave me a day's shooting. He was an old friend of my uncle's, who, as a young man, when my grandfather was at the Paris Embassy, used, in pre-railway days, to race Lord Norreys (as he was then) in post-chaises from Paris to Calais. He once beat him by sending on ahead and hiring all the horses at the various posting-places on the way, but would take no money from him, having won his wager by such sharp practice. I got an occasional day's shooting in Bagley Woods, which belonged to St John's, through the kindness of Ludlow Bruges, the Bursar of that College, whom I had met at Guisachan, Sir Dudley Marjoribanks' place in the Highlands. Sir Dudley was afterwards created Lord Tweedmouth.

Lady Churchill was also kind enough to ask me to luncheon once or twice at her beautiful home at Cornbury; and I occasionally called on Lady Catherine Weyland who lived not far from Oxford. A laughable incident occurred here. A friend and I had ridden over there one winter afternoon and were having tea; he was a small man with very thin legs and a long nose. A small folding chair collapsed beneath him. He sat there struggling to disengage himself, tea-cup balanced in hand, his booted legs between which his long nose projected, waving in the air. It was getting dusk and Lady Catherine, who was short-sighted, could not imagine what had happened and sat peering at him through her *lorgnon*, whilst I was convulsed with laughter. It made it all the more awkward for him as he had never met her before. Amongst other places to which we rode out were Blenheim, Brill, Abingdon and Dorchester, with its beautiful abbey.

Eynsham was a favourite resort of ours; in summer we sometime
went there by the river in fours, and occasionally a large party in
brake to dine there, returning late at night.

My heart not being strong, I was not allowed to train for th
Torpids, though I enjoyed going on the river; sometimes havin
pleasant picnics at Nuneham or on the Cherwell. I occasionall
played cricket but not continuously. After my first summer term
my Father was pleased when I told him that I played in the Second
Balliol Eleven, but his satisfaction was modified on hearing that there
were only twenty-one men in the College playing cricket that term

Miss Rhoda Broughton, the novelist, lived in Holywell with he
widowed sister, Mrs Newcome. I used to go to tea there. She had
a quick wit and a sharp tongue and was excellent company. He
tea-parties were pervaded by three turbulent pugs, named Cupid
Psyche and Sluttikins.

Besides Miss Broughton's, several other pleasant houses were ope
to me whilst I was at Oxford. Amongst these I may mention that o
Mr Butcher (brother of J. G. Butcher, who was for many year
M.P. for York, afterwards Lord Danesfort); he had married Miss
Trench, a very beautiful woman, and had collaborated with Andrew
Lang in his prose translation of Homer's *Odyssey*. Many authoritie
consider this the finest rendering of that work; in any case it was a
great achievement and was widely and warmly welcomed when it
appeared, so that I was greatly surprised when he told me that he had
only received for it eleven shillings and sixpence from the publishers,
the cheque for which he framed and hung in his room.

I also now and then went to tea at Professor Max Müller's house
near the Parks, where, as well as at that of Mr and Mrs Humphry
Ward, one met many interesting people. Max Müller was a cheerful
little white-haired man with spectacles who always took a lively
share in the conversation, and Mrs Ward, who was afterwards so
well known as a novelist, was an extremely kind and agreeable woman,
whose easy and friendly manner had the gift of putting young men
quickly at their ease.

Mr Charles Cavendish Clifford, for many years Liberal M.P. for
Newport in the Isle of Wight, a life-long and intimate friend of my
Father, often asked me to dine at All Souls, where I spent many an
enjoyable evening in the most agreeable society. He was one of the
Fellows of the *ancien régime*, elected long before the day of the devastat-

ng Parliamentary Commission of 1853, and had a comfortable set of rooms in the back Quad. Amongst others of the "unreformed" Fellows I remember Lord Bathurst and Mr Inge, both very old men—born in the 18th century. Mr Inge was notorious for the number of waistcoats which he wore simultaneously; it was said that in the hottest weather the minimum number was three. Mr Clifford pointed out to me the junior Fellow mixing the salad in Hall before dinner, a solemn duty incumbent upon him and in the nice mysteries and traditions of which he is carefully initiated by his predecessor . . . "*et quasi cursores.*" At All Souls it was a custom that no guest should drink until invited to take wine by the Warden or some Fellow. Mr Clifford, being very absent-minded, often forgot to go through this ceremony, so I had to sit through some of the earlier courses without raising my glass to my lips, until one or other of the Fellows noticed my woeful plight and brought me welcome relief. Mr Clifford, amongst other bequests, left my Father a very handsome Florentine cabinet. He was indirectly connected with my Father through the fifth Duke of Devonshire, and was a tall man, with pronounced features and a patriarchal white beard. His speech was drawling and hesitating, but his mind keen and active, and he had a talent for writing graceful verse and prose of no mean order. Notable among his prose works was a delightfully humorous account of a tour in Iceland, entitled "Travels by Umbra."

He once addressed a political meeting at Bodmin, held in support of my Father when he represented that borough, and in which I also took a humble part. This happened to be at one of the frequent occasions when the House of Lords were engaged in their customary sport, now happily curtailed by the Parliament Act, of mangling Liberal measures. "How long, gentlemen," he thundered, "how long will you suffer your liberties to be wantonly trampled under foot by a callous and irresponsible oligarchy!" (Immense applause.) After the meeting my Father congratulated him on his speech, but said that he wondered whether his audience had quite followed that part about the irresponsible oligarchy. "I don't know," said Clifford dreamily, "I'm sure I don't know; I hope they did; I believe they did. Anyhow" (brightening up), "they understood that it was a term of opprobrium."

He had a pretty villa at Ryde, in the Isle of Wight, where, on one of my visits, I met Lord Coleridge, the "silver tongued" Chief Justice.

A feature of All Souls dinners was the potent audit ale, served i
small round silver cups with the cheese. Long before the war, c
course, a German princeling dining there ridiculed the smallness c
these cups. "That is not the way that we in Germany drink bee
etc. etc." The extreme strength of the ale was explained; but to n
purpose. He called for a tumbler of the largest size, had it fillec
swigged it off, and, I am glad to say, collapsed and was carried ou
head and heels. The All Souls Common Room was one of th
pleasantest in Oxford, particularly cheerful being the semi-circula
table facing the fire, with people sitting round the outer side, and wit
a baby tramway to pass the wine to and fro. I often played tenni
with Sir William Anson, later to become Warden, and with anothe
Fellow, Mr Prothero, afterwards Lord Ernle—whilst among m
hosts with whom, in later days, I passed many a pleasant Saturday t
Monday at this most delectable of Colleges were my old Ballic
friends, the late Dick Farrer, George Curzon, Cecil Spring Rice an
Arthur Hardinge.

From time to time I attended afternoon service at Magdalen or Nev
College, at both of which the music was superb. One day afte
shooting at the butts I went to the New College service, being give
a place on a long, heavy, oaken bench. I was very tired and mus
have drowsed for a second, as I swayed backward against the benc
which fell with a resounding crash. I at once looked sharply to righ
and left, as though trying to discover the culprit, and thus escapec
detection.

CHAPTER XII

I LOSE A GREAT FRIEND

IN the Long of 1878 I went on a reading-party to Dalry in Kirkcud-
brightshire, with Shoobridge and Mr McCunn as our coach. On
arriving at Parton, the station for Dalry, some nine miles distant from
that village, we found that the coach did not leave till several hours
later. We therefore decided on walking, and asked the station master
to see that our luggage was sent on, as there was no cloakroom.
The station master looked doubtful, rubbed his chin and finally
announced with true Scottish caution: "Weel, I'll see tae pittin' it
on, but, mind ye, I'll no be responsible for't!" Needless to add that
every bit of it arrived safely. In similar circumstances an English
station master would have merely said: "That'll be all right, sir,"
whilst an Irish one would have sworn by all his Saints that the trust
would be the one and only object of his thoughts, and the luggage
would probably not arrive at all.

Close by our inn was the home of Dr and Mrs Sellar, he being
Professor of Latin at Edinburgh University. One of their daughters
afterwards became Mrs McCunn, but I never found out whether this
was the consequence or the reason of Dalry having been chosen as the
locale of our reading-party. McCunn afterwards got a Professorship
at Liverpool University, and amongst other works published a most
interesting book on the ethics of citizenship. One day we were taking
a walk and came to a field surrounded on three sides by high, roughly
built, stone walls and on the fourth by a sheer cliff, some 20 feet high,
at the foot of which ran a deep and turbulent stream. Climbing one
of the walls we were crossing the field when, at the bottom of a little
valley in the middle of it, we saw a bull who evinced signs of displeasure at our presence. Shoobridge and I retired in good order
towards the wall, but McCunn, prompted by I know not what
demon, danced about and yelled at the bull, who thereupon trotted
briskly towards him: McCunn ran, the bull ran, we all ran. Having

a certain start Shoobridge and I first reached the wall and scramble
over; McCunn was less lucky in finding a climbable place, but we sa
a hole cut in the bottom of the wall for sheep to pass through an
shouted to him to make for it. He dashed at it and began to squee
through, but by now the bull was close upon him. At the critic
moment he stuck fast, his hinder parts exposed to the full fury of th
animal. Shoobridge and I each seized one of his hands, put one fo
against the wall, and somehow hauled him through by main forc
though not without considerable damage to his person and his cloth
ing. Just as we got him through the bull came up with an enormo
crash against the part of the wall where he had been but a mome
before. It was one of the closest shaves I ever saw!

A neighbouring laird, Mr Greig, invited us several times to dinne
It was at his house that we heard some Spanish songs charmingly giv
by Miss Ashton, the late Lady Bryce. One evening, at dessert, M
Greig was carefully watching the progress round the table of a bott
of rare old Château Lafite and the way in which it was received by h
guests. The butler whispered to one young man, who did not kno
claret from cider: "Château Lafite, sir?" The youth nodded assen
"No, Jackson, no!" shouted Mr Greig. "You do *not* give Lafite 1
Mr —— He's eating preserved cherries! Give him some '
Julien." The poor young man looked hopelessly dazed. He ev
dently could not make out why his host should get so much excite
over all these French names. Neither could he understand what th
said French names meant. It was all Hebrew to him!

One afternoon at the Sellars', Alfred Myers, who was their gues
gave a reading of his "Agamemnon." It was all very magnifice
and imposing, if, perhaps, just a thought tedious, when the litt
Scotch maid burst in and addressed her mistress: "If ye please, Men
the rat-catcher's come!" No more "Agamemnon" that afternoo

At the end of our reading-party I spent a few pleasant days wit
Lord and Lady Selkirk at their pretty home, St Mary's Isle, whic
was not very far from Dalry. This house was raided by Paul Jone
the celebrated American privateer.

My coming of age in 1879 was celebrated by my aunt, Lady Maria
by a dinner to about thirty of my relations at Alford House.
responding to the toast of my health, after some conventional remark
of the usual kind, I said that one of the most serious results of comin
of age was becoming responsible for one's debts. I added tha

COMING-OF-AGE, 1879

Back Row (*L. to R.*) ARTHUR HARDINGE, WALTER ROPER LAWRENCE,
HAROLD BOULTON, LEONARD SHOOBRIDGE, W. RADCLIFFE
Front Row: HON. G. N. CURZON, RENNELL RODD, G. LEVESON GOWER,
L. to R.) R. R. FARRER

whatever debts I might now have were of course not recoverable at law, unless it could be proved in Court that they were such as might be deemed to be for necessities in my position of life. I was sure, however, that my Father would scorn to stand upon a legal quibble of this kind, and that rather than see me morally dishonoured would cheerfully liquidate whatever debts I might have incurred. This completely took him in, although everybody else saw that I was having a joke with him. He drew me aside and anxiously asked the amount of my indebtedness; when he found that I owed nothing at all, it was amusing to watch the conflict between his relief at this assurance and his annoyance at my having, as he put it, "played upon his feelings." As a matter of fact I left Oxford without a penny of debt and it was only afterwards that I ran into debt for a few hundreds in consequence of the inadequacy of my allowance for the life which my Father expected me to lead in London.

My coming of age was also recorded by a photograph taken by the kind leave of the Fellows, in their garden, with as a background one of the few remaining portions of the picturesque old buildings of the College. I was the centre of a group of friends[1] all busily engaged in tormenting me in different ways. I am happy to think that after this lapse of so many years, my friendship with all of them is undiminished, the only severance of our comradeship having been by the hand of Death.

The group consists of George Curzon, Leonard Shoobridge, Rennell Rodd, Arthur Hardinge, Walter Lawrence, William Radcliffe, Harold Boulton and Dick Farrer, none of whom are living except Rodd (now Lord Rennell).

Two of my other friends died whilst still at Balliol, young Collier and Eustis Johnston. Collier was drowned at Sandford Lasher, which has claimed several victims. The whole College followed his funeral to Holywell Church, where in later years Strachan Davidson was also laid to rest. He had a good voice and sang French songs with much effect and feeling. He was a relation of the late Hamilton Aïdé, who was well known in Society for his varied talents. Aïdé's father was a Greek gentleman who married an English lady. He died in Paris leaving her and her little boy in a state of destitution, from which my grandmother, then Ambassadress, was happy to be able to relieve

[1] By the kindness of the Fellows, one copy of this photograph now hangs in the Senior Common Room and another in the Bursary.

them. Hamilton was a clever painter in water colours, and a writer of sketches in prose as well as of songs, some of which he set to his own music. He knew the whole theatrical, artistic and literary world and gave pleasant receptions in his rooms in Hanover Square. Shoobridge and I went with him to one of the Bayreuth festivals, travelling afterwards through the district known as the Franconian Switzerland to Rothenburg, that marvellous mediæval town, where my two companions took a number of sketches. Aïdé good-naturedly gave Shoobridge several useful hints for his work.

Eustis Johnston was the other of my friends whom I mentioned as having died whilst at Oxford. He succumbed to typhoid contracted at Dinard, where he had gone in the Long of 1878 to read with E. T. Cook, afterwards Editor of the *Daily News*. Our friendship began at Eton, where we were at the same House. He was, like all his family, strikingly handsome and an excellent musician, with the highest spirits and the sunniest, merriest of natures. He was an only son, and his early death at the age of twenty was a terrible tragedy. His father was a director of the London and Westminster Bank, whilst his mother came of the well-known family of Eustis of New Orleans, who were partly of French extraction. An uncle of his was Senator for Louisiana and at one time American Ambassador in Paris.

I wrote to a friend on October 18, 1880, nearly two years after Eustis' death:

"Yesterday I wrote a long letter to Mrs Johnston, my poor friend's mother. It is quite touching to see how eager she is that I should write often and at length to her, and I do so, although I fear my letters must awaken painful recollections. I have never seen her since his death, yet now, strangely enough, through much correspondence, know her more intimately than before. She is a brave-hearted woman.

"It is quite startling the number of dreams in which I see and seem to talk to Eustis, and there nothing is changed! he is the same gay, light-hearted spirit he always was, and never a touch of sadness or melancholy in those dreams, always the brightness of full friendship shining through them. And then, when I wake, the fulness of the loss comes with new vividness upon me, and in the depth of the night I cry like a little child.

"I do not think that any friend of mine was ever—I will not say so dear to me—but was ever so thoroughly in harmony with me as to all ways of thought and all views of looking at things as he was.

"With Eustis I used to talk for hours into the night, and though little points of difference arose we argued them out with each other, and ended by agreeing, and with that agreement which is not the result of weariness or being defeated in argument, but with one that is the outcome of full and free consent. Not only our hearts but our minds were one.

"Yet I cannot cease thinking of those long talks during which we got to know every thought, every half thought, that passed through the other's mind. They seem to me like bright, tender sunsets, the strong yet soft hues of which one remembers years afterwards. Sometimes the recollection of these talks and of him brings me great happiness and calm, but too often it ends in passionate grief. Even now the tears are welling up in my eyes so that I can scarcely see to write. Oh! my friend, my friend, why did you go away? Shall I ever have such a friend again?"

Clinton Dawkins, who has also passed away, and who married one of Johnston's charming sisters, was another of my intimate friends. He afterwards occupied many high and responsible positions. My Father, when paying me a visit at Oxford, wanted a rubber of whist, so I collected Dawkins and another man. "Dawks," as he was known to us, was quite a novice and played at that time, like many other able men, an execrable game. When he had left my Father reflectively observed to me: "I don't think that I ever met anybody who played quite such bad whist as your friend Dawkins," a remark which, at imminent personal risk, for he was eminently a man of his hands, I hastened to repeat to him. A few months later my Father and I were staying at Hawarden with Mr Gladstone, who good-naturedly made up a rubber for his benefit, the fourth being a young Parsee lady. After the rubber my Father said to me: "I think that that young Parsee lady plays even a worse hand than Dawkins." I thought it only fair to him to tell him when we next met of this modification of my Father's unfavourable judgment, which strangely enough only moved him to further wrath—and a painful scene of violence ensued. Soon after leaving Oxford he and I took a pleasant little summer tour. After seeing Haddon Hall we walked down the valley of the Dove to Burton-on-Trent, whence we rowed through Nottingham to Newark, bathing here and there on the way. We ended our trip by a visit to the beautiful Southwell Minster. Dawkins became a Civil Servant and was Private Secretary to Mr Cross, Secretary of State for India. Later on he went to Peru as representative of the Peruvian Corporation, in which capacity he had to supervise the service of the Peruvian debt. Lunching in a restaurant at Lima he overheard a conversation between some Peruvians at a table near-by but screened from observation. One of them said that he was going to Europe, and when asked his reason for doing so said: "Oh! there's nothing more to be done in this infernal country, since that damned fellow Dawkins has come here, who don't know the meaning of the word *diñero* (dollar)!" A remark which he took as an unsolicited testimonial to his incorruptibility.

It was the custom to make up bathing parties near Callao and the President once asked him to join one of these. Another of the party was the Finance Minister, who playfully splashed the President's wife. The President called on Dawkins to protect her, an opportunity which he joyfully seized, as the Minister had been very troublesome of late by delaying the signature of certain necessary documents, on various frivolous pretexts. Dawkins, always a man of action rather than of words, promptly seized the Minister and ducked him; letting him up he asked: "Will you sign those papers?" and when he equivocated ducked him again. At last the Minister reluctantly promised that he would send them that same afternoon, but they never arrived. The next morning Dawkins sent him a message that he "was looking forward to the pleasure of having another bathe with His Excellency," and the papers, duly signed, were immediately returned. He was also Financial Adviser to the Egyptian Government, in which post he greatly disliked having to wear the official fez and the regulation frock coat of rather peculiar cut, which he said made him look like a cross between a Mohammedan and a High Church curate. Whilst at Cairo he joined a party which went to visit the great Barrage, by which the outflow from the different mouths of the Nile is regulated. Among the visitors was the beautiful wife of a high financial authority who has since been created a peer and became an Ambassador. Clinton, like everyone else, was captivated by her charm, but was slightly disillusioned when she asked him to explain to her the exact effect of the Barrage upon the Suez Canal. I afterwards told him that a lovely woman had a perfect right to mix up the North Pole and the Equator if it were her pleasure to do so.

He then became Financial Member of the Government of India, and after being made K.C.B., accepted a post of great responsibility as London partner of J. P. Morgan. Unfortunately a period of great financial difficulty supervened and he fell seriously ill, in consequence, as his friends fancied, of worry and over-work. After a temporary improvement, he resumed work to which he devoted longer hours than his doctors thought prudent; this occasioned a relapse, which was followed by his untimely death in the prime of his age. His numerous friends missed him sorely, for in him was found a singular but characteristic combination of marked abilities, untiring industry, a most lovable disposition and an iron strength of will.

In 1879, when we went Head of the River, we gave a ball. Stewards were elected, of whom I was one, who were adorned with a gorgeous sash of the College colours, against the size of which I vainly protested both on the ground of ostentation and expense. Its chief advantage was that it enabled one to ask a girl to dance without the formality of an introduction. The ball was a great success. One of the most noticeable figures was Ahmed Ali, an Indian Mohammedan, a good-looking fellow enough, who utilized the opportunity to sport a striking if somewhat fantastic costume, which was much to the taste of the ladies. I remember once asking him what a "Yogi" was, and he answered: "Oh! he is a poor foolish heathen man, who spends all his life meditating by himself on a stone." Once on our way to London he saw an advertisement of Huntley and Palmer's Reading Biscuits. "I must get some of those," said he. "I suppose they are particularly suitable for reading men." Another instance of the many pitfalls of our elusive language for the unsuspecting foreigner!

Abdul Kassim, a Persian, was another of our oversea imports. He was extraordinarily intelligent, as is evidenced by the fact that he passed an examination brilliantly six months after he had begun to study our language. At a dinner at the Master's he sat next my Father and, finding that he was an M.P., asked him whether he did not think it unfair for constituencies of only a few hundred voters to enjoy the same political power as others with as many thousands of electors. My Father cordially agreed, but confided to him that he represented one of these unduly favoured constituencies and jokingly asked him as a personal favour not to lay stress on the fact. This reduced poor Kassim to a great state of confusion, as he feared that he had unwittingly been uncivil. On his return to Persia he was made Governor of some town of importance (I think it was Meshed), where Curzon met him again during his travels: he told me that Kassim's great intellectual powers were quite neutralized by his unconquerable timidity, which reduced him to such a state of nervousness as completely to paralyse his ability to take a decision and to act upon it.

When I came up two other distinguished Orientals were at Balliol, the Japanese noblemen Hachisuké and Iwakura, whose names the scouts playfully metamorphosed into "Hutchysukey" and "Highwakaroo." They both ultimately attained high official positions in their own country.

The presence of these exotic students and of other foreigners at Balliol was the topic of many jokes in less favoured Colleges, which unseemly merriment we attributed to secret envy at their inability to attract them within their own precincts. One of these legends ran that some Balliol men wearing their College blazers were wrecked on a cannibal island, and were about to be led to the slaughter-house when their blazers were recognized and themselves rescued by the chief, who was also a Balliol man!

But, joking apart, I cannot help thinking that it is good policy to invite young foreigners to pass a year or two within our walls, thus giving them an opportunity to gain some idea of English life and institutions in general and Oxford life in particular, and incidentally to form friendships with Englishmen of their own age. When I say "Englishmen" please do not suppose that I exclude Scotsmen, Welshmen or Irishmen, but "Briton" is in this connection an awkward word, although infinitely preferable to that horrible Americanism "Britisher."

My last year at Oxford I spent in lodgings at 4 Turl Street, as already mentioned. One advantage of being in lodgings was that one was excused from attending early chapel. An undergraduate who had found it more than usually difficult to get up in time for this ceremony was congratulated by his tutor on going into lodgings "where the weary are at rest." "Yes," he replied, mindful of many gatings, "and where the wicked cease from troubling." My rooms were pleasantly situated, there being no buildings opposite from which one could be overlooked. The garden of Lincoln, beautiful in summer with copper beech and laburnum, was at the other side of the street, flanked to the left by that College's picturesque buildings and to the right by the church of All Saints.

When we were going down for the Easter Vacation in 1880 Shoobridge and I gave a luncheon to Curzon, Rodd and a few other friends. Shoobridge had to leave the first to catch his train when, as his luggage was being put on to the hansom, a demoniacal inspiration came to George Nathaniel. Seizing a big plate of ripe oranges he proceeded to bombard the party in the street. A scene of indescribable confusion ensued. Oranges burst all over the place: the horse pranced wildly and was with difficulty prevented from bolting; Shoobridge was picking up his hat in the gutter; the maid screamed; the cabman swore; passers-by, according to their disposition, looked either angry or amused, and finally the cab clattered off plentifully bespattered with orange juice.

An eccentric cleric had at this time acquired a certain notoriety. His name was Lyne, but he chose for some reason best known to himself to be called "Father Ignatius." He had established a monastic community at Llanthony Abbey, not on a very solid basis, as I have heard that the brethren, whilst he was absent on his preaching tours, not infrequently found themselves in a state of positive want. He affected monastic garb. I went to one of his meetings held in a disused music-hall in Holywell Street. Whilst exhorting us to the pursuit of what was good, he inadvertently pointed upward, that is to the ceiling. His gesture was unluckily directed towards the painted representation of a lady with flowing golden locks who held a timbrel and liberally displayed her personal charms.

Another evening I was dining with some friends at Christ Church. After dinner we adjourned to the Town Hall near-by, where the "Father" was to deliver a discourse. He gradually worked himself up into a great state of excitement, waving his arms about, rolling his eyes and shouting himself hoarse in impassioned denunciation of pretty well everything and everybody, *more ecclesiastico*. Of gentle persuasion, much less of reasoned argument, there was not a trace. Descending from the general to the particular, he indulged in a violent attack on my College and all its works, shouting out "Ichabod!" several times over. This of course delighted my Christ Church friends, who dug me in the ribs and plied me with light banter. Noticing this he proceeded to give his remarks a still more personal application and pointing at me a finger trembling with excitement exclaimed: "There sits one who, etc. etc. etc." Whereupon I got up and rejoined: "Well, he's not going to sit here much longer," and, suiting the action to the word, left the room. I have never witnessed a more pitiful or puerile display, which I can only compare to the ravings of a corybant.

CHAPTER XIII

LAST DAYS AT OXFORD

ON Valentine's Day in 1880 I played a trick upon my two aunts, Lady Marian Alford and Lady Granville, and it was some time before they discovered the author. I got small terra cotta busts, such as were hawked about in those days, of Mr Gladstone and Lord Beaconsfield. These I packed up, and had delivered by hand in London, getting a friend to address them and to copy out the lines which accompanied them. Mr G.'s bust went to Lady Marian, with the following verses:

> Though faction's rage our lot doth part,
> Though different far thy views from mine,
> Believe me, this Bulgarian heart
> Beats but for thee, my Valentine.
>
> "W. E. G."

Lord Beaconsfield's bust was sent to Lady G., accompanied by these lines:

> Suffer him, gentle lady, still,
> Who long hath worshipped from afar,
> Who long hath been, though 'gainst thy will,
> Thine own, thy country's guiding star.
>
> He who doth power despotic wield
> To Beauty deigns to bow the knee;
> Accept this bust of Beaconsfield
> And let him still thy beacon be!
>
> "B."

The authorship was, after much mystification, finally traced to me by it suddenly occurring to somebody that I was nephew to both of the

ladies. I afterwards heard that my little hoax came to the ears of both
Lord B. and Mr G., and was received, characteristically, by the former
with amusement, whilst I regret to say the latter was, also characteristically, a little put out.

At the General Election which took place in the spring of 1880,
the Liberals contested both of the seats of the town of Oxford, the
representation having been previously divided between Sir William
Vernon Harcourt and a Conservative; the result was that two Conservatives were returned. Hereupon, I blush to say, I addressed an
anonymous communication to Sir William. I hasten to add that
this is the only one that I have ever sent or ever mean to send; also
that it only consisted of a single line of Hesiod,[1] which may be
translated:

> "Foolish ones, nor do they know how much more the half is
> than the whole."

In the Summer Term of 1880 (or possibly of 1879) a representation
was given in our Hall with marked success of the "Agamemnon" of
Æschylus. This effort has been so often and so well described that I
will not attempt a regular account of it, but will confine myself to two
incidents. Cecil Spring Rice was acting the part of one of Clytae-
mnestra's maidens. He was part author with Beeching, who afterwards became a Canon of Westminster, of a series of epigrams on
members of the College, which was known as "The Masque of
Balliol" and of which I have given in an appendix as much as I can
remember with the kind help of my friend the late Leonard Huxley.[2]
Cecil arrived rather late at a dress rehearsal after a game of lawn
tennis and omitted to change completely, trusting that his long white
robes would conceal any incongruities of costume. He forgot that
at one moment he had to kneel down to spread a strip of crimson
cloth for the entry of the Queen; and in doing so displayed a length
of leg in grey flannel trousering which was anything but consistent
with the garb of an Argive maiden.

The other incident was at the very opening of the play, where
W. L. Courtney, then a Don at New College and who subsequently
edited so capably the *Fortnightly Review*, was enacting the *rôle* of the
Watchman, perched aloft on a battlement to give notice of the return

---

[1] Νηπίοι, ουδ' ισάσιν οσω πλέον ημίσυ παντος.

[2] See Appendix.

of the Greek fleet. At last, after long and weary watches of the night, he descries the anxiously looked for signal of the distant beacon fire, and hails the end of his labours by joyful greeting of the welcome blaze. Alas! the distant beacon had to be lit behind the scenes and amid the hushed stillness of the audience was heard the "scratch, scratch, scratch" of the match which obstinately refused to ignite. For a moment the awe-inspiring tragedy was perilously near turning into comedy and the "buskin" was nearly replaced by the "sock"!

All his many friends were delighted when Rennell Rodd won the Newdigate Prize for English Verse with a very fine poem on Sir Walter Raleigh, a subject which specially appealed to him, as is shown by a life of that hero which he wrote in later years. His gift of poetry is of a high order, as is evidenced by the numerous volumes of verse which he has published at intervals in the times of leisure allowed by his varied, strenuous and brilliant diplomatic career, which may be said to have culminated in his achievement, when Ambassador at Rome, in largely influencing Italy to enter the Great War upon our side. His prose works are also of much interest, including a Life of the Emperor Frederick of Germany and a History of the Frankish and Latin Dynasties in Greece.

We all flocked to the Encaenia to hear him recite his Prize Poem, which he did very well and with much applause.

J. D. Rogers, a Balliol Scholar, a most amusing companion and a fine musician, delighted in playing unexpected pranks. The Scholars had to read Lessons in turn in Chapel, and once Rogers proceeded to read in an even and unemotional voice a particularly lurid chapter of Leviticus, prohibiting a number of offences in a rising scale of enormity. Needless to say that the Chapter was not that appointed for the First Lesson. When the catalogue of proscribed offences had mounted to an intolerable pitch, the Master intervened and said: "I think that will do, Mr Rogers." He was afterwards gated for a month in spite of his declaration that his mistake was purely involuntary.

Many years after going down I attended a College Dinner in London, at which most of those present were senior to myself. The Chairman (of whose name I am not sure, but think that it was Davenport) had presided over these banquets for a good many years. Rogers had to propose the toast of his health. He began by saying that he had vainly tried to discover from the Chairman's contemporaries anything to his disadvantage, or even to his advantage, and alluding to what he called his "perpetual Presidency" happily quoted the lines:

> "*Sedet, aeternumque sedebit*
> *Infelix Theseus.*"

("There sits unhappy Theseus, and will for ever sit.")
I recall two amusing examples of the less successful efforts of candidates for the Newdigate.

One competitor who had previously failed with his poem on "The Death of Sir John Moore," tried his luck the next year when the subject was "John the Baptist." He began as follows:

> "Erst it was mine in sounding verse to tell
> How Sir John Moore before Corunna fell;
> But now a holier theme I've hit upon
> And 'Saint' instead of 'Sir' precedes the John."

The other aspirant to the bays had to wrestle with the subject of "The Hebrides," and began his poem thus:

> "Far, far away amid the Western seas
> There are some Isles, men call them Hebrides;
> The people there are poor, they've got no wood,
> They can't build ships, they only wish they could."

Rennell once consulted me as to the terms in which he should make a character in one of his longer poems express disbelief of a certain statement. I accordingly humbly suggested the following:

> "Know then, that 'ere such prophecies come true,
> The heavens I'd picture green, the grasses blue,
> Radder[1] as beardless or the Dicker[2] dumb,
> Charteris as friendly or the Cuss Boss[3] glum.
> Nay, all these things I sooner would suppose,
> Rennell would change his burning verse for prose,
> Or the sweet Shooer[4] lose his length of nose.
> Sooner the Laxer[5] would go down in weight,
> Sooner the Pammer[6] cease to sway the State,
> The Brodder[7] care no more for Irish land,
> The Lymmer[8] social problems understand,
> Forbes's[9] fair form dissolve in throes of love,

146

> Or bearded Pickering murmur like the dove;
> Sooner than this should happen I could guess,
> That Strachan[10] would blossom out a buck in dress
> And Jowett waste his days in idleness."

The following notes are required to explain the Balliol nicknames in the above poem:

[1] The Radder, William Radcliffe, author of the celebrated History of Fishing. [2] The Dicker, Dick Farrer. [3] The Cuss Boss, George Nathaniel, afterwards Lord Curzon. [4] The Shooer, Leonard Shoobridge. [5] The Laxer, myself. Etymology: Leveson, Loose 'un, Lax One, Laxer. [6] The Pammer, W. W. Palmer, now Lord Selborne, then just entering on a political career. [7] The Brodder, St John Brodrick, afterwards Lord Midleton. [8] The Lymmer, Lord Lymington, afterwards Lord Portsmouth. [9] W. H. Forbes, a Balliol Fellow of austere aspect and ascetic habits. [10] Strachan Davidson, Dean and afterwards Master of Balliol.

Spencer Pickering, mentioned in the last line but three, was a science man, a study generally known to us with scanty reverence as "Stinks." He invented a mechanical device known as "Pickering's water toy." In order to stimulate its sale just before Christmas, a number of us mapped out certain of the London districts of which we each undertook a section, and called at all the toy shops within each area, asking for it. If, as was generally the case, the shop was ignorant of its existence, we expressed pained surprise that a shop of such reputation should not have in stock what was undoubtedly quite the best, most instructive and ingenious plaything of the season. It is to be hoped that our campaign led to satisfactory results.

Cardinal Newman preached a sermon in the Catholic Church at Oxford in 1879 or the early part of 1880. A great concourse flocked to hear him, myself among the number. I was far from the pulpit and could not hear a word that he said as his voice was very feeble. He looked worn and weary. Shoobridge was also there, and next to him sat Professor Huxley, whose son Leonard was a fellow undergraduate of ours at Balliol; the thought crossed my mind as to whether the Cardinal would have ever attended a lecture given by the Professor.

In 1878 I took a Second Class in Classical Moderations, whilst in the summer of 1880 I also got a Second in Greats, or Litteræ Humaniores. In the latter examination Lewis Nettleship, a Balliol Don, was one of the examiners. He afterwards told me that my fate hung in the balance between a First and a Second, that he himself thought I ought to have a First, but that, as a Balliol Don, he judged it better to stand aside: to this I answered that it was the first time that I had regretted that he was a Don at Balliol. As a matter of fact in my case I do not think that my missing a First greatly signified, although of course it was a disappointment. The only time that it made any difference to me was years afterwards when I applied for a vacant Civil Service Commissionership, a post which entails the duty of arranging and supervising examinations for entrants into the Civil Service. Sir Henry Campbell-Bannerman, then Prime Minister, told me that he would personally have been ready to give it me, but that he feared that political opponents in Parliament and in the Press would criticize this particular post going to a man who had missed his First. "Even if they knew better," he said, "they would not be able to resist the temptation of saying, 'Here is this post being given to a Second Class man because he is a Party hack,' and the worst of it is that they will be careful to spell 'Second Class' with a small 's' and a small 'c,' and even if they know the difference themselves, they will hope that the public will not." He was probably quite right, but he very kindly made amends a few months later by offering me the Commissionership of Woods and Forests, an office now known as that of the Crown Lands, which is really a more accurate and comprehensive, as well as comprehensible, denomination.

Before I could take my Degree I had to pass my Greats Divinity Examination, and in October 1882 obtained leave from Mr Gladstone to return to Oxford for a week to prepare for it. He had appointed me Assistant Private Secretary in June 1880; and I took up my duties the day after my *Vivâ Voce* Examination for Greats. Fortunately enough my friend Shoobridge was in a similar, although a worse, predicament, inasmuch as he had not even passed his Mods. Divinity, which is equally essential for passing Moderations. Indeed, when he went up to Macan of Christ Church, who was afterwards Master of University, for his *testamur* in Greats, he was asked for his Mods. *testamur*, which he produced. "Where is your *testamur* for your examination in Moderations Divinity?" he was asked. But when Macan heard that he had never gone up for it he said: "But you cannot have passed your Mods. without having previously passed your Mods. Divinity."

'But I *have* got my Class in Mods.," said Shoobridge. "My name appeared in the Class lists two years ago." "This is all very awkward and very unusual," said Macan. "I really don't know what to do about it." Shoobridge solved the problem by suggesting that he should now go in for his two Divinity examinations, first Mods. and then Greats, and if he passed them, let bygones be bygones. Macan, whilst saying that it was all very irregular, sensibly accepted the suggestion, and Shoobridge eventually passed his two Divinity Examinations one after the other and so emerged from his troubles. The fact was that not only Shoobridge, but both the College authorities as well as the examiners, had forgotten all about the Mods. Divinity Examination. In view of this imbroglio I may refer to a very sensible suggestion recently put forward in the Press by Sir Daniel Hall, himself an old Balliol man and one of the leading experts on scientific agriculture. He advocated substituting a compulsory pass examination in the elements of agriculture for that in Divinity. I hope more than I expect, that his proposal may find favour in the eyes of the University authorities.

Shoobridge and I took rooms in the Corn and had a capital time. Most of our friends were still at Oxford, there were no lectures to attend or other College obligations, and we had plenty of time for recreation, and I got some riding as I brought my mare with me, as well as tennis, whilst our impending examinations were not of a character to cause us anxiety.

We both came up for Commemoration Week in 1881 and took rooms in the Corn, but not the same as those we had in the following year. Returning from a ball at about 4 a.m. we found that, whilst the outer door, of which we had the latch-key, was unlocked, an inner one was fastened and ringing proved ineffectual. Our rooms were on the first floor and one of them faced the street and had a broad window-sill, whilst the window was wide open. Discovering a fire-escape near-by we accosted a policeman, explained our predicament and satisfied him of the truth of our story by opening the outer door. He thereupon lent us a hand to wheel the fire-escape into position and took it back again after we had clambered up into our rooms. The passing of half a crown may have helped matters, and it is too long ago for this admission to injure his career.

Looking back at my Oxford days, whilst I was naturally sorry to miss my two Firsts, I am not sure that, on the whole, a man may not get more good out of the time that he spends at the University by taking part in its numerous and varied interests and activities, than by the exclusion of everything else but his studies and keeping his nose perpetually to the grindstone and so obtaining the highest academic honours. That is, provided that he also reads continuously and seriously so as to widen his knowledge and cultivate his taste; and also if he does not propose to devote himself to the teaching profession in after life; although even here, I fancy, certain Governing Bodies and Head Masters of schools attach nearly as much importance to an athletic as to a scholastic record. But quite apart from all this, these three or four years at a University have an enormous effect in moulding a man's character by other influences than those of the lecture-room. The large freedom and independence which are his, within certain limits, and the corresponding sense of responsibility which they entail, the wide choice he has of making friends of congenial tastes whether in his own or in other Colleges, men older as well as younger than himself: the friendly mixing of men from many schools, of different religious and political ideas, and of widely varying social status—all this tends to the shedding of prejudices, to the acquisition of a broader outlook, and not only to the toleration but to the recognition and comprehension of views that are not one's own. I do not know whether I shall be thought to be attempting to combine two mutually exclusive attributes, when I say that my ideal of a University education is that it should make a man into something of a philosopher and at the same time a man of the world. I am, moreover, strongly sensible of the imperceptible but all powerful change which these four years wrought in myself: and all the while I was unconscious of the gradual change which was at work, as one is of the corresponding change in the tissues of one's body. I can only gauge it by comparing the enormous difference of my point of view on a number of subjects when I joined the University and when I went down. I came to Oxford a lad: I left it a man.

This, at any rate, I can say for myself; my years there were not only some of the happiest in my life, but they have left me with an enduring sense of deep love and obligation to the University for her many and wonderful gifts, which I know I can never hope to repay.

CHAPTER XIV

10, DOWNING STREET

My Father wished me to get into the Foreign Office and the idea appealed to me. But when he suggested that I should put in "a little work" in preparation for it "in my spare time," as he put it with unconscious irony, before I had got through my Greats, I drew the line. The suggestion throws a vivid light of his conception of reading for Greats. I humoured him by paying a visit to W. Baptist Scoones, the well-known coach for F.O. and the diplomatic service, and arranged to cram with him when my Greats were over. But the General Election in the spring of 1880 upset all these plans. Mr Gladstone became Prime Minister and had arranged to take his wife's nephew, Spencer Lyttelton, as one of his Assistant Private Secretaries. At Lord Granville's request he very kindly agreed to take me for that post, my uncle taking Spencer as his own Secretary until a vacancy should occur in Mr Gladstone's secretarial staff. So all my dreams of F.O. and of a diplomatic career melted into thin air. At the time I was inclined to regret this, as a diplomatist's life has many attractions, but considered it wiser to accept without demur the responsible position. I have often thought how very different my life would have been if the Liberals had not won the 1880 election. I should certainly have tried for the F.O. and, if I had got in, should have stuck to it. A diplomat's career, or that of a F.O. official, has one advantage over a politician's, not being at the mercy of a capricious electorate. On the other hand it is no profession for a man who is not wealthy, as is so often seen in the case of those of small private means, who have been so much hampered by the high obligatory scale of expenditure which that life entails. On their retirement, after serving with distinction, they find themselves left with sadly straitened resources. As to my chances of success in the F.O. examination I cannot speak with any confidence. The proportion of nominations to vacancies was much smaller than now; I think there were about three nominations for every vacancy, whilst one had the further chance, that if one did pretty well in an examination without getting in, the authorities sometimes gave one the next vacancy without the necessity of further competition.

My uncle jokingly said that if he were Foreign Secretary when I came up for examination he would find out beforehand which of his friends had the stupidest sons, and would then try to persuade them that their young hopefuls had a natural gift for diplomacy and that he would give them nominations. Pitted against such competitors he thought that perhaps I might be able to squeeze in.

As it was, I took up my duties as Private Secretary the day after my *vivâ*. I should have liked a week or two's holiday after my hard work, but had to go into harness at once, since Mr G. was Chancellor of Exchequer (1880–81), as well as Prime Minister, being desirous of remedying as far as was possible the bad financial position which was a heritage of the late Tory Government, and work was consequently heavy. I found myself in a new and unaccustomed world in which I had to cope not only with the "damned dots" immortalized by Lord Randolph Churchill, but with such weird and mysterious topics as "worts," "mum" and "inkle." One day when I took some papers to my Chief, he wheeled round in his chair and asked me quite suddenly: "What was the Sugar Duty in 1842?" I said I would look it up. He seemed at first rather surprised that I could not give him an immediate answer; then remembering that I had only taken up this particular job a week or two before he laughed good-naturedly and said that obviously I could not be expected to know.

The following are extracts from a letter:

"10, Downing Street,
"Whitehall,
"August 12, 1880.

... "My work is now lighter as my Chief is ill, and I can generally get away by five or soon after. Theoretically I arrive at ten, and did so whilst we were at high pressure. Now it is generally between ten and eleven. When the Budget was on I had to wade through endless wildernesses of figures and statistics, and particulars about 'drawback' and 'plant' and 'worts' and every other kind of horror, in wordy letters from brewers and wine merchants and hardly ever got away before 7 or 7.30.

MR. GLADSTONE AND HIS PRIVATE SECRETARIES
HORACE SEYMOUR, SPENCER LYTTELTON, G.L.G., E. HAMILTON

"I used to go to balls and was so afraid of being supposed to have come uninvited, as I often did not know my hostess by sight, that I took my invitation in my pocket. About a month ago I was regularly seedy: however I did not knock off but stuck to it and now am all right again for the present. However if you hear of me ill with fever don't be surprised, for the smells on the staircase are 'hoffle' and Barty Mitford,[1] of the Office of Works, says all the drains are wrong and that there is a big cesspool in the garden, but as the Government has come in on a policy of retrenchment they are too economical to do anything and possibly myself and colleagues may be among some of the unnecessary expenses to be 'retrenched.'"

About a year later I had an even worse attack of fever which kept me in bed for some time. Both of these illnesses as well as Mr Gladstone's were, I am convinced, caused by the insanitary state of 10 Downing Street, which was only put right after Sir William Vernon Harcourt became Chancellor of the Exchequer and insisted on the system of drainage being thoroughly overhauled.

"The other day I was Godpapa to a very small cousin; it was not very amusing, except my Uncle always did the wrong thing at each point of the service."

The said "small cousin" is now Vice-Admiral Earl Granville, C.B., D.S.O., Governor of the Isle of Man, and about 6 feet 2 inches high; a very able and popular member of the Service, who did excellent work before the last war chasing Arab slave dhows in the Red Sea, and equally good work against the Germans later on. He married Lady Rose Bowes Lyon, Lord Strathmore's charming daughter and sister to Her Majesty the Queen.

The letter concludes with two sketches, one of my dog Jock, the other of myself, inscribed "Ye Private Secretarie of Ye Premier, doing ye country its businesse, as he will appear at ye Streete of Downinge during ye monthe of September. Alacke!"

Sir Arthur Godley, who had previously been my uncle's Private Secretary, acted in the same capacity to Mr Gladstone when I entered on my duties at Downing Street, the other members of the secretarial staff being Eddy Hamilton, Henry Primrose and Horace Seymour.

[1] Afterwards Lord Redesdale.

Godley was later created Lord Kilbracken and was one of the finest scholars of his generation; he was succeeded as Chief Private Secretary by Hamilton, son of a former Bishop of Salisbury, who eventually became Secretary to the Treasury and G.C.B. Hamilton collected a great number of fine engravings of previous Prime Ministers, which he bequeathed as an heirloom to the Prime Minister's official residence. He was nicknamed "The Cob," partly on account of his strong, compact little figure and partly on account of his cheeriness and great capacity for work. He was a general favourite. He had a suite of rooms at the top of 10 Downing Street, and returned his friends' hospitality by inviting them to see the annual Trooping of the Colours on the Horse Guards Parade. He and Godley were Oxford men and both were exceedingly kind in initiating me into all the branches of a Private Secretary's work, which, like Sam Weller's knowledge of London, are "extensive and peculiar." Godley, when he was with my uncle, met Miss James, the daughter of Sir Walter James, of Betteshanger, whom he afterwards married. Sir Walter was a neighbour of my uncle at Walmer Castle. Lord Granville had a high opinion of his judgment and frequently consulted him on political matters. He was subsequently created Lord Northbourne. His son left the Liberal Party on the question of Home Rule and later was so much incensed by Mr Lloyd George's drastic financial policy that he announced that he would have an ox roasted whole and distributed among his neighbours when that statesman should be driven from office. But being more of a patriot than a partisan, when Mr Lloyd George, as Prime Minister, rallied his fellow-countrymen so magnificently to a vigorous and ultimately successful prosecution of the Great War, the ox was sacrificed to celebrate the Prime Minister's triumph instead of his defeat. My uncle enlarged Walmer Castle by the addition of several fine rooms over the Gateway and was enabled to do so very successfully from an æsthetic point of view. Three Cinque Port Castles had been erected by Henry VIII, not far distant from each other; Walmer being the southernmost, Deal in the middle and Sandown to the north. Here Sir William Hutchinson, Governor of Nottingham Castle for the Parliament during the Civil War, was imprisoned and died after the Restoration. Sandown had become a ruin from the encroachment of the sea, and as all the Castles had been built at the same time and of the same stone, my uncle got leave from the Office of Works to utilize the ruins of Sandown for the enlargement of Walmer with the happiest effect. Lord G. asked me to write a Latin inscription placing on record this addition to the Castle, which I accordingly did, but not before it had been submitted to Godley for his revision. It stands over the Gateway and only a few years ago I asked the Secretary of the Office of Works to prevent its being hidden by ivy.

To return to Eddy Hamilton; he was several years my senior at Oxford and was a Christ Church man; he introduced me to a number of his friends and contemporaries, and got me elected to a delightful society called the Wilton Baggers, which was speedily Spoonerized into "Bilton Waggers." The President was Lord Pembroke, and we had a very tasty ribbon—red, white and blue. Every year we had a dinner during the Eton and Harrow match, nearly all of us being Etonians. We also had an annual river excursion, when we rowed down in eights to Windsor, and a cricket week at Wilton, the President's beautiful home, of which perhaps the cricket itself was not the most brilliant feature.

Eddy died several years later of a terribly painful and trying disease, borne with the utmost fortitude and serenity.

Henry Primrose, nicknamed "The Colonel" for no better reason that I could discover than that he had a fine moustache, was not with us for long, as he went to India as Private Secretary to Lord Ripon when he became Viceroy. He returned to Mr Gladstone when Lord Ripon's term of office ended and was subsequently made Head of the Customs and later of the Inland Revenue. In after years he suffered from a severe illness which had a sudden and tragic ending which will be in many people's recollection. Only a few days before his death I played several rubbers of bridge with him at his son's flat and noticed nothing which foreshadowed this calamity, by which I was all the more painfully saddened and impressed.

Horace Seymour was a delightful personality; he was brother to Lady Spencer, the Red Earl's wife; "Spencer's Fairy Queen" as the Irish called her with native gallantry. Horace married Miss Romilly and was subsequently made Deputy Master of the Mint, where I used to visit him from time to time as I greatly enjoyed his society and that of his charming wife and beautiful daughters. When he was gazetted K.C.B., I wrote to congratulate him and was rather surprised at getting no answer, but was horrified on learning that he had died suddenly either just before or just after the announcement of his honour in the newspapers, but in any case before his investiture. King Edward, with his customary thoughtful kindness, conferred the title of "Lady" on his widow.

When Primrose went to India he was succeeded by Spencer Lyttelton, under the agreement previously mentioned. He was Mrs Gladstone's nephew, his mother having been her sister. It was from Mrs Gladstone's brother, Sir Stephen Glynne, that she inherited the Hawarden estate. The two families of Lyttelton and Gladstone had invented a curious cryptic language called Glynnese, of which the late Lord Lyttelton compiled an amusing glossary. This was freely used amongst themselves and their intimates and occasionally bewildered the uninitiated. As an instance of this at a Foreign Office reception which Mr Gladstone did not attend as he was very tired and not very well, the Russian Ambassador asked Mrs Gladstone why he was not there. "Well," she said with one of her confidential winks and nods, "the fact is, he's rather dragging his leg." Now in Glynnese this meant to be a little below par, not quite up to the mark. The poor Ambassador, however, took it literally, and cabled home in code that the Prime Minister had had a slight paralytic stroke. Other happy expressions in Glynnese which occur to me are: a "rebound," i.e. a statement (generally of a pleasant or flattering nature) made by A. to B. of C. and repeated by B. to C.; an "old shoe," which meant a friend so old and intimate as to make you feel perfectly at ease in their company; "wizzy," a mixture of something strange and disagreeable: a "groutle-hole," a place into which things were shoved away, more or less in a state of confusion: "the passing pigman," an equivalent of "the man in the street"; to "benumb" was Glynnese for to condole; and to do a thing "high-gee" was to do it on the spur of the moment. Spencer was what the French would call "an original," not perhaps universally popular in the way that his brother Alfred was, but greatly loved by his close friends. He was tall and slim, with a short black beard, curly dark hair and of a pale complexion. He was really shy and self-conscious but masked this under an abruptness which sometimes verged on rudeness. He never hesitated to express his views of men and things in the most direct and caustic terms, and appeared at times singularly wanting in consideration for other people's feelings. When he was once charged with this he dismissed the subject with: "They oughtn't to have such feelings!" So that was the end of that! He had a comfortable income derived from property left him in New Zealand, where there is a town bearing his family's name. I have heard that he did many acts of benevolence and spent a substantial part of his income in charity.

He had a way of blurting out short sarcasms with delightful abruptness. We worked in the same room at Downing Street and on my expressing disapproval of something in pretty emphatic terms: "George," said he, "your meaning is obscure and your language profane." Like all his family, he was the very essence of directness, straightforwardness, and of crystal-clear integrity. I have always had a sneaking idea that the Lytteltons have all been trying to make up with might and main and with conspicuous success for the scandalous immorality of their notorious ancestor, whose name became a byword for iniquity and who even succeeded in shocking his 18th-century contemporaries, in itself no mean achievement.

The only other Lyttelton who deviated from the family type was Spencer's uncle and namesake, who was extraordinarily witty, and was often at Walmer, as he was a great favourite of my uncle's, although I have an idea that Lady Granville did not greatly relish his visits on account of his general freedom of language and behaviour. Once when I was there he mercilessly and rather unkindly chaffed my cousin Mary, then a very small girl. She, being unaccustomed to that sort of thing, was at first bewildered but gradually became exasperated, and at last turned upon him and gave him, in her own childish language, as good as he brought. Lady G. at once saw her opportunity and said: "Mary, it is no reason why, because other people do not know how to behave, you should do the same." He was once staying with the eccentric old Lord Crewe, the uncle of the present lord, who had a good deal of shrewdness behind his vague and absent-minded manner. Lyttelton bet one of his fellow guests that he would knock down a valuable china vase from the mantelpiece without incurring any rebuke from his host. This he accordingly did, whereupon Lord Crewe rang for the footman and told him to sweep up the fragments. Lyttelton thought that he had won his bet, but after a minute or two Lord Crewe rang the bell again and, on the servant reappearing, said: "Tell Mr Mason" (the butler) "to order the carriage round to take Mr Lyttelton to the station in time for the next train to London." "But I'm not going, dear Lord Crewe." "Oh! yes you are."

When Lord Crewe had a party at Crewe Hall, he asked a number of his guests separately whether they would like to go for a ride. They all accepted and gathered in the Hall, assuming that they were to make up a party. No horses appeared at the appointed hour, and one of them espied his lordship disappearing at the end of an avenue on a white horse, having presumably realized that he had offered the said horse to each guest.

When his home was burnt down his lordship remarked: "Richard" (his brother-in-law, Lord Houghton) "will no longer be able to complain that Crewe Hall is cold."

Once on a visit in Scotland, his host, whose house was far from the railway station, asked him to give a lift to an impecunious young fellow guest. Lord Crewe was so friendly that the young man was emboldened to ask him for the loan of £100. To which Lord Crewe replied: "It has been very agreeable to me to enjoy your company, but it is not equally so to lend you £100."

When the younger Spencer Lyttelton was at Eton he was Captain of the Eleven and a very bad one, because, as somebody said at the time, he was much more interested as to what would be the next anthem at St George's Chapel at Windsor than in trying to discover a good new bowler or in other ways strengthening his team. He was devoted to music and had a good baritone voice, and belonged to a touring amateur society of vocalists called the Magpies, but his singing was spoilt by a heavy manner and lack of animation. He told me that when he became my uncle's Private Secretary Lord G. suggested that he should learn shorthand, which he did at some trouble and expense, but he was never called upon to give proof of his proficiency. Sir Reginald, afterwards Lord Welby of Allington, Secretary of the Treasury, who came of an old Lincolnshire family, was a great coiner of nicknames, and dubbed him "Il Spenseroso."

Welby was of a rather grim and sardonic aspect and demeanour. As deputy guardian of the public purse, he came into frequent and generally successful conflict with the spending departments, especially with the War Office and Admiralty, whom he denominated the "Red and Golds" and the "Blue and Golds," whilst I regret to say that he did not shrink from calling the Household Cavalry the "Tin Bellies." He did not altogether escape retaliation as to nicknames, for when he was to be made a Peer and people were wondering what title he would take, somebody maliciously suggested that Lord Cutemdown would be appropriate. This was in the happy days

when the First Lord and the Sea Lords of the Admiralty were not the
final arbiters of the number of millions which were to be piled on to
the back of the over-burdened taxpayer, times of low taxation and great
prosperity, and before the era of a political Rake's Progress, when the
poorer a nation is and the worse its trade, the higher mounts taxation
and the more crushing are the burdens.   Welby was a most amusing
companion and a fine scholar, he turned out capital Latin verses on all
sorts of topical subjects in a variety of metres; he did sterling work as
Alderman of the L.C.C., especially in connection with finance.   The
dinners at his comfortable house in Stratton Street were delightful,
and he once told me that the average price of the contents of his cellar
was sixteen shillings a bottle.

Sir James Carmichael afterwards joined Mr G.'s staff of secretaries.
At Downing Street I worked in a queer little room which looked
as though it had been somehow knocked together to utilize an odd
vacant space.   It was on the ground floor, looking on to the leads
which were over the garden, if garden it could be called, being a sort
of gravelled space with a few trees in it, although in the north-east
part of it there was a plot of turf.   My room had, if I remember
aright, a corrugated iron roof, and the temperature in hot weather
was appalling.   I think that it was in the late summer of 1880 that the
thermometer never fell below 90° for a whole week.   During this
hot spell a lot of "flimsies" came from the Foreign Office referring to
the enforcement of the provisions of the Berlin Treaty by which the
territory of Montenegro was enlarged and a sea port given to that
gallant little Principality.   Mr Gladstone desired a précis made of
these papers, which, as their nickname implies, were copies of telegrams and despatches made on thin tissue paper.   I was very tired,
as it was not long after my Greats and I had not only been working
from ten to seven every day, but as often as not dancing till three or
four o'clock every night.   I accordingly sat down to make the précis
in my shirt sleeves, but unluckily was tempted by a big arm-chair.
The next thing I knew was Mr G. himself in the room, asking when
the précis would be ready.   The window was wide open and the
draught caused by his opening the door caught all the flimsies up into
a wild whirl, blown about like autumn leaves.   I felt like the sentry
caught sleeping by Napoleon.   But he was very good-natured.   At
first he looked a little vexed, but quickly changed and said with a
smile: "Well, I daresay you *are* very tired."   The curious thing about

this contretemps is that this was the only time that I ever remember his coming into one of the secretaries' rooms in the whole five years that I was in his service. It was an unfortunate moment to have chosen.

I greatly regret that I did not keep a diary from the time I began my work with Mr Gladstone. The reason was that I doubted whether it would be quite honourable unless I informed him of my intention. Had I been a little older I should have done this, telling him at the same time that I should never publish any part of such a diary without the leave of his heirs and family, but I shrank from the possibility of his regarding me as a sort of privileged spy and feared that it might diminish his confidence in me. I am sure now that I was wrong, and these scattered reminiscences would be infinitely more valuable as well as more interesting if they had had some such solid foundation to rest on, instead of only one's memory aided by a few casual documents.

Each secretary took his turn for attendance on Sunday mornings for the despatch of any urgent business; we had to be at Downing Street by ten o'clock, and were hardly ever kept there for more than half an hour, if as long. On one of these occasions after the necessary business had been despatched, Mr G. asked: "Where are you going to church?" I had had a very heavy week both of work and of dancing, had overslept myself and got down to Downing Street without any breakfast. I had cherished the pleasing prospect of breakfasting at Brooks's after leaving No. 10, and possibly having a nap before luncheon; but from the manner of his inquiry I felt it impossible to confess to such a programme, so weakly compromised by saying that I had not made up my mind. "Oh! well, come along with me; we will go to Marylebone where Canon Barker preaches an excellent sermon." So off we went at four miles an hour in a blazing sun (it was in the dog days), whilst on the way my Chief regaled me with historical and ecclesiastical disquisitions. During the course of these he asked my opinion of Fra Paolo Sarpi, whom I had never even heard of, but who, as it turned out, was the historian of the Council of Trent. He stopped short in his stride, perfectly horrified at my confession of ignorance. "What! Never even heard of him!" I had to remind him that I had taken my Schools in Greats and not in History, and learnt a lot about the historian before we reached the church. By the time the "excellent sermon" was over I was feeling faint from hunger, and began to scheme how I could slip away, but he insisted on taking me back to Downing Street for luncheon, still at four miles an hour, and commented delightedly on the efficacy of a combination of devotional and physical exercise in promoting my appetite, for I ate like an ogre.

When at Holmbury on one of his frequent visits, he praised the sermon which we had just heard, and which I did not think remarkable. Nor did my Father, who said: "Well, Mr G., I never heard you listen to any sermon without saying it was a good one." "And I never heard you," he retorted, "listen to any which you said was good; that is to say if you ever listened at all, which I am inclined to doubt."

John Bright also heard the same preacher. My Father asked him what he thought of the sermon. "If I had been in the pulpit, I think I should have tried to get more of a grip on the congregation!" which he undoubtedly would have done, for though the sermon was not so bad in its way there was not much "grip" about it.

John Bright on one of his visits to Holmbury gave offence to James Russell Lowell, the American Minister (for it was before the representative of the United States at the Court of St James's became Ambassador), by inadvertently speaking of American "subjects." Lowell, the mildest and most courteous of men, flared up at once and proceeded to deliver a miniature Fourth of July oration about Americans being "citizens" and not "subject" to anybody or anything except God and the laws which they themselves had made, and much to the same effect. All of which was slightly ridiculous, especially when addressed to such a pronounced democrat as J.B.

Another time, whilst still an undergraduate, I asked Lowell whether he had been at a University in America: he answered "Harvard," adding: "It is a very old University, over two hundred years old!" I did not turn a hair, but he quickly caught himself up and said: "At least what we in America call very old."

On December 4, 1880, a great meeting was held at Hanley, in the Potteries, at which my uncle, as Foreign Secretary, defended the measures taken by the Government to enforce certain of the provisions of the Berlin Treaty, in conjunction with other Powers, who were acting together in a combination known as the Concert of Europe. I was introduced to this assembly of some 5,000 people as the son of their former Member: my Father having sat for Stoke-upon-Trent from 1852 to 1857. I only spoke for some six or seven minutes, but managed to say what I wanted, which was a message of goodwill from my Father, who congratulated the North Staffordshire Liberals upon having three such excellent representatives as Mr Craig, a coal owner who sat for the Northern Division of the County, Mr Woodall, a protagonist of Female Suffrage, and Mr Broadhurst, a working man, the two members for Stoke-upon-Trent; these last both held posts in a subsequent Government. I was, as might be supposed, pretty nervous, but contrived to make myself heard, and my uncle was much pleased at shouts of "North Staffordshire" being raised at the end of my speech, by which the audience signified the hope that I might be chosen as candidate, together with Mr Craig, for that Division of the County. I gratefully remember some good advice given to me by my uncle in the matter of public speaking. He told me not to speak too fast; to look at the furthest man in the room and try to make sure that he could hear what I said; if I found the audience noisy or inattentive to lower my voice slightly instead of raising it in an attempt to shout against them; not to gesticulate, but to throw all the power of expression which I could command into my voice and my countenance; and lastly not to drink water, or, at any rate, if I moistened my mouth, not to swallow the water, which only tended to make the throat drier.

After this *début* in political oratory I resumed my work at Downing Street with occasional short holidays. On December 14 in that year (1880) I was shooting at Lord Pembroke's at Wilton, after another shooting-party at Gorhambury, Lord Verulam's. From Gorhambury we went over to a ball at Mrs Gerard Lee's at Luton Hoo, where I met with a catastrophe. I was dancing the barn dance when I got entangled in a woman's train and fell heavily, luckily not dragging my partner with me, the floor was very slippery and I slid several yards in a sitting posture, terminating my career just in front of the Prince of Wales. He congratulated me on inventing a new figure in the dance, and I answered that I could not do better than "place myself at His Royal Highness's feet." Lord C——l, an Irish Peer who had taken too much champagne, pinched a girl at supper; she naturally screamed, which caused some excitement and a little scandal.

My work at Downing Street was mostly routine. Every day's vast correspondence had to be opened, classified, and docketed. Letters and papers were folded into as near as possible a uniform size about two-thirds the width of a sheet of note-paper, the docket, consisting of date, name of correspondent, and a brief résumé of contents, was written at the back of the letter, if there were space for it, if not on a covering piece of paper folded round the communication. The correspondence was then divided into bundles, according to subjects, a précis of answers being suggested. Letters of importance were similarly dealt with, the only difference being that we used our judgment in deciding which letters Mr G. would prefer to answer himself. He generally confirmed our suggestions, but occasionally made slight alterations in our proposed answers. The formal resolutions of support from political associations, etc. etc., could nearly always be replied to by means of a lithographed form to which you only had to add the date, "Sir," "Gentlemen," or "Madam," as the case might be, and your own signature. These forms covered an enormous percentage of the whole correspondence. One was known as "Ack. receipt," which explains itself; another as "R.I.," which stood for "regret inability." This was in use for all requests which were inadmissible. It covered begging letters, suggestions that Mr G. should advertise a patent food or medicine, deliver a lecture in support of a charity, give a post to the deserving nephew of the applicant (generally a lady), etc. etc. Its laconism was admirable and all-embracing. "I am desired by Mr G. to express his regret that he is unable to meet your wishes." In the case of begging letters which had some semblance of justification the form of refusal was modified: "Mr G. regrets his inability to subscribe to objects with which he has no local or personal connection." Then there were the "Thanks" for resolutions of support passed by political bodies, not of outstanding importance. "I am desired by Mr G. to thank the Association of so-and-so for the resolution passed by them on the 2nd inst., which you were so kind as to forward to him." We got to have a special "flair" for madmen, although we were occasionally taken in. When you had made up your mind that a correspondent was mad, you had further to classify him as "dangerous" or "harmless"; the letters of the former being forwarded to the police. I only remember one of the former cases leading to anything, and the result proved very inconclusive and unsatisfactory. A man wrote threatening to break the windows of No. 10. I was not sure whether he was a madman, or a man who wanted to draw attention to a grievance by a threat of forcible methods. These two categories being apt to overlap, I sent the letter to Scotland Yard. Shortly afterwards I went to my cousin Brownlow's, at Belton in Lincolnshire, for a week's covert shooting. On the night of my arrival a telegram was handed to me, to my inexpressible disgust, requiring my presence at Bow Street the next morning at 10 a.m., to give evidence that I had forwarded this wretched letter to Scotland Yard. So I had to journey back to town by a night train. The next day I was kept in court all day whilst a man was being tried for trying to kill his wife, and at the end of the day I was told that, after all, my presence would not be required, as the police authorities had decided not to prosecute. Of course it was the best day's shoot which I had missed!

One madman wrote in Greek from the Island of Cephalonia, and as I was "last from school" his correspondence was turned over to me, and, since I failed at first to spot him as a lunatic, I amused myself by answering him in his own tongue. He then, after enlarging upon the advantages of cementing the good relations existing between our two countries, suggested as a happy means to this end that he should marry Princess Beatrice; he enclosed his photograph which would scarcely have forwarded his suit, as I rarely saw the portrait of a more villainous cut-throat.

The letters answered by Mr Gladstone with his own hand were more numerous than might be supposed. These were all copied into a big book and indexed, and I have often thought what a store-house of interest and information these books must contain and regretted that at any rate a selection from them has never been published. His correspondence ranged over a marvellously wide ground, especially when it is remembered that he was at the time Prime Minister, and, for the first year of this Administration, Chancellor of the Exchequer; besides politics it embraced questions connected with art and literature, especially if Homer or Dante were the subject. He was a good Italian scholar, though not so good at French; once he made a speech in Italian at Florence, and the Italians who heard it declared that it was extraordinarily good, the only criticism being that it was just a little archaic and couched more in Dante's style than in that of the present day. His knowledge of German was, I believe, very slight, but this was not unusual in men of his generation.

Whenever a Church dignitary happened to die—and we used to say that we thought that they did so on purpose to spite Mr G.—

he whole business of State seemed to be put aside whilst he poured
orth a perfect avalanche of letters inquiring at great length and in
ninute detail as to the comparative merits and claims of various
lergymen for preferment. In fact he seemed hardly able to give
is full mind to any other matter, however weighty or urgent, until
his Bishopric, Deanery, or even Canonry were filled. This made
s look longingly at the practice of Lord Palmerston who, when
rime Minister, handed over all his Church patronage to Lord
haftesbury. Mr G. was, moreover, so far as politics were con-
erned, rigidly impartial in his ecclesiastical appointments. I had all
ut said "too impartial," by which I mean that if a clergyman had
nown himself active on the Liberal side it almost seemed as though
his put him at a disadvantage. Since no corresponding feeling
ctuated Conservative Prime Ministers, to say the least of it, with
egard to clergymen of their own political views, there was not much
nducement to an able and ambitious clergyman to espouse the cause
f Liberalism.

At first Mrs Gladstone, with the help of one or both of her daughters,
sed to send out invitations to garden-parties or evening receptions.
On one memorable occasion it was matter of comment that one of
hese receptions was very sparsely attended; indeed, people began to
vonder whether some new schism had suddenly broken out within
he Party; but someone happened to notice that nobody was there
vhose name began with a letter which came later in the alphabet
han K, and a day or two later all the invitations addressed to people
vhose names began with a later letter than K were found stuffed
ehind a cushion on a sofa.

Mr Gladstone, on one occasion when the Prince of Wales was going
o dine with him, thought that my uncle's chef would provide a better
linner than his own and asked for the loan of Béguinot, which was
f course willingly granted. The Prince, on being asked by my uncle
few days later how he had enjoyed his dinner, said: "Most interest-
ng, my dear Granville, most interesting and agreeable; very pleasant
eople and capital talk; but the dinner! my dear Granville! the dinner!
Very different from what one gets at your house!" My uncle was
mused but discreetly held his tongue.

Mr G.'s varied and voluminous correspondence was in itself a
iberal education. It included letters from his colleagues in the
Cabinet, from prominent supporters and opponents, legal and

ecclesiastical dignitaries, heads of departments in the Civil Servic
from Viceroys and Governors of Colonies, from Ambassadors an
Ministers and from distinguished foreigners. His own letters to th
Queen were extraordinarily interesting. He wrote Her Majesty
letter describing the proceedings of each sitting in the House
Commons, besides one after every Cabinet meeting, his letters bein
always couched in terms of the most courtly deference. I remembe
once after a specially tiring and harassing debate witnessing a sigl
which to me was peculiarly pathetic. Mr Gladstone, paler even tha
usual and looking worn out with fatigue, sat late at night writing h
letter to the Queen, unmoved by the habitual taunts and insults whic
were being hurled at him by the Opposition; and I could not hel
wondering whether the Royal recipient of that letter at all realize
the depth and fervour of devotion with which the Crown and th
Royal Family were unceasingly served by the greatest of her Minister
in circumstances which might well have discouraged a less magnan
mous and high-minded statesman.

One of the duties of the Private Secretaries was to go round th
room after a Cabinet had been held and to collect and destroy an
scrap of paper or even of blotting paper which might give a possibl
clue to the Cabinet's deliberations. I cannot say that I ever foun
anything of importance, my chief "finds" being caricatures (generall
of their colleagues), though perhaps these might have had a marke
value with the Press under the heading: "Ministers as seen by eac
other." Besides Mr G.'s own correspondence, one also saw the letter
addressed by our representatives abroad to the Foreign Secretary
both official and unofficial, of which the latter were often the mor
illuminating as well as the more amusing.

In 1883 I made a bet of two and sixpence with Eddy Hamilton
then Chief Private Secretary, that the big book in which copies wer
entered of Mr. Gladstone's letters would not be exhausted befor
the Government fell or, in other words, that a new book would no
have to be begun before a change of Administration.

In result, I lost my bet, as a new letter book was obtained in April
1885, just two months before Mr. Gladstone's resignation.

The old letter book with the bet recorded on its fly-leaf is now i
the British Museum.

A great deal of business was also transacted *vivâ voce*, and I thu
gradually got to know most of the Private Secretaries of othe

Ministers, as well as many of the Heads and leading men in the various Departments. What was further very valuable was that one acquired a knowledge of how business of State was transacted, as well as what may be described as intra-departmental methods, and incidentally a certain knowledge of men, both in the aggregate and also of the characteristics of notable personalities.

One of a Secretary's many duties is to act as a "buffer," by interviewing people whom his Chief either does not want or has not time to see. This occasionally implies a certain capacity to "suffer fools gladly," although of course those whom we saw could be described as comprising "all sorts and conditions of men." I remember a Monsieur Taschard, who favoured us with a good deal of his company, in the hope, I suppose, that some of his views might somehow filter through to our Chief. He was a big, excitable man; an Alsatian of considerable property, who after the Franco-German War had opted for German nationality and thus incurred a good deal of unpopularity in France; very unreasonably, as it seems to me, for if the Francophil Alsatians had emigrated *en bloc* to France, the two annexed Provinces would have been stripped of French sympathizers and "swept and garnished" ready for the "seven devils to enter in." Anyhow, Taschard was not a happy man, as the French disliked him whilst the Germans mistrusted him. His chief idea was that Great Britain should avert another war by getting Alsace-Lorraine neutralized. It was my difficult task to persuade him that we could hardly undertake this thankless office without getting ourselves disliked by both French and Germans, and that too without the faintest prospect of success. I once asked him how such a neutralized State was to be defended. He suggested a force of Swiss mercenaries, to which I rejoined that the Swiss were all far too busy, making watches, running hotels and acting as waiters to join such a force. However, all his persistence and tediousness were forgiven him for the sake of his most charming and beautiful daughter, who was a universal favourite. Another of my visitors was an unknown Australian who sent me in his card and, on being introduced, asked, without preliminaries, how much a Peerage would cost him. At first I took him for a lunatic, but found that he was, in his way, quite sane. When I intimated as frostily as I could that Peerages were not thus bestowed, he airily waived the matter aside and proceeded: "Well, Baronetcies, then? Round about what sort of figure would they rule?" I told him that they would not rule round any kind of figure, whereupon he looked very knowing and said: "Of course, I understand; you come into this too; it's only fair you should have a bit of a rake-off. Now, as man to man, if it's a go, shall we say one per cent on the total price?" As man to man, I said that it was a "go" but a go of a different kind, as I rang for the messenger to show him out. He left with a look of mild and pained surprise, as though sorry to see that a man could be so unbusinesslike and so neglectful of his own interests.

This story of attempted bribery reminds me of another. When my Father was M.P. for Bodmin, and before posts in the Civil Service were obtained by competitive examination, a constituent asked him to try to get his nephew a place in the Post Office. My Father accordingly applied to my uncle, who was then in the Cabinet, but without much hope of success. A nomination, however, was forthcoming, which so delighted the nominee's uncle that in his letter of thanks he enclosed a cheque for £500, which of course my Father returned. Back came the cheque with a letter explaining that, as the writer had not made any promise or even suggestion of payment if the nomination were obtained, it should not be regarded as a bribe but only as an expression of gratitude. My Father again returned the cheque, whereupon he received a third letter asking him, since he felt a scruple in accepting it, to regard it as a gift for "his dear little son," an excellent suggestion which I regret to say my Father found equally unacceptable. When he told me the story years afterwards I pointed out to him that, even if he had thought it right to decline the gift for me, he was morally responsible to make it good. He thought I was serious and again declined.

For a little while after I became Secretary I found that some people, mostly women, showed considerable ingenuity in their efforts to extract news. One favourite method was to ask suddenly whether such and such a thing were true, in the hope that one would be betrayed into either confirming or denying it. I found the best way to answer questions of this kind was to say: "How very interesting! And what is *your* opinion?" This was a form of the good Scotch method of answering a question by another.

I generally lunched with my Uncle Granville, when his family was in town, at 18 Carlton House Terrace, the last house at the south-east corner of the Terrace. It took no time getting across the Horse Guards Parade, leaving Downing Street by the door in the garden wall and getting into my uncle's house by the back way which gives on to the Mall. The luncheons were pleasant as one met many diplomats, distinguished foreigners and leading politicians, whilst I and the children generally had a game of drawing-room cricket afterwards, the ball being a soft woolly one and the wicket a tambourine placed on one of the dining-room chairs; in these games we were often joined by Tommy Sanderson, my uncle's Secretary, afterwards created Lord Sanderson, known familiarly in the Foreign Office as "Lamps," from the large spectacles which he wore. Once at Walmer in some charades in which he had to personate an acrobat he gave offence to Lady G. by appearing in his under-shirt and drawers, and she would not be mollified by my assuring her that that was the nearest approach to a professional acrobat's correct costume which could be attained.

CHAPTER XV

CLUBS, COMPLIMENTS AND A STALK

My first Club was White's, which I joined in 1880. The Committee a few years previously had, very inconsiderately, refused to provide a convenient smoking-room, which resulted in the Prince of Wales, who was devoted to his cigar, leaving the Club. His friends started the Marlborough, and many of them followed the royal example and left White's for the new Club. One curious custom from ancient days survived at White's, namely, that if ten or more members put down their names any day before twelve o'clock, a "house dinner" was provided gratis. I attended one of these on the night when my cousin, Lady Cowper, was giving a ball at her house in the north-east corner of St James's Square, and a number of us who were going there put down our names for one of these house dinners. It did not, however, prove quite so cheap as might have been supposed, as one was expected to drink a good deal of wine "for the good of the house," whilst there were subsidiary charges for lights, attendance, etc. In 1881 I was elected to Brooks's, in which Club there has always been at least one member of our family ever since it was founded in the middle of the 18th century; and soon afterwards I resigned my membership of White's, as it seemed not worth while to belong to two Clubs just opposite each other, whilst Brooks's being at that time a purely political club, I there met most of my friends who were Liberals. This state of things was ended by the Home Rule split in 1886, and although the dissentients at first still called themselves Liberals, this was a position which could not long be maintained and they became Tories in name as well as in feeling. In 1887 matters came to a crisis. Sir William Harcourt, who was not a member of the Club, was dining there as a guest on the night when Mr Goschen was beaten, as a Dissentient Liberal at a bye-election in Liverpool. On hearing of this, Sir William loudly gave vent to his exultation and prophesied that before long all the rats would be driven from the

2ND EARL GRANVILLE, K.G.

FROM A SKETCH BY G. RICHMOND, R.A., AND FROM A WATER-COLOUR

House of Commons. This language was naturally not calculated to please such of the aforesaid "rats" who happened to overhear him, and resulted in the blackballing of several Liberals of unexceptionable standing. At the following ballot the Liberals retaliated by pilling some Dissentients of equally good position and an unhappy deadlock seemed to have been reached. Before the third ballot Lord Granville, who was then leader of the Party in the House of Lords, took the unusual but eminently salutary course of making an impromptu speech to the assembled members. He pointed out that this was by no means the first time upon which the Party had been divided, and further, that through and despite all these divisions the Club had remained one of the Party strongholds and had probably been an indirect means of ultimately reuniting the temporarily discordant elements; he further urged that, if a policy of mutual exclusion were to prevail, the Club must inevitably shortly cease to exist, and that if it were really thought impracticable that Liberals and Dissentients should continue in joint occupation of the premises it would on all grounds be preferable to sunder their connection in an amicable and businesslike manner rather than to indulge in this puerile and suicidal warfare. He told me that he had never been so nervous in all his life before making a speech; but it was very well received and the mutual blackballings promptly ceased. Indeed one member half jocularly complained to me that it was now impossible to black-ball an undesirable candidate as his exclusion would be attributed to political motives. At the present time the Club has quite lost its historical political character and Conservatives are elected just as freely as Liberals. A few years after becoming a member of Brooks's I was elected to the St James's, a delightful Club, as one met Foreign Office and diplomatic friends there, as well as the foreign diplomats. I was once in the outer hall with Harry Cust, most brilliant and best beloved of mortals; we looked through the glass door into the morning-room which faces Piccadilly and I was going in when he pulled me back. "Don't, George; there are too many Bolivians there!" I did not join the National Liberal Club when it was founded, as two Clubs were quite enough for a busy and not over wealthy young man. On the Home Rule split the same situation arose as at Brooks's, only instead of mutual pillings a violent debate ensued at a general meeting which, after heated recriminations, resulted in the secession of the Dissentients. In the middle of

November 1887, my friend, Herbert Gladstone (afterwards Viscount Gladstone), who was indefatigable in his efforts to keep the Club afloat, made a strong personal appeal to me, which I could not resist, to become a member. I was a little dashed a fortnight later when I learnt that several hundred new members would be elected without having to pay an entrance fee, especially as I had to pay one yearly subscription on November 20, 1887, and another on January 1, 1888. However, I suppose it was all in the day's work. During the time that I was the unpaid Government representative on the Ecclesiastical Commission, I found this Club very handy for luncheon before going on to the House for my duties as Whip; and it was, moreover, a capital place to entertain one's constituents. The only other Club that I belonged to in those early days, besides the Guildford County Club and the M.C.C., was a short-lived and, on the whole, rather hectic experiment of a musical and artistic character, called the Lyric, near Leicester Square. The M.C.C., to which I was elected in 1881, is, in my opinion, the best money's worth that you can get in Clubland, especially for one who, like myself, is fond of the old game of tennis as well as of cricket, and in the pavilion on the days of great matches one has many opportunities of renewing acquaintanceships dating from Eton and Oxford days. I find that I had forgotten two other Clubs of my youth. The Burlington Fine Arts Club in Savile Row, whose excellent annual exhibitions are so widely known, I gave up after a few years, as I had neither the leisure nor the means to become a collector. The other was the Cosmopolitan, to which I was elected in 1881, chiefly out of compliment to my Father, who was one of its oldest members. This was an unusual sort of Club, as it only met twice a week, on Wednesday and Sunday nights, opening about 10.30 p.m. and remaining open for about three hours or so. On Wednesday nights, in those days, the House did not sit, as it was the Private Members' day, when the House met at noon and rose at six. It was, therefore, the great day for political dinners and people came on afterwards to the "Cos." The method of election was unusual, but worked well. At the beginning of each season a paper was circulated to each member bearing the names of candidates and of their proposers and seconders, mention being also made of the number of vacancies. Each member could vote for as many candidates as there were vacancies, and did so by underlining the names of those of his choice. He was forbidden to sign his name. At the first meeting of the season, which was generally well attended, the committee made out a list of the votes which the various candidates had received, those who got most being elected. In the event of a tie for the last place, a ballot of the members present was held on the spot. If, after four years, a candidate did not receive a certain minimum of votes he automatically disappeared from the list. The merit of this arrangement was that nobody was ever blackballed, and the most that an unlucky candidate could complain of was that the claims of others had been considered superior to his own. I was lucky enough, owing to my Father's popularity, to come in at the head of the list, an election which a friend of his, with more good will than knowledge of French, declared to him was quite a "*succès d'estime*." The meeting-place was very handy for my Father and myself, as it was held in Watts's former studio, in the narrow part of Charles Street, near the chapel in John Street, Mayfair, and only three minutes' walk from our home in South Audley Street.

The home of the Cosmopolitan was of singular construction, as, apart from two tiny rooms on the ground floor, it consisted only of one very large room on the first floor lighted by a skylight and without windows. Nearly the whole of one of the walls was occupied by an immense picture by Watts, representing an incident in one of Boccaccio's *Decameron* Tales, wherein the spirit of a girl who had jilted an admirer is depicted as flying from him in a state of complete nudity, whilst he on horseback urges on a pack of savage hounds in pursuit. The tale runs that another young man in a similar unfortunate predicament witnesses this terrifying manifestation, and invites a party, including the damsel who had played fast and loose with his affections, to picnic in the woods at the spot where the apparition takes place. The young woman was so much impressed by what she saw that she repented of her obduracy. It was a current joke in the Club that each of the figures had only one leg, and such indeed was very nearly the case, but it was a fine picture for all that. A laughable occurrence took place at the Cos. The method of admission was by rapping at the front door which was opened by a commissionaire. An over-zealous policeman noticed that the place was only open two nights a week, and the absence of windows giving it an air of mystery, a police raid was organized, under the impression that it was a gambling hell or something worse. The police obtained admission, silenced the amazed commissionaire, and leaving a guard at the front door the inspector and the rest of his men crept up the stairs and cautiously opened the door of the big room. Behind this was a very broad and high Chinese screen, representing every variety of torture, the gift of a member, who presumably did not care to have it in his own house. The inspector dashed round the corner of the screen, calling out, "In the name of the law!" but instead of seeing an orgy in process, he was confronted by a score or so of elderly gentlemen quietly conversing over their whisky and soda and cigars. Amongst them were a Bishop, a Judge or two, several Ambassadors, many Peers and M.P.'s, and the Home Secretary! The inspector's retreat was more hurried than dignified, and I doubt whether he got the promotion for vigilance and acumen on which he had confidently reckoned.

The subscription was very low, only two guineas, but yielded an income far exceeding the Club's very modest requirements. In consequence, tea, coffee, tobacco, mineral waters, brandy, whisky and gin were supplied gratis to members and their guests. When Wednesday nights ceased, from a Parliamentary point of view, to be a "*dies non*" (if I may be allowed such an Irish bull), the Cos. began to decline. It finally migrated for a few years to the rooms of the Alpine Club in Savile Row; whilst its last expiring efforts took the shape of a series of sumptuous annual dinners paid for out of the surplus funds of the Club. I well remember an instance of Beerbohm Tree's wonderful vivacity and vitality. We had been dining at a Pilgrim Club dinner and I brought him along to the Cos., and can vouch that he poured forth at the two places a flood of intensely interesting and brilliant conversation without intermission from eight o'clock till one in the morning, to the delight and admiration of all who were privileged to hear him.

The Breakfast Club was another institution which flourished in the 'eighties and 'nineties, although founded some years earlier. It consisted of about a dozen members, who, during the season, entertained each other alternately once a week in their own houses. The only guests admitted were foreigners or distinguished Colonials, but when a member was giving a breakfast he was allowed to have his son, or sons, at the table. I profited by this regulation and heard much good talk at these pleasant reunions. Amongst the members were Lord Dufferin, Lord Wolseley, Lord Aberdare (at one time Home Secretary in Mr Gladstone's Government), Henry Cowper (Lord

Cowper's brother), Sir Mount Stuart Grant Duff (at one time
Governor of Madras), Lord Reay (afterwards Governor of Bombay),
and Mr Venables, who when a boy at Westminster broke Thackeray's
nose in a fight and who, if I remember aright, edited the Annual
Register. There were also Sir James Lacaita, Lord Lansdowne, Sir
T. Erskine May (Chief Clerk to the House of Commons and author
of the well-known work on Constitutional History), Sir Frederick
Pollock, Lord Arthur Russell, M.P., the first Lord Acton, Lord
Carlingford, Sir George Trevelyan, Mr Goschen, Laurence
Oliphant, Lord Herschel, Mr Robert Duff, M.P., Sir Robert
Herbert of the Colonial Office, Lord Courtney, Sir Alfred Lyall (the
well-known Indian administrator and writer), the first Lord Loch
and Lord de Tabley. Of this distinguished company I believe there
are no survivors. Cecil Rhodes came, as a guest, to a breakfast held
at my Father's house, and sat at his right hand. My Father found him
difficult to get on with, and when he asked him if he were going to
be long in England, got the not very gracious reply: "Not a moment
longer than I can help!" The only other time that I met him was in
the train, on our way to a Saturday to Monday party at Lord Roths-
child's at Tring. He scowled at me all the way, and as I could barely
get an answer out of him when I spoke, I gave it up as a bad job. He
may have been delightful to those with whom he was intimate, but
could not be described as having a happy manner with chance
acquaintances.

I witnessed a similar instance of bad manners at Walmer Castle,
when Count Herbert von Bismarck (the great Bismarck's son) was
my uncle's guest. At the end of dinner he announced, quite
gratuitously, that the liqueur brandy in English country houses was
so bad that he always took a bottle with him when he went on a visit,
and, suiting the action to the word, produced a flask from his pocket.
The rudeness was all the more noticeable as my uncle was then Foreign
Secretary, whilst his own father was Imperial Chancellor. Sir George
Dasent, a man of infinite jest, who was a Civil Service Commissioner,
and whose witticisms were heightened by being delivered with a
jerky manner and in a high falsetto voice, rejoined: "Very natural
indeed; I do the same; only I always take two bottles." "What!
No! *Two* bottles!!" was the Prussian's astonished exclamation.
"But where is your flask?" "Well, to tell the truth, it's in my
bedroom. I know our poor host's brandy is shocking; quite un-

drinkable; but he's an old friend, and I have to humour him by pretending I like it, though I have to go to my room afterwards to take the bad taste out of my mouth by a swig at my own!" All this in front of my uncle who was perfectly delighted, whilst the heavy German boor took it all in and never for a moment suspected that fun was being poked at him.

Sir George once told me that Lady Dasent was "very strict, very strict indeed," which in fact she was. "Why, when we have friends to stay with us she insists on the luggage of the men and women being put into separate lumber rooms!"

On another occasion he horrified Mr Gladstone by his account of Disraeli's cynicism à propos of the Royal Academy Exhibition. He said that they had met in Bond Street and that Dizzy had told him that he had just come from the Private View. "Such a collection of miserable trash, my dear Dasent, it would be hard to conceive. Horrible! Horrible!" The same evening Disraeli made the chief speech at the Academy Dinner, in some such terms as the following: "It is some compensation to a jaded Minister, worn by the burden and the cares of State, to leave for a moment the fevered atmosphere of political conflict, and to seek momentary refreshment and spiritual solace in the contemplation of the triumph of British art displayed on these walls by the glowing masterpieces which I see hung around me on every side." When Dasent concluded this story with the comment "Rather comic, wasn't it?" Mr Gladstone, instead of being amused like the rest of the company, became pale with indignation and his great eyes flashed, as he rejoined: "Comic! Do you call that comic? I call it devilish!" There you have the two men in a nutshell.

Dasent was an Icelandic scholar and translated some sagas: he also wrote an amusing collection of essays entitled "Jest and Earnest," and another called "Bubbles from the Brünnen of Nassau."

In February 1881 I attended my first levée at St James's Palace which I thus describe to a friend:

"It was a beastly squash on the stairs and an officer ran the spike of his helmet into the cheek of a fat, podgy little man in front of him, who waxed exceeding wroth, whereat all the company did fall a laughing. I made my bow with grace and self-possession to four successive Royalties and then went home. *V'là tout.*"

On July 1, Mr Gladstone sent the following letter to my Father

which I reproduce with some hesitation on account of its too complimentary terms.

"July 1, 1881.

"MY DEAR LEVESON,

"A year has now passed since your son joined my staff of
Private Secretaries. In this respect, he was brought, I must say,
into extremely good company; but this is only saying in other
words that the standard is high, and the test of competency and
capacity severe. This being so, I think it may please you to know
from me in writing what I have already stated to you more generally
in conversation, that he has stood that test admirably, and has made
or proved himself thoroughly well qualified for the nice and exacting
duties of a good P. Sec. to a Minister. And all his qualities make
him not less agreeable to his colleagues than he is valuable to me.
I should rejoice on every ground if an opportunity were to offer
for advancing him beyond his present position, in which it seems
hardly just that he should much longer remain, though, were he to
pass these walls, he would leave many regrets behind him.

"Believe me always,

"Sincerely yours,

"W. E. GLADSTONE."

In September of the same year I got a holiday and went to Scotland,
amongst other visits I paid one to Sir Dudley Marjoribanks at Guisachan, near Beauly, whence I wrote to Shoobridge on the 8th of the
month, describing my deer-stalking experiences:

"The stags unfortunately prefer to hide themselves in recesses of
the mountains, instead of remaining at a lower altitude where they
would be more accessible to a sportsman who is not in the best of
condition. Having therefore climbed '*non sine sudore*' to the top
of Ben Beastly-Grind (or some such name), one is informed after
a due interval of spying with telescopes, 'Aweel! the stogs ha'e
just feedled awa' to the co-o-rries wast of Ben Straddlekin, so we
wull just go roon' by yon glen, and then wull keep up acrost the
scaur, an then wull aye follow the bur-r-rn to the top o' the beeg
hull, an' may be there'll just be a gr-r-rand chance o' seein' them
there.' Then we tramp off again, tramp, tramp, tramp; then
heather and stones get into my boot and hurt my right heel, and

then when that has been rectified, the other boot begins to gall my left instep. When I am thoroughly blown a ghillie is seen wildly gesticulating at the top of a neighbouring peak and thus delivers himself in Gaelic, 'Hoosh, wash, skornoch, striddlevan skeeach kooroo!' or somewhat to that effect. The other stalker then addresses me, 'We'll need to be rinnin' up yon slope-like to cut them aff, the deers are fiddin' (feeding) op the hull.'

(N.B. Angle of "Yon slope-like": _1_)

"If clinging on for dear life to a sheer precipice and slowly and painfully swarming up it can be fairly called 'rinnin',' I rin, and on reaching the top in a state of utter prostration behold the stags disappearing over another hill about half a mile further on. Then, after a consultation, the head stalker asks, 'Wad ye be likin' your lunch the noo?' I jump at the proposal, as this is a part of the stalk which I thoroughly enjoy; but on offering to light a cigarette, am told 'Ye must na' smok', the dee-eers wull smull it!' Then another long stalk, then a sudden halt, and down we all go into thick black peat mud in which you sink nine inches. Intense excitement of which I cannot discern the cause. First Gillie (excitedly), 'Killi-bannin bishwallashy, toorillooral kin bang floobah!' Second Gillie (still more excitedly), 'Yah bool faramallaloo koom pigwash!' Stalker (dubitatively), 'Agool kan foh!' First Gillie (inquiringly) 'Igollo? 'Stalker, 'Clang': then to me, 'They're just lyin' doon the noo, so we'll need to do just so whiles they move again.'

"Down in the deep black mud sits a sportsman wet through his breeches.

"'Hating the stags and the stalkers, abhorring the hills of the Highlands!' Then midges devour me. I plead vainly for a cigarette. 'Na, na, ye must na' smok'!' Then I wave my hand-kerchief in maddening irritation. 'Hoots, sir, the hinds will be seein' ye!' Resignation to misery! A fine subject for a Fable after the manner of Æsop. 'The sportsman and the midges.' After sitting in mud and midges for two hours a thick mist super-venes which changes into a drenching drizzle, through which a nine mile ride on a Highland pony forms a suitable conclusion to this most enjoyable day."

This episode recalls an incident which occurred at the house of a great Scotch landlord, who owned one of the finest forests in the

untry. A guest was enjoying an after breakfast cigar on a bench
the garden, which happened to be near the window of his host's
dy, which was open. Quite unwillingly he overheard the follow-
g conversation between his host and his head stalker, as by the time
at he realized that it concerned himself, he feared to reveal his
esence if he moved away. Stalker: "And for what will your Grace
wishful to-morrow?" "Well, Mr —— (the man outside) might
e to go on the hill." "Wull it be for a wa-a-alk or a stalk, your
race?" "Oh! I think that he would enjoy seeing the beautiful
enery. You understand, McGregor?" "I do that, your Grace."
t luncheon his host asked Mr —— whether he would like to go for
stalk the next day, and was thus answered: "I should enjoy a stalk
ry much; but as far as a walk is concerned, I am not sure that I
ould not prefer the beautiful view you get from the path by the
rn just over the Castle." The hint was taken, but the guest was
t invited again.

CHAPTER XVI

SPANISH MISSION

On October 1, 1881, I left London at the age of twenty-three, as attaché to the Mission of which my uncle, Lord Northampton, w the head, which was commissioned to invest the King of Spai Alfonso XII, with the Order of the Garter. With the exception the officials from the Heralds' Office we were practically a fami party, consisting of my uncle and his two elder sons, Lord Compte and Lord William Compton (the latter being then a diplomat Philip Currie of the Foreign Office (afterwards Lord Currie), wh was Secretary to the Mission; Colonel Alick Elliot (afterwards Major-General and K.C.B.), a *beau sabreur* who had distinguishe himself greatly in the charge of Balaclava and whose sister ha married my uncle; Lord Downe, who looked magnificent in his Li Guards uniform, and my cousin Lady Margaret Compton, wh afterwards married Sir Henry Graham, who was Clerk of the Parli ment. The Heralds' Office was represented by the Garter King Arms, Sir Albert Woods, a short, grey, stoutish old gentleman, qui ignorant of French, but profuse in his declarations that he woul "always do his duty"; the Lancaster Herald, Mr G. E. Cockayne, a elderly and rather melancholy man with a long beard; and Blu Mantle, Mr E. Bellasis, a young and friendly person whose featur were wreathed in a perpetual smile. Our company assembled ver early in the morning at Victoria, where we were marshalled by ou Swiss courier, Werner, who decorated our luggage with distinctiv badges of red, blue and yellow tape; by which precaution I do no think that a single piece went astray during the whole of our journey in itself no mean performance. I found these badges so convenier that I kept them on my luggage after our return, and nearly paid penalty for doing so as, when I was going down to Holmbury fron Charing Cross next year, my traps were nearly whirled away wit the belongings of a party whom Werner was at that moment escortin

om the same station on their way to Italy. It was a very close shave
ndeed! Werner was an excellent courier and a man of great
olubility and resource.

We were all in tearing spirits and there was a good deal of bally-
agging in the train between Elliot, Downe and Willie. Minnie had
 huge paper wrapper (originally used for packing up a long stick)
nd laid about her with this in much the same fashion as a huntsman
vould use his whip with an unruly pack of hounds. On leaving the
ailway carriage this was attached to Elliot's coat-tails, who descended
n to the platform with much "presence" and only became aware
f the trick by the merriment of the bystanders.

To quote from my journal:

"We keep steadily an hour late, they say that the French engine
rivers are allowed a certain fixed maximum of coal; if they can save
ny on the journey it is their perquisite, so they will not put on extra
oal to make up for lost time.

"We saw 'Divorçons!' at the Palais Royal, all except Minnie, who
leaded fatigue, which perhaps was as well. Chaumont took the
art of Cyprienne; she has got fat and ugly but the acting was through-
ut first rate. The French people are lucky in not being saddled with
 Lord Chamberlain, who, as the 'Figaro' remarked, 'veille à ce que
 public ne s'amuse pas trop.'

"Oct. 5. Walk with Currie to the Embassy, where in the
Chancellerie we find Tom Legh" (now Lord Newton) "and Gerard
owther" (afterwards created a Baronet). "Tom Legh and Sheffield
ave just made a fine hash of it between them. A lovely lady, of a
ertain age, presents herself yesterday at the Embassy and asks to see
heffield, who, polite as ever, presents himself and finds himself
lking to a most charming English lady, calling herself Mrs Sinclair,
ho gives verbal references to all sorts of distinguished people, talking
f them in a way which seemed as if she knew them quite well; had
st come from an out of the way provincial town, was going with
er daughter to Russia and—requested a passport. 'What ho! Tom
egh!' cries Sheffield, and, hey presto! the passport is drawn up.
heffield bows to the lady, opens the door for her; she smiles
aciously, expresses thanks and sails away. Scene 2. A messenger
om the Russian Embassy two hours later. 'A dangerous Nihilist,
ladame So-and-so, calling herself Mrs Sinclair' (a description of her

tallying exactly) 'is in Paris and will probably call for a passport fo Russia. If she does, please refuse it and let us know.' But the bir had flown; telegrams were fired off to the frontier and we are all i a state of excitement to know whether the lady and her 'daughter will succeed in smuggling through a choice selection of bombs an dynamite as a little offering to the Emperor of All the Russias.

"I bought a stout cane for the moderate sum of four francs, the lad who sold it assuring me that it was '*propre à assommer un taureau*,' statement which I was quite willing to take on her word.

"*Oct.* 6. On leaving Bordeaux we change carriages into da saloons, a Frenchman occupies one of these and firmly refuses t budge, to all explanations that the coupé was '*loué*' and '*réservé*' h turns a heedless ear and when we suggest to the officials that the should remonstrate with him they shrug their shoulders and say '*Impossible, Monsieur, c'est un Député.*' Hurrah for '*Liberté, Egalite* etc!' So he succeeded in resisting eviction and secured his 'fixit of tenure.' What an Irish M.P. he would have made!

"Willie much chaffed for investing himself in a coat with a ver pronounced waist, long tails, and altogether fearfully and wonderfull made. He has an idea that it makes him look like a Frenchman.

"Before reaching Menoux we get into the regular Landes country passing on a dead level through miles and miles of pine woods plante by the Government, who, they say, spend £80,000 a year in this way Currie said that when we took the plantation of Cyprus in hand w had to employ a Frenchman to direct operations, as he was the onl person who could be found to do it satisfactorily. At Menou Elliot nearly reduces a French General to a fit of apoplexy by mistakin him for the Chef de Gare, and we left him swelling visibly on th platform looking as if he were going to burst instantaneously; how ever, I don't think he did, as we did not hear the report of the explos ion. We have taken to call Elliot '*Mon Maréchal*' before the foreigner as we think it adds to his importance. Willie alone detracts from th effect by addressing him as '*Mon Caporal*,' which he deems a mor appropriate title.

"On arriving at Biarritz we find a number of fashionable people o the platform, conspicuous among whom was the traditional 'Auguste or 'Hippolyte,' with a very small billycock, very tight-fitting coa and very loose trousers, a butterfly tie all over his chest, a gun slun over his shoulder and a pair of white lawn tennis shoes!

"When near Miranda Elliot told us that Lord Lonsdale, when travelling in this part of the country with a tutor at the age of eighteen or nineteen during the Carlist War, slipped away and offered his services to Don Carlos, who accepted them. Before long he was in command of a brigade and on one occasion distinguished himself by covering the retreat of the army.

"*Oct.* 7. Some amusing extracts from the 'Figaro.'

"(1) '*La fureur de la Chambre*' (House of Commons) '*contre ces révolutionnaires ne connut pas de bornes; ainsi, dans un mouvement d'indignation expulsa t'on MM. Parnell et Bradlaugh, malgré la vive opposition de leurs compatriotes irlandais.*'

"(2) '*Autre violence commise dans le Comté de King*' (King's County).

"(3) '*Le théatre du Lycée appartenant au célèbre comédien Swing*' (Irving).

"*Madrid.* After luncheon I went off to a barber's, no one could talk anything but Spanish, but I made myself understood with much pantomime, some bad Italian, three or four Spanish words and some laughter on the part of the hairdressers.

"Walking home we noticed a number of mounted gendarmes. They always seem to run in couples, a fact which Elliot accounts for by their not being trusted alone.

"After coming back to the Hotel de Paris in the Plaza del Sol, a big open place in the middle of the town, we heard the sound of music and revelry downstairs, which we were told was occasioned by a *réunion* in the café of bull fighters and ladies of the town, but we were not allowed to go as it was thought *infra dig.*

"*Madrid, Oct.* 8. I heard an amusing story about the *octroi*, which imposes a local duty on all sorts of comestibles, especially upon spirits. A distillery was established just outside the *octroi* boundary and prospered exceedingly. The men and women employed in it slept in Madrid and went out every morning to their work. One evening as they were returning home, some of the *octroi employés* were attracted by the buxom charms of several of the young women, who were remarkably finely developed. One tried to snatch a kiss, but his playful *badinage* made him suspect the super-natural firmness of the damsel's bosom. She was hurried off and handed over to a female searcher, who found too large false breasts of tin, naturally full of brandy, strapped on to her person. A tremendous general hue and cry ensued, the girls running like hares in every direction with the *octroi* men after them, for every woman was similarly equipped. After this fortuitous discovery the profits of the distillery considerably decreased.

"*Madrid*, *Oct.* 8. An old gentleman, a certain Col. Fitch, called; he is about eighty and has lived in Spain all his life; he fought in the first Carlist War, though I am not clear on which side, and is now one of the features of Madrid. The greatest pleasure you can do him is to die here, as he has the management of the English Cemetery, and not only gets the excitement of ordering your funeral, but also the fees, which are an object to him as he is not well off.

"At six we rehearsed the investiture. Fitzroy Langley, of our Embassy, was king and had a beautiful paper crown, whilst Minnie, as his consort, had a smaller one.

"On the day of the ceremony the chambermaids at the hotel were invited to have a look at Minnie before we started for the Palace. She wore a very smart Paris 'creation,' and the head chambermaid said that she looked quite '*como una Madrileña*' (like a lady of Madrid), which I suppose was, in her opinion, the highest compliment which she could pay her. I acted on the suggestion by buying her a beautiful high tortoiseshell comb, such as Spanish women wear to hold up their mantillas above their heads, but not even this succeeded in making her look very Spanish, with her fair hair, blue eyes and fresh complexion.

"For the investiture I am, as we used to say at Eton when picking up sides for a game of football, 'last choice,' and have to carry the hat and feathers. The hat is of black velvet and somewhat of the Beef-eater shape, adorned with ostrich feathers.

"Señor Zarco, a grandee and one of the King's Chamberlains, dined with us and made himself agreeable. He told me of a curious custom prevailing at the Court. In the tenth century a King of Spain was out boar hunting, when a ferocious boar rushed at him and would have gored him had not two faithful hunters thrown themselves between the beast and his sacred person. These men came from a village near by, since called *Espinosa de los Monteros* (E. of the Hunters), and the King was so much pleased at having been rescued that he issued an Edict that the inhabitants of this village should ever after have charge of his person and of those of his descendants. There were only fifteen families in the village but they were all made nobles and twelve

men of these families have ever since then taken turn to guard the
King by night. Every night two of them arrive at the ante-room of
his bed chamber, and one sleeps in the armchair whilst the other paces
up and down until one o'clock, when he is relieved by his companion.
Their days are free, and each one gets £120 a year, out of which they
have to find their uniforms. They also have sole charge of the
monarch's body after death until it is buried. Señor Zarco told me that
he once had to escort the corpse of one of the sisters of a former King
from Madrid to the Escorial. This was before the railway was made
and he had to sit in uniform for thirteen hours in the coach. These
Monteros walked all the distance (rather less than 40 miles) as an escort.

"After dinner I talked to Mr Cockayne about the Heralds College.
Their number is thirteen and they are nominated, very conscientiously,
by the Duke of Norfolk. It is not much of a post financially, being
only worth £16 a year. They had each to be in residence for two
months in the year at their College, which lies between St. Paul's
and the river. They have very good chambers but their post is
otherwise a sinecure.

"*Madrid, Oct.* 9. We went over our Legation which is in a very
tumble-down condition, but the rooms themselves are good, although
now quite unfurnished. In the chancery there were some amusing
sketches of the reign of 'King' Layard (Sir Henry Layard, the celebrated excavator of Nineveh, a former Minister at Madrid), who
appears from them to have been by no means a popular monarch.
Photographs of all the former members of the Legation are hung up
in affectionate remembrance. In one room an attaché was shot at
from outside during a Revolution, the bullet being visible imbedded
in the wall. A palace just in front of the Legation was burnt down
during one of these riots, and the staff were disappointed at the
Government rebuilding it, as it will darken their windows. Captain
Ruffwell, of the Intelligence Department, who has been sent out to
attend the ceremony and to report on the Spanish army, was here,
having only just arrived.

"After luncheon we went to the bull fight. I was curious to note
the variety of vehicles, some old shandrydans drawn by eight mules
or ponies. There must have been about 6,000 people present. Our
box was very comfortable and held eight people, so we just filled it.
The bull-fighters were splendidly dressed and I hear that the three best
spadas are to fight to-day. Their clothes fit very closely and are

covered with spangles and tassels. After the course has been cleared by two Alguazils, the whole company march across the arena and make their bow to the President, who throws down the keys which open the gates of the pens where the bulls are confined. It is a cruel sport, as the poor bull is scientifically tired out before they venture to go near him, besides which he has the disadvantage of being dazzled by leaving the darkness of his pen for the blaze of light in the arena. I should not mind the risk the men have to take, but I hated the cruelty to the horses, poor blind-folded hacks stationed around the arena to be helplessly gored by the bull. Much skill, it is true, was displayed, but I shall never go to see this revolting spectacle again. One of the *spadas* had been a lawyer, he now maintains twenty dependents. A *picador* (a horseman) prodded the bull too low down and was fined by the President amid general cheering. They say that two or three men are killed every year, to which I can only say 'Serve them right!'

"*Madrid*, *Oct*. 10. Currie, Willie and I left early and spent the day at the Escorial; an impressive but gloomy pile, the description of which I will spare my readers.

"*Madrid*, *Oct*. 11. The great day of the Investiture has arrived. We all look most imposing. Uncle William in an Admiral's uniform; Downe in that of the Life Guards; Elliot as a Staff Officer; Charlie as a Deputy Lieutenant; Willie, Currie and myself in diplomatic uniforms with knee breeches; Sir A. Woods gorgeously attired in a flowing mantle reaching to the ground, with the Cross of the Garter embroidered at the side, he bore a sceptre and looked almost regal. Cockayne and Bellasis in tabards and white legs, looking like the Knaves in a pack of cards. Elliot and I started first. I had some difficulty in keeping the Hat and Feathers on the cushion, as it was top heavy and always threatening to tumble off. A splendid coach and four awaited us, the horses richly harnessed and decorated with plumes. Six footmen in wigs, three-cornered eighteenth-century hats and long staves walked by the side of the carriage. Every now and then two mounted officers galloped up and down for no particular reason, and returned for the same cause, but were much impressed with their own importance. The other coaches followed ours, the two last with six horses each and my Uncle sitting in the last of all. The streets through which we passed were full of people. On arriving at the Palace yard we found a line of infantry and hussars down the middle, with a band playing and lots of spectators. We were then deposited alternately at two side entrances, my Uncle being alone allowed to go up the central one. We halt at the foot of the stairs and wait for him, and, on his arrival, file up the staircase. I was at the head of the procession and had to be whistled back as I mounted the staircase with too much rapidity for the dignity of the occasion. The rest of the Mission followed in pairs (like the animals going into the Ark). At the head of the staircase we were received by two Big Wigs and proceeded to an ante-room to the strains of 'God save the Queen.' We pass between two lines of the body guard, a fine set of men with cocked hats and pikes. On reaching the ante-room we are met by Zarco and halt for a few minutes. The door is then thrown open and the Ambassador announced.

"The King was a little bit of a man but had a pleasant face. The Queen had a good figure and was well dressed, but I regret to add that her complexion was not all that could be desired. The Grandees were anything but grand in appearance; short, ugly, stupid looking and fat, such should I say were the most appropriate epithets. The women were better looking but rather badly dressed, so far as I could judge. The audience seemed much interested in the ceremony, and, when it was finished, we all backed out bowing and marched downstairs in the same order as that in which we had come up, I at the head of the procession. We drove home in state. My Uncle had to start off in uniform to pay two official visits, which were immediately returned, whilst we got into our ordinary raiment as soon as possible. The whole business took about an hour and a quarter.

"*Oct.* 12. We spent a delightful day at Toledo, with the beauty and picturesque situation of which I was much impressed, as also with its Roman and Moorish remains.

"*Madrid, Oct.* 13. My Uncle and I stroll about the Buen Retiro, a park situated above Madrid. From one point one gets a good view over the plain to the South. All the *beau monde* seemed to be there. The equestrians amused me not a little, their main idea seeming to be to stick their feet as far through the stirrups as possible, to sit well forward and to drag heavily on the curb, thereby causing their unhappy steeds to caper in what, I have no doubt, their riders thought was a graceful fashion.

"At 7.30 we dine at the Palace; the same galaxy of footmen lining all the stairs. My Uncle presented each of us to the King and Queen, who spoke a few gracious words before we went into dinner. On one side I was seated next to a General who had won the battle of Tetuan in Morocco in 1869 and had commanded the Spanish forces in Cuba for four years. Unfortunately he could only speak Spanish, but by the greatest of good luck I had gone that very same morning to see an excellent panorama of the Battle of Tetuan, so proceeded to make the best play possible with my very recently acquired information. The conversation proceeded somewhat as follows: I, with a deep bow and in (probably) execrable Spanish, '*Una grande vittoria, Tetuan.*' The General beams all over his face and bows in return. I, '*La infanteria?*' in a tone of interested inquiry. The General, 'Ah! yes, the *infanteria!*' illustrating the movements of the infantry with the help of a lot of crumbs. I listen with rapt attention, and when the exploits of the infantry seem to be exhausted, I proceed, '*Y la caballeria?*' The General, 'Why certainly, the cavalry'; and their achievements are dexterously indicated by an arrangement of forks. I resume, '*L'artilleria?*' The position of the batteries was then demonstrated by wine glasses. I exclaim, '*Nada los Moros.*' ('The Moors were nothing'; i.e. beat to a frazzle.) This last effort of mine sent the General into paroxysms of delight. I afterwards heard that he told someone that he was quite enchanted to find that the Battle of Tetuan was so well known in England that its details were familiar even to a civilian of that nation, and that he thought that I had shown a remarkable grasp of the various details of strategy which had brought about that memorable victory.

"My other neighbour spoke French and was an agreeable man. He was a Marquis and a Grandee, and seemed to have more go about him than most of his peers. He had formerly been a Deputy for the Asturias, but at the last election had been beaten by a Liberal by a small majority. He now sits, by virtue of his rank, as a Peer. He told me that Grandees may be candidates for the Chamber of Deputies. The *Progresistas*, or Liberals, are now in power. The Opposition consists of *Moderados*, or Conservatives, and of Republicans, broken up into a number of sections, some favouring a unified and some a Federal Republic; but he added that the Republicans were few in numbers and hopelessly divided. The dinner was excellent and quickly served, whilst a band of the Halberdiers played very well all the time. After coffee in the drawing-room we were all presented to the Infantas, the King's sisters. (It was my great privilege when I was Comptroller of Her Majesty's Household to be attached to the service of the Infanta Eulalia, when she came to London, I think in 1892. I showed her over the Houses of Parliament and other places of interest, and shall not readily forget the charm and beauty of that most gracious lady.) The Colonel of the Halberdiers, as a conclusion to this most agreeable evening, then took me round the State Rooms and we left at about 11.30.

"*Madrid, Oct. 14.* At 1.30 we drove to the Palace and were ushered up to the private apartments. Their Majesties received us very graciously, and the baby (a little girl of thirteen months) was brought in, a pretty enough child, accompanied by two nurses, one English and the other a Spaniard with much bravery of national costume, black velvet, big silver buttons and red silk. The King and Queen were quite at their ease and talked away and laughed freely, which, it is said, they do not do before Spaniards. The rooms are small but prettily furnished and very snug, the King insisting on showing us everything, including the bedroom. To wind up he took us to his study, where he produced photographs of himself and of the Queen, and we were allowed to choose one of each, which they signed. There was a good deal of chaff about a huge cigar, about four and a half feet long and as thick as one's two hands could clasp. It had come from Cuba and smelt very good, the King offered it to Downe (whom he would call Major Downe) to smoke on his way home. He rather embarrassed my Uncle by a number of questions about our Navy, from which he had retired ages ago, I should think before the days of steam or of ironclads, and he had to confess that he was as ignorant of modern naval developments as the veriest landlubber. The Queen admitted to Minnie that she hated the bull-fights, but had to attend as it would be as much as her place was worth if she absented herself. She made the curious statement that whenever she felt particularly sick at the proceedings she fortified herself by eating sandwiches, which seems a strange remedy for nausea. ('Stay me with flagons, comfort me with apples, for I am sick.') There was no time to see the Royal Stables, so leaving my Uncle and Currie (who had been respectively presented with the First and Second Class of the Order of Carlos III, the most distinguished Order in Spain) to pay their p.p.c. visits to the Minister of Foreign Affairs, the Marquis Vega y Armijo, we returned to the hotel where we changed our clothes and said good-bye to the Heralds, to Charlie, Downe and

Elliot, who were going home. The Order of Carlos III has a pretty ribbon of light blue and white and my Uncle wore it constantly on State occasions when he got home, until he was made a Knight of the Garter a few years later, when Carlos III was generally relegated to the obscurity of his wardrobe.

"A Spanish paper in an account of the Mission made a sad hash of our names. We were described as Lord Northamton (without a 'p'); El Señor Downe; Sir Voos (Sir A. Woods); M. Fritz (Fitzroy Langley); M. Courrie and Lord Villian (Willie, who was promptly christened 'The Villain'). This was excusable in a foreign paper, but we were positively amazed at a long account of the proceedings in *The Times*, simply crammed with the most extraordinary howlers. This, I am sure, would be quite impossible at the present day, when *The Times* is a model to the whole journalistic world, not only for the exceptional interest of the news which it gives, but for the correctness and elegance of expression which characterize its articles."

The mistakes were so funny and so numerous that I hope I may be excused if I reproduce a notice of them which appeared in *The World*, of Oct. 19, 1881; *The Times* Letter, which was dated from Madrid on Oct. 11, being published in their issue of the 12th; I have a copy of both of these and can personally vouch that the mistakes signalized by *The World* are all as given textually in *The Times*. The only way in which I can account for this strange production is that there was probably ill-feeling in their staff against the management at that time, and that the errors were purposely concocted and somehow eluded the vigilance of the reader.

Punch, in the issue of Oct. 22, 1881, had a clever black and white caricature by Harry Furniss, rather on the same lines as *The World's* criticism.

THE WORLD. Oct. 19, 1881

"It is so long since Boabdil breathed his last sigh and the Arab took his last farewell of Spain, that the few incoherencies their illustrious descendant has admitted into the description of the great ceremony at Madrid, with which he entertained the readers of last Wednesday's *Times*, are really very pardonable. Thus when we read that the Marquis of Northampton and Sir Albert Woods *quietly* followed, we do not conceive the rest of the Embassy as leaping and shouting out of their hotel, each waving his particular share of the precious insignia over his head like a diplomatic Bacchanal. Nor do we understand Sir Albert to have been clad *only* in a scarlet mantle and white knee-breeches as the text might seem to specify; nor, for the credit of England, would we really believe the Marquis to have told the King that our Queen had commanded him "to express her *sentiment oi* most sincere friendship," nor to declare that she prayed for the *hapbiness* of his Majesty. Again, we are quite ready to make all allowances when we read that the King replied, *sdaeking* in Spanish, that he *cordailly* reciprocated her Majesty's kindness, and sincerely wished her constant *happinest*. And though at first we learn with some surprise that the *Ribaud* was handed to the Lord Chamberlain, and *laetly* the hat and plumes and star, we gather a general idea of the meaning even as we do when we are told that the Marquis, immediately after the ceremony, paid an official visit to the *Primeer* and the Minister of State for *Fereign* Affairs. But when we are gravely told, as a proof of the high appreciation of which this mark of English friendship is held throughout Spain, that the evening papers generally comment on the ceremony in *uncomplimentary* terms, we cannot but feel that something or somebody must be seriously wrong, a feeling which is not much diminished by the announcement that the invest-ment of the present King's grand-father, *Perdinand* VII, was shorn of its full honours, and that it was nearly *three centuries* before *the last* Spanish Monarch received the honour. He must indeed have lived to a ripe old age, this *Perdinand*."

"On October 15 we arrived at Cordova, where we were enchanted with the beauties of the Mesquita, or Moorish mosque, now converted into a Church, for which purpose 400 out of the original 1,200 lovely marble columns of every colour, brought from France, Italy and Africa, had been barbarously removed; but, as is my rule, I refrain from inflicting 'guide-book' on my readers.

"Bull fights were held in the Market Place here before the new bull ring was built. I hear that the *spadas* get £300 for every fight, of which they clear £200, and as they fight every Sunday and often on week-days, the chief exponents of the art must earn a great deal of money; but they hardly ever keep it as they generally squander it wildly and live very hard. One of the first *spadas* in Spain has an excellent house at Cordova.

"On October 16 we reached Granada at 8.50 p.m., where a telegram was awaiting Currie saying that his Father was seriously ill with pneumonia. He started early the next day and we were all very sorry to lose him, as he was a most delightful companion.

"Lunching at a restaurant we tried to get some butter, which is here a practically unobtainable luxury. Willie thought that he was giving effect to our wishes by calling to the waiter '*Burro!*' but the waiter glowered ferociously at him and we were not surprised later on, when we were informed that '*burro*' was Spanish for 'donkey' and not for 'butter,' the name of which is '*manteca*,' a word derived from the Arabic.

"On October 17 and 18 we thoroughly explored and delighted in the beauties of the Alhambra, and of the Generalife, and admired the manifold glories of art and nature which combine to make Granada one of the enchanted places of the world.

"On the 19th we went on to Seville, mindful of the old jingle which tells you:

> "'*Chi no he visto a Sevilla*
> *No he visto a maravilla.*'

('He who has not seen Seville has not seen a marvel.')

"After a very bad dinner the men of the party went off to a public ball, but only as spectators. The dances were all national, the performance moderate, though one or two girls gave signs of promise and one young man displayed prodigious activity. They were mostly dressed as ballet girls but one or two were in peasant costume; the men all wore national dress and there was a great clatter of castanets. I was the only one of our party who had put on evening clothes, whereupon a number of girls, supposing me to be the most important member of it, shoved their handkerchiefs one after the other on to my knees before they took the floor. It is customary to acknowledge this attention by returning the handkerchief with a five peseta piece wrapped inside it. This operation, whilst flattering to one's self-esteem, became after a time a strain upon one's purse, so when we got home I insisted upon my Uncle re-imbursing my expenditure, with the exception of one piece of five pesetas, as I argued that I had made these disbursements to sustain the dignity of the Embassy. The girls were quite young, the eldest being not more than seventeen, whilst there were some little tots of not more than six or even five.

"*Seville, Oct.* 20. The Cathedral is a building of splendid proportions, the Gothic architecture of which has been less defaced by later barbarisms than is usual. The beautiful painted glass is said to be the best in Spain. In one of the Chapels there is a huge picture by Murillo of Our Lord as an infant appearing to a Saint in a monk's dress. In 1874 a Spaniard and an American had a false key made of the chapel gate, cut out the Saint and took him off to America. The theft was not discovered for a fortnight as the picture was usually veiled by a curtain. A great commotion ensued when the robbery was detected and some fifty persons connected with the Cathedral were arrested on suspicion, including some of the Canons and at one time they even thought of arresting the Archbishop. Some five months later the picture was sold in America to a gentleman of the name of Chouse for £50, who, when he learnt its history, very honourably sent it back to Seville and gave information which led to the arrest of the culprits. The American was claimed by his Government and given up. The Spaniard was found one morning poisoned in his prison, foul play being suspected on the part of certain great personages to prevent awkward revelations. Since then six fierce bull-dogs are let loose every night in the Cathedral, who only know two men and would tear any one else to pieces. One night they nearly killed an unhappy Canon, who went to sleep in the vestry. He only awoke as the last gate was being shut, and made for it at the top of his speed, but the dogs were quicker and, regardless of his ecclesiastical dignity, had begun to worry him when their keepers rushed up and rescued the poor devil at the last moment.

"*Seville, Oct.* 21. A story is connected with a big bathroom below the Palace which was used by Maria Padilla, the mistress of Pedro the Cruel. All the courtiers, to flatter their master, used to drink some of the water when she had finished her bath. One, however, steadily refused to do so and, when Pedro asked him the reason, answered cleverly enough: 'Sire, if I tasted the sauce, I might be tempted to try the partridge.'

"*Seville, Oct.* 22. We went to the huge cigar manufactory which is under Government management. It is a great ugly building with large courts and staircases, the walls very white and the red-tiled floors very dirty, in fact a wilderness of whitewash. To judge from its size and style it must have originally been built for some kind of palace. A gentleman strolled along before us with his hands in his pockets and a cigar in his mouth, and, without paying the slightest

attention to us, sauntered slowly through the whole place, we following meekly like so many sheep. On arriving at the place where the
girls were working an old woman came up and accompanied us on
our round. She was as garrulous as our previous friend had been
silent. There is a succession of huge rooms, or rather barracks, with
long tables running down all their length and women working away
at the cigars. Six thousand of them are employed, and a good work-
woman is said to be able to roll 300 cigars in four hours. They only
work from 11 to 3. The process was not very inviting as they
stuck the cigars with a horrid kind of black glue. Some were very
pretty and all were picturesque. The smell of tobacco was overpowering. A great proportion of these ladies had babies in their
arms or elsewhere, and the old woman assured us that the fathers were
not always spotted with certainty. She pointed out a young girl of
fifteen and a half who, she said, was already the happy mother of two
children.

"*Oct.* 23. In the train I travelled with a gentleman, who was a
Deputy in the Chamber and was on his way to visit his constituents.
At the stations he was greeted by large and enthusiastic crowds, bands
of music, flags, flowers, cheering and every symptom of popularity.
I congratulated him and said that there did not seem much doubt as
to his re-election. 'Ah! You might think so,' he replied, 'but I
quite expect to be beaten.' 'But you seem very popular,' I answered;
'why do you suppose you will not be re-elected?' 'Oh! I'm
popular enough, but that does not secure one's return. You see, in
Spain there's a custom of "turn and turn about" and as I have been a
Deputy for a longish time, many voters who are quite friendly to me,
and in fact share my political views, think it is only fair that my
opponent should have his turn. But in spite of this I should, I think,
probably be re-elected, as I believe that most of the electors really
prefer to have me as their Deputy.' 'But then what is the difficulty?'
'Well, you see, my party is not now in power, and naturally the
Government does not want me to get in.' 'But how can they prevent
it if the majority of voters want to return you?' 'Oh! there are a
number of ways; of course all the local officials know that the
Government wants me to be turned out and they take steps accordingly.' He then enumerated a series of ingenious and irritating
devices which the aforesaid officials would resort to. One of the
most effective was to fix the polling place in a hay loft approached by

a step ladder at the foot of which was a fierce bull-dog in charge of a man who when a voter hostile to my friend appeared, hauled the bull-dog off by a chain to his kennel, but, when one of his supporters presented himself, let the animal loose. I thought of the unfortunate Canon in Seville Cathedral and began to appreciate the difficulties of an Opposition candidate in Spain.

On October 27 I arrived in London, after a most interesting and enjoyable three weeks' tour in Spain.

When Lord Northampton was made a Knight of the Garter, Sir Albert Woods, the Garter King-at-Arms, informed him that he would have to pay a fee of £400. In his letter inclosing his cheque my uncle said that at first he feared that there had been some mistake and that, instead of having been made a K.G., he had been appointed to the Order of the Golden Fleece.

Elliot, who was a good-looking man, made a large drawing of the Investiture, in which everybody was savagely caricatured with the exception of himself; his own portrait being, if anything, rather flattered. My Father hated all caricatures and told me afterwards that when it was being passed round the tea-table at Ashridge, he was very nearly tearing it to bits. He restrained himself with difficulty, and when Elliot pointed all our portraits out to him in turn contented himself with asking, with reference to the portrait of the artist: "And who is that silly, conceited looking fellow there?" This occasioned a move from the tea-table.

CHAPTER XVII

COUNTRY VISITS

I figured in a group cartoon representing a number of M.P.s in the inner lobby of the House of Commons, which was published in *Vanity Fair*, 1886. I took this as a compliment, although my pictorial presentment was anything but complimentary. In this cartoon I was talking to the late Lord Chaplin (then Mr Chaplin) and to Bobby Spencer, who was then one of my colleagues as a Whip.

On May 6, 1882, I write to a friend:

"10, Downing St.

"We live in troublous times, nobody knows what is going to happen next; whether the Whigs are going against the Government or the Radicals; whether the Irish will vote for or against the Government; whether Freddy Cavendish will be opposed and if so whether he will be beaten; what the Government are going to do and when they are going to do it; whether there will be a dissolution if F. Cavendish is beaten: in short nobody knows anything at all.

"On Thursday I was in the House from 4 to 7 and heard poor old Buckshot's resignation speech and those following it."

Lord Frederick Cavendish, a son of the Duke of Devonshire and brother of Lord Hartington, had just been appointed Chief Secretary to the Lord Lieutenant of Ireland and had in consequence to be re-elected. It was only a few days after this letter was written that the barbarous murder of Lord Frederick and of Mr Burke in Phoenix Park, Dublin, horrified and stunned the public. This sentiment of horror was intensified by the fact that he had taken up the difficult post of Chief Secretary with the hope of instituting a policy of conciliation. Had he succeeded, Ireland for the next few years might have had a happier and more peaceful history. He was of a lovable disposition and he and his wife (who had been one of Lord Lyttelton's numerous family) had been visiting my Father at Holmbury exactly a week before he was killed. He spoke to me then of his hopes of being able to do something for the good of Ireland during his term of office.

"Buckshot" was Mr W. E. Forster, so nicknamed as he had advocated the use of buck-shot for dispersing riotous assemblies, as being sufficient to inflict serious punishment without great risk to life. He had, as a young man, been indefatigable in voluntary relief work during the Irish Famine of 1845.

"10, Downing St.

"*June* 3, 1882.

"Politics, save Egypt, a little brighter. Outrages in Ireland going down and things running smoother in the House. Egypt though is a sad muddle. On Friday I go to Oxford till Tuesday to play tennis, see some friends who are still there and go to a ball given by Vincent's Club.

"To-night I dine in uniform at 10 Downing Street, as guest of the Chancellor of the Exchequer, together with the chiefs of the various Departments under him. The Prime Minister entertains the Prince and noble peers upstairs."

"Wilton House, Salisbury.

"*July* 23, 1882.

"The last month has been an enormously busy one, no one knowing whether one was standing on head or heels; telegrams, despatches, summonses for Cabinets, Cabinet letters, cypherings and decypherings, questions in the House with answers thereto to be prepared; numerous resignations, expeditions, alarums and excursions. And the worst of it is that, like the poor woman in the Bible, after all this one is 'none the better but rather the worse.' Then besides working all day, I have generally been dancing all night, winding up on Friday with a capital ball at Marlborough House, where I stopped till four. I am bound to confess that I am not like some men who groan from weariness of spirit whenever they 'have to go' to a ball; but then I make it a strict rule never to go to, or at any rate never to stay at, bad or even indifferent balls. This makes a great deal of difference, as it gives one off nights now and then and keeps one fresh and keen. Then again the more I dance the more I like it, and also because one gets to know one's partners better, and is able to talk to them with greater ease, or at all events with less difficulty.

"So much for the *Vanitas Vanitatum* called Society, so much abused and yet so much appreciated. It is all over now though, and London will be left to the owls and the bees, the M.P.s and the hard-worked and under-paid officials; everyone else having gone to Goodwood or some similar resort of pleasure.

"At D. Street we are all rather tied by the leg at present in consequence of the sudden appointment of our Chief of the Staff, Godley" (afterwards Lord Kilbracken) "to a Commissionership of Inland Revenue. No new man has been appointed as No. 4 yet; so we none of us can make any definite plans for the autumn holidays. I shall prepare myself to stay in town all autumn, running down to Holmbury for a few days whenever I see a chance and the coast is tolerably clear.

"This is a lovely spot, with heavenly gardens; full of grand trees and streams in every direction reminding one of the rivers that flowed through Paradise."

"10, Downing St.
"*Aug.* 12, 1882.

"Our secretarial arrangements are all finished, Godley took his final departure to-day and Spencer Lyttelton comes in to-morrow; he and I are to divide Godley's salary, which comes to £200 each, a very brave sum and that will help my poor Father to provide for his thriftless son." (This £200 was composed of £100 from the Treasury vote, and £100 from Mr Gladstone's private purse.) "It is very pleasant to be earning something for onself, however ill one does it; one feels lifted out of the crowd of idlers. So I am off for my holidays in about half an hour's time; I shall probably be at Holmbury for about ten days, when I move northwards. I hope to go for ten days to the Grahams who have taken a lovely place in the south of Skye. I shall then go on to Lady Ashburton's in Ross-shire, returning here about the middle of next month."

"Armadale Castle, Skye.
"*Aug.* 27, 1882.

"I have just arrived in this distant region by gradual steps from the South. Worcester was my first stage, where I stayed a few days at the Deanery, where my Aunt (Lady Alwyne Compton) has been busying herself greatly over the artistic department of a local exhibition. The needlework was good; nice old Italian and Spanish embroidery and fine Flemish lace. Mr Lowell, the American Minister was there; he is always agreeable and amusing.

"Then I went on to stay with the George Howards at Naworth, an old Border Castle with beautiful woods and glens and a river all round it. We saw the site of a camp on the Roman wall and had a splendid walk home by the river, seeing some Roman inscriptions on the cliffs by the river, which they used as quarries.

"From Oban I came on here yesterday by boat, after a bleak, stormy passage of seven hours, starting at 7 a.m. We passed through glorious country, a succession of headlands, bays, sounds and mountains, of every conceivable shape and colour." (Professor Blackie was on the boat. I had previously met him at Oxford in the rooms of my friend, D. G. Ritchie, when the latter was a Fellow of Jesus. He in vain tried to persuade me to study Gaelic. An exuberant sort of person, over given to paradox and somewhat of a "poseur.")

"Armadale looks across to the main-land and is embowered in woods. The Sound of Sleat, being land-locked, is providentially calm, so that sea-fishing may be pursued without the usual disadvantages. There is some grouse shooting but no Forest, and a cheery party of about fourteen people, mostly family."

My host was Mr William Graham, a Liberal M.P. for Glasgow; he had a large family of talented daughters (his only son having died as a boy). Two of the Miss Grahams married respectively John Horner (my predecessor as Commissioner of Woods), and Major Herbert Jekyll, both of whom were subsequently knighted and were at Armadale at the time of my visit; Horner, in fact, was accepted during my stay there. Jekyll and I went out shooting rock pigeons in the most inaccessible spots in cliffs overhanging the sea, and I remember being far more solicitous not to fall than to bag the pigeons, which came out of holes in the cliff at a pace of about sixty miles an hour!

Thence I went on to Loch Luichart, Louisa Lady Ashburton's place in Ross-shire. It is near the railway which runs from sea to sea, from

Dingwall to Strome Ferry. Lady Ashburton's only child, Maisie Baring, afterwards married to Willie Compton who became Lord Northampton in 1897, was greatly loved by all who knew her, to whom her long illness and comparatively early death were a sincere sorrow.

Lady Ashburton was an imperious old lady, of strong evangelical views, extremely emotional and given to occasional outbursts of anger. She was a Miss Mackenzie of Kintail. She had a yacht at Strome Ferry and we went for a cruise of two or three days, visiting my cousins, the Brownlows, who had taken the Applecross shooting on the mainland opposite Raasay. When we were passing Kintail, which had belonged to her ancestors, poor Lady Ashburton dissolved in tears, not only because the home of her fathers was no longer hers but because of the indignity of its having been bought by an Australian hat manufacturer who was also called Mackenzie, although apparently no connection of her own. To make matters worse he had adopted the "style" of her family and now called himself "Mackenzie of Kintail." One night at dinner the piper was perambulating round the house, making those weird sounds which are considered an appropriate accompaniment to a Highland repast. She suddenly became very angry and sent for him. "She held him with her glittering eye" and in the manner of a Tragedy Queen said: "How dare you!" We none of us knew what it was all about but the poor piper did and looked ready to sink into the earth: he humbly implored forgiveness, attributed his misdeed to forgetfulness, and vowed he would never so offend again. It turned out that he had thoughtlessly played the march of some rival clan, who had indulged in mutual throat-slitting with the Mackenzies some four hundred years before. When Dick Farrer was at Loch Luichart, Lady A. and I walked down with him to the station to see him off, a distance of about a mile. We were rather late and were still some way from the station when the train was seen approaching. "Run, Donald," said Lady A. to a gillie who was carrying Dick's bag, "run and stop the train"; as if it were the most natural thing in the world. Donald ran accordingly by a short cut, leaping over every obstacle and emitting loud yells, and the train complacently stopped quite a longish time, so that "Her Leddyship's frien'" would have time to get on board.

Her butler, an old Highlander, was never really at home in the English language, which he had almost entirely acquired from intensive study of the Bible. This was noticeable from his style of speech, and I remember his announcing the carriage one day in the following fashion: "Behold, I say unto thee, the chariot awaits thee!"

In London she gave me a general invitation to drop in to luncheon at Kent House, which is now the home of Sir Saxton Noble, and once I called and asked the butler, at lunch time, whether she were at home. He looked perturbed, but finally admitted me. I found that his embarrassment arose from the fact that a revivalist meeting had just been held and that the participators were sitting down to what they did not regard as a light repast.

In October of this year I accompanied my Father to Bodmin, where I made a speech of twenty minutes at one of his meetings. His constituents received me very kindly. Eddy Hamilton showed a report of this in a local paper to my Chief, who was kind enough to send it back with a note: "Capital, except the last bit." The last four words were characteristic, as the "last bit" was a vehement attack on Mr G's calumniators and detractors. He further was so good as to add that it was "a prophetic speech"; whilst to the editorial notice which concluded "everybody was delighted," he paid me the high compliment of adding: "I too am delighted but not surprised."

In November, when, as previously mentioned, I spent a week in Oxford to read for my Greats Divinity Exam., which I passed, I was invited by my old College Debating Society, the Dervorguilla, to make them a speech, and gave them one on the subject of Co-operation, with which they were good enough to say they were pleased. Two rather amusing things took place during this Divinity Exam. A man was asked to give a list of the Beatitudes and headed these by "Blessed is he that putteth away his wife, for it shall be restored to him an hundredfold." Another, on being asked why St Paul appealed to Cæsar, said: "Because he was a Cæsarean."

In 1883 I paid a visit to Lord Ducie, at Tortworth in Gloucestershire. He lived to a great age, being nearly a centenarian when he died. His son, Moreton, had been at Cheam with me and both he and his father were my fellow members at Brooks's. Lord Ducie was a great stickler for punctuality and I remember our delight when he was once two minutes late for dinner. I am ashamed to confess that I could not resist, in spite of Lady Ducie's mute appeals, looking at my watch as he came down the stairs into the hall where we were all assembled, and I am sorry to say that my bad example proved contagious, but he was very good-humoured. "Ah! well; we're all human I suppose!" was his only comment upon this lapse from his own standard of perfection.

Count Piper, the Swedish Minister, was one of the party, a vivacious and entertaining little man, who came of a great family. One afternoon we visited the village school, where the children greeted him by a hearty rendering of a song beginning "The hardy Norseman o'er the foam," a compliment suitably acknowledged by the Count; but when we were walking home it became clear that the ditty had not been happily chosen. "These Norsemen, these Vikings," exclaimed the little man, "they were all robbers; they were bad men; they stole all our treasures. My own forefathers' castle, they burnt it. The wine they did drink; the men they did kill, and to the ladies they were very, very —— rude!" The last outrage seemed rather a bathos, but we remembered that the Count had to modify the vehemence of his indignation in consequence of the presence of several girls.

He also told us of an old family tradition that one of his ancestors had made a compact with the Devil. He apparently had had this in common with the recently denounced Vikings, that he was a "very bad man," and had led "a very high life." The Devil had presented him with a golden chain and promised him and his descendants earthly prosperity so long as the chain was preserved in the castle, but woe betide them if it were ever removed. All went well until a sceptical Count Piper in the eighteenth century said it was all nonsense and took the chain to Stockholm, whereupon the castle was very properly and promptly burnt down. Since then the chain had been religiously kept at home with highly satisfactory results.

CHAPTER XVIII

TRAVELS IN GERMANY
1883 and 1884

ON July 17, 1883, I went for a fortnight's holiday to Germany with Rennell Rodd, who was in high spirits as he had just come out first in his examination for the Diplomatic Service, which was then distinct from the Foreign Office. From Cologne we went to Gerolstein, a queer old village, where we were disappointed on visiting the old castle by moonlight, not to be favoured by a glimpse of the ghost of the fair Grand Duchess, whom Offenbach has made known to all the world.

This recalls a story of Schneider, the beautiful and gifted actress who interpreted the title role of the comic opera of the "Grande Duchesse." The First International Exhibition which was held in Paris took place towards the end of the Second Empire. On the Opening Day Schneider drove up in a magnificent equipage to the entrance reserved for Royalties and persons of high official distinction. When the officer commanding the guard asked for her pass, she said: "*Mais, comment donc, Monsieur, ne reconnaissez vous pas la Grande Duchesse de Gerolstein?*"[1] He saluted, the guard presented arms and she passed through triumphantly. I suppose such an incident would have been impossible in any other country and at any other time.

Similarly my uncle, Lord Granville, who was a Commissioner of the First International Exhibition held in London in 1852, was stopped at the entrance on the Opening Day, having forgotten his ivory pass. He explained who he was, but the Cerberus at the gate only smiled and said: "That won't do, my man, we've had fifteen Lord Granvilles here already."

From Gerolstein we walked through the lovely Eiffel country, down the Kyll valley to Kyllburg, some sixteen miles; from Kyllburg we

[1] "But surely, sir, do you not recognize the Grande Duchesse de Gerolstein?"

went by train to Trèves, that delightful old town on the Moselle, celebrated for the Porta Nigra, the Amphitheatre, the Palace of the Roman Governors and other antiquities of that period.

I like the old local drinking song, with its rollicking chorus:

> "*Trevir metropolis, urbs amœnissima,*
> *Quæ Bacchum recolis, Baccho gratissima,*
> *Da tuis incolis vina fortissima*
> *Per dulcor.*"[1]

We next bought a boat to take us down the Moselle to Coblentz for the modest sum of sixteen thalers (about forty-eight shillings); as we sold it on reaching our destination for half that sum, our transport expenses over some hundred and fifty miles only cost us twelve shillings each, a pretty modest outlay. Our craft was not much to look at, but "a good 'un to go." It was a huge, roughly built boat with one seat in front. Our luggage went amidships; our two oars were about as long as big walking-sticks with great boards at the end, whilst our rudder was at the end of a pole about as long as the boat; we were further equipped with a primitive baler which also had to do duty as a stretcher. Some wags started us badly by directing us towards a weir, but we managed to pull up in time and retraced our course with some difficulty by punting and hauling. We christened our boat with a bottle of Piesporter, calling her *Die Probe* (the Experiment or Trial), and although she at times justified both of her English names, she served us well and brought us safely to the end of our journey.

At Die Quinte (the fifth Roman milestone from Trèves) we ferried three working people across to some ironworks, who were equally surprised and pleased when we refused their money. One old lady asked from what part of Germany we came and, when Rennell told her that we were English, seemed much amused, wagging her head and repeating in patois: "*Nä, nä, dass will i' gar ni' globen.*" ("No, no, I won't believe that!") We passed through a succession of corn-fields, vine-clad slopes, hills covered with brushwood or bright purple heather, deep orchards, groves of walnut trees, water meadows, little

[1] O Mother city of Trèves, most delightful of towns,
  Who worshippest Bacchus and to Bacchus art most dear,
  Give to thine inhabitants the strongest of wines
    And the sweetest.

white villages with slate roofs and queer old gables and arches and the inevitable church spire. The riverside varied immensely, willows and osiers, banks of bright yellow flowers, sometimes too, though more rarely, cliffs falling sheer down to the water. We alternately sailed (with the help of our umbrellas) when the wind was fair, rowed, or drifted, taking turn and turn at the helm. Now and then we had slight difficulties of navigation: sometimes a strong head wind quite neutralized the force of the current and one had to scull with might and main to stop the boat from going backward: once we had trouble with a swinging ferry, the chain catching first on my head and arm and then on the rudder pin, the stream running so strongly that I had a great job to get it off. It was delightful to go whirling down this immensely powerful stream, and rare fun shooting past the break-waters, of which there were many. You steered the boat out a little towards the main current and then, just as you came to the break-water, turned her sharply in and round it you were swung by the force of the stream. We only stuck once but soon got clear again. We took our lunch with us and bathed whenever we found a convenient back-water, sleeping at the little villages and towns on our way. Rennell had been reading in this district for his exam. during the previous summer, and as he talked German fluently had made many friends who were all delighted to see him again.

We passed Berncastel and Traben to Starkenburg, at which last place a Countess Loretta more than five hundred years ago ran a chain across the river, caught the Archbishop of Trèves, who was sailing down it, and held him up for a goodly ransom. At Alf we were Jacks ashore and walked up the lovely little valley of the Ues to Bertrich, a watering place some five miles from the river. Here we took baths of hot springs, more for cleanliness than for hygiene. We had, however, to enter our names in a book, together with the malady with which we were supposed to be afflicted. I entered mine as "elephantiasis," wondering what the local Æsculapius would think of this when he made his weekly perusal of the records. The iron in the water was so strong that it caused some old rubs on my shins to burst out bleeding afresh, but the general effect was exhilarating.

The next day we walked up the Marienberg to the ruins of a convent on the high ridge which makes the great curve of the river before you get to Alf. From the top you got a good view of both sides. An Archbishop of Trèves in former days heard an evil report of the nuns in this convent, so he sailed down one day, and moored his barge and invited them all to dinner. As soon as they were aboard he slipped his moorings and shipped them off in spite of all remonstrances, to be transplanted or disseminated elsewhere.

I think it was at Alf that I made a sad slip in German. We had heard of a fine old Gateway and were looking for it when I asked a man whether he could tell us *"Wo findet sich der alter Thor?"* meaning to ask "Where is the old Gateway?" I should have said *"Das altes Thor,"* as *"das Thor"* "the Gateway," is neutral. What in fact I did ask him was "Where is the old fool?" *"der Thor"* in the masculine being "the Fool," so it was not surprising that he raised his eyebrows, shrugged his shoulders and answered: *"Herr Je! es giebt so viel!"* ("Good Lord! There are so many!")

At Beilstein, a picturesque place with a population nearly wholly Jewish, I remember the arbour of an inn, overlooking the river. It was constructed out of an old tower and a terrace trellised with vines stretched beyond it. Our hostess, a lovely Jewess, gave us excellent coffee and insisted on presenting us with a number of capital apricots which she made us gather from a lordly tree. A great thunderstorm burst over the valley, the thunder echoing from hill to hill. It was followed by a wonderful sunset, broad spaces of orange sky glowing beneath heavy clouds and above the dark blue hills.

On July 25th we were saddened by the news of the sudden death on the 21st of our great friend, Dick Farrer. He had been suffering from tuberculosis but we had not thought the end so near. As it was impossible to get home in time for the funeral we decided to pursue our journey. We had only written to him on the 24th.

At Brodenbach we rose at five o'clock and started off up the hills, with half a bottle of wine each and ham sandwiches, for a miscellaneous *"Jagd,"* or shooting-party, organized by the village notabilities. Our party included Herr Wagner (the Jaeger or gamekeeper), Herr Probst (our host), a cousin and namesake of his who had had three fingers shot away before Metz, the Schoolmaster and the Tax Collector. Rennell was armed with a weapon fearfully and wonderfully made, which held a ball cartridge in one barrel and a cartridge of shot in the other. The disadvantage of this being that Rennell tried to bring down a stag with small shot and aimed the deadly bullet at the derisive jay. Our dogs were a motley lot and got off on the scent of an old grey fox, Rennell and I being reproved for not shooting at him.

The "hounds" returned in about an hour dead beat and were not of much use for the rest of the morning. Our bag consisted chiefly of rabbits, a few hares, a pheasant, some thrushes and wood pigeons, a lot of jays and a squirrel or two. We saw recent marks of roe deer but did not come across any. Altogether it was very good fun and quite unlike any other shoot that I have ever taken part in.

WITH LEONARD SHOOBRIDGE, 1884.

From Cologne, after visiting the Sieben Gebirge (Seven Mountains), we went up the Rhine, diverging here and there to explore on foot several of the lovely valleys on either side of the great river, the course of which we followed as far as Heidelberg. Here we found ourselves short of funds and were agreeably surprised at the hotel keeper accepting our cheques without the slightest demur. Thence we followed the valley of the Neckar up to the picturesque town of Würzburg, where we enjoyed the Stein-Wein in the quaint squat bottles, called "Box-beutel," and bathed in the River Main. At Bamberg we found, after buying our tickets for Nürnberg, that we had exactly two marks left between us, and great was my companion's indignation when he found that I had bestowed one of these on a porter who was attending to the luggage of a charming lady with whom I had scraped a very hasty acquaintance. The disbursement was unlucky as it turned out that she was travelling in a direction diametrically opposed to our own, whilst we had not the means to alter our destination. The result was that we had to put up with half rations of the sausage and rolls and lager beer which were to sustain us until we reached Nürnberg, to my companion's no little dissatisfaction. Nor was he mollified by my declaring that self-sacrifice was the essence of chivalry and reminding him of the efficacy of the widow's mite. He only insisted that whilst I got all the smiles he only had half the sausage, and that half of the widow's mite belonged to him. A painfully narrow-minded view! Nürnberg, in spite of a general prevalence of evil odours, at that time no rarity in German towns, was delightful and much less spoilt than it is now. In the Burg, amongst other fearful instruments of torture, we saw the "Eisene Jungfrau" ("Iron Maiden"), a horrible hollow iron machine made in the semblance of a woman, studded in the inside with sharp spikes; the victim was placed inside it and the two halves gradually closed upon him (or her). The woman who acted as cicerone told us that it was last used in 1806, the victim being "*eine Dame die ein kleines Kind bekam*" ("a lady who had had a baby.")

An American lady and her daughter were being shown round at the same time as ourselves. The mother did not wish to visit the Torture Chamber but her daughter insisted. On seeing the "Jung-frau" the girl was upset and saying that she felt sick, wanted to with-draw, but met with an "*Eisene Mutter*." "No, Sadie, you dragged me in here, and here you're going through with it, sick or not sick."

Thence we went to Regensburg where we saw the room in the Rathhaus where confessions were extracted by torture up to 1803. In this town, called by the French most inexplicably "Ratisbon," we also saw the Walhalla building, which for hideousness compares with the War Memorial at Rüdesheim on the Rhine. From there we journeyed to Praha (called "Prag" by Germans), where we were joined by Rodd, who got leave from his post at the Berlin Embassy. The Czech element was fully noticeable in the Bohemian capital, where one met with the greatest civility when one's English nationality was known. Whilst in Bohemia we always talked English or French, and even if one's hearer did not understand one, which was seldom the case, he invariably took one to somebody who did. We were told that had we spoken German we should probably have got no answer. Rennell wrote a beautiful little poem, since published, on the old Jewish cemetery at Prague, a weird place, the gravestones leaning at every angle close together, red and grey in colour, with Hebrew inscriptions and of great antiquity.

Thence we travelled to Aussig, where we went by steamer down the Elbe through Saxon Switzerland, a district remarkable for its strange basaltic formations, to Dresden. Here we came across the inimitable Harry Cust and for a few days had a rollicking time with him. One night we heard "Mignon" at the Opera, when there ensued a curious comic-tragic episode productive of much irrepressible laughter on our part in the midst of grave Teutons who stared at us in astonished dismay. I can best describe what happened as recorded in Shoobridge's diary. "To picture it imagine that you are an Italian Count, that you have lost your daughter, wandered in search of her with a harp, forgotten your own name, got into your own house by mistake; somebody mentions your name, and you stand up in your rags and shout it out 'Cipriani!' loud enough to split the ears of your ancestors' portraits. Don't you feel rather foolish? Count Cipriani certainly looked so and not the less as staggering to his dressing-room with arms outstretched he returned in gorgeous apparel possibly rather dusty and unaired."

To quote again from the same source: "At the Zoo we made a lengthy study of a most delightful party of monkeys whose sitting-room is a large semi-circular cage open, so that for spectators there is an airy auditorium and for the inmates there are retiring places for sleep by night and the recruiting of harassed nerves by day. A most exciting life is led in this cage, but good nature prevails, the peculiarities of the hermit are tolerated and gentle side episodes of parental affection undisturbed. But to lead a successful career learn to swing from a rope on to the wall, run along it by centrifugal force and alight on another rope. Then there is pleasure in looking over your shoulder at your pursuer and you can eat a nut and even let your tail hang down in momentary security. There are possibilities of subtle diplomacy in the assumed unconsciousness of your tail not at all to be neglected. But if you are tailless and human it may be well before you imitate in your bedroom your remote cousins in their cage in company with two other friends one of whom is apparently cracking nuts and the other crawling along the floor with the intent to pinch him, to see that the door is locked. Otherwise the door may be opened by a waiter and the form of a German Count appear who inquires after the Herr Cust. The Count is assisting the Herr Cust to find a German family to live with, of which according to him there are two classes, in one of which the drains smell and the family talk German and in the other the drains do not smell and the family talk English."

A *contretemps* occurred during the same visit to the Zoo. Outside the elephant house I bought a particularly large and luscious pumpkin, which I presented to "my Lord, the Elephant." Unfortunately it did not seem to be his particular brand of pumpkin, as, after conveying it to his mouth, he expressed his disapproval by extending his trunk and snorting vigorously in my face. It took days to dispel the "*bouquet d'éléphant*" which clung to my clothes and my person.

I suppose because of our high spirits our quartet caused infinite merriment to all in our neighbourhood, the waiters could hardly serve us for laughing; little boys and grave elders joined in the universal hilarity. When we were photographed in a group the photographer could hardly do his job. Our last dinner was one of rather sad hilariousness. We commend Harry to the porter, a man of many tongues and of a wise countenance, and are regarded as an excellent joke. The same impression prevailed at the railway station. We had a final tremendous rag in the railway carriage; exhausted by the fray I got out to refresh myself with beer, to which I treated the guard, as is the habit of the land. Suddenly a bell rings; flight on the part of most, choking on mine, the guard alone is unmoved: "*Bleiben sie doch ruhig, mein Herr, dass ist nur die Reisende zu schrecken.*" ("Be easy, sir, that is only to frighten the travellers.") The last episode is that Cust's hat gets under the carriage; as the train moves off into the night towards Berlin we hear him imploring us from the platform to tell him how to ask for it.

At Berlin we only stopped for one night. Rennell told us an amusing story of his chief, Sir Edward Malet, who had dined with him in his hotel where he was staying before he had taken lodgings. They sat up rather late in Rodd's room talking and smoking and when Malet wanted to leave they found the front door bolted and the porter vanished, as there were very few guests at the hotel and they were all, presumably, within its walls for the night. Rather than hunt for the porter and disturb the whole place to get the front door unlocked, Malet elected to drop from Rodd's window into the street, as his room was on the ground floor; but unluckily dropped into the arms of two policemen, who were not unnaturally suspicious of such a method of exit. They were deaf to his explanations. "The British Ambassador, indeed! That's a pretty story! Ambassadors don't behave that way, my fine fellow! You must come along with us!" When Rodd protested from his window that it was all right they thought he was an accomplice. Finally they could only be persuaded of Malet's identity by accompanying him to the Embassy, seeing him admit himself with his latch-key and be recognized by a sleepy and startled night porter.

Having secured copies of the *Spectator* during my five weeks abroad, I was able to pick up on my journey from Berlin to London the main lines on which politics at home had run whilst I was away, and so to be more or less prepared for my three months' campaign in North West Staffordshire before the General Election.

CHAPTER XIX

WORK AND PLAY

ɪɴ the course of 1883 I was chosen as second Liberal candidate for the Borough of Much Wenlock in Shropshire, which was then represented by Mr Cecil (afterwards Lord) Forester, a Conservative, and Mr Alexander Hargreaves Brown (subsequently Sir Alexander), a Liberal. It was a curious borough, as it was scattered in separate fragments all over that part of the county, the reason for which was, I believe, that in its extent it conformed to the area of the estates originally belonging to the Abbey of Wenlock. This circumstance added to its interest as it enjoyed the borough franchise as settled by the Reform Act of 1867, and thus comprised in its roll of voters a number of agricultural labourers, whose status was exactly the same as that of those in other country districts who were only enfranchised by the Reform Act of 1884. This fact, which was reproduced in the case of a few other similar boroughs, was a powerful argument in favour of the extension of the County Franchise, as it was logically maintained that it was absurd to concede the vote to labourers who happened to live on one side of a road within the boundaries of a borough and at the same time to hold that another set of labourers living on the other side of the road were unfit for the privilege. Amongst the electors were also miners, workers in iron and steel, and potters, for the Coalport Pottery, at one time famous for the beauty of its ware, was within the boundaries of the Parliamentary borough. One reason why I was chosen as candidate was on account of the largely preponderating interest possessed by my uncle and my Father in the neighbouring Lilleshall Company, whilst the head of my family, the Duke of Sutherland, at that time nominally a Liberal, was the owner of Lilleshall Abbey and of extensive property in its vicinity. In a letter to George Curzon I described my first public appearance in connection with my candidature at the annual dinner of the Wenlock Farmers' Club early in November, where I was entrusted with the toast of The Labourers. My political opponents were in the majority but treated me with courtesy and good humour; one of them suggesting in a speech that I looked as if I wanted to rape St Milburga, the patron Saint of the Borough. In my reply I indignantly repudiated so ungallant and sacrilegious a project, saying that I understood that these matters were always carried out more agreeably on a basis of mutual consent, and adding that from what I had seen I had hopes that the lady might not prove unwilling. A strenuous week of canvassing and public speaking followed.

Lord Granville wrote to me on November 9, 1883:

"I wish you joy of what seems to have been a very great success. I read your speech with very great pleasure."

Amongst my supporters were Mr Milnes Gaskell, of Wenlock Abbey, who had married Lady Catherine Wallop, sister of my Balliol friend, Lymington.

A very old friend of our family, Mr Edward Cheney, lived at a place called Badger, within the constituency, but he took no part in my brief campaign, nominally on account of his age, but I fancy that his real reason was that he was not in sympathy with the Liberal programme of the day, although he did not wish to pain my Father and uncle by pronouncing himself as hostile to my candidature. He clung to old-fashioned tricks of pronunciation; pronouncing balcŏny "balcōny" (in the Italian way); Rome he pronounced "Room" (as Shakespeare did); cucumber, "cowcumber"; tassel, "tossel"; wrap, "wrop"; garden, "gyarden"; yellow, "yaller"; gold, "goold"; and so with many other words.

Once when I called on him in his house in Audley Square (which would be more properly designated Audley "Recess"), he warned me never to make a joke about Americans, Catholics or Jews: "In the first place the joke would probably be a bad one, and in the second you would as likely as not tread on the corns of somebody who is listening to you, unless you are on the most intimate terms with all your audience."

Lady Marian Alford, who was very unpunctual, was once leaving Holmbury in his company for London. She started from our home very late and they missed the train. Old Mr Cheney was angry, but concealed his ill humour from my aunt. However, he went up to her footman, who was standing on the platform a little way off and

sked: "Is her ladyship *ever* in time for the train?" "Her ladyship
always in time for the next," was the witty reply, which would
em to indicate that the footman's real vocation should have been
iplomacy.

I did not go to the poll, as by the Redistribution of Seats Act, which
ccompanied that for the extension of the County Franchise, the
orough was abolished and the County cut up into Divisions, each
eturning a single Member. Mr Hargreaves Brown, as sitting
Member, contested the Wellington Division, which had absorbed the
orough, in the General Election of 1885 and won the seat; whilst in
884, after withdrawing my candidature for the soon to be abolished
orough of Much Wenlock, I was chosen as candidate for North
taffordshire. My withdrawal furnished my opponents with a joke,
s they declared that in withdrawing I was only following the Govern-
nent's example, and that whilst their policy was to scuttle out of the
oudan, mine was to scuttle out of Shropshire. However, they
aughed best who laughed last.

Early in December, 1883, I went to shoot at Somerley in Hampshire,
he home of Lord Normanton, whose eldest son, Somerton, had been
n Eton housemate and friend of mine. I recall the wonderful sunsets
here, which were said to be due to the dust floating in the earth's
pper atmosphere as a result of the recent vast volcanic eruption of the
sland of Krakatoa, near Java. We had wonderful wild-duck shooting
long the banks of the Avon. The procedure was as follows. All
long the river bank for a long way ran a screen some seven feet high
nade of wattled rushes. At intervals this was broken by a series of
what I can best describe as pens, which had a similar screen about four
nd a half feet high on the side facing the river; the screen at the back
eing again of seven feet and gradually sloping down to meet the lower
ront screen at its two ends where it joined the high continuous screen
unning along the river front. At a distance of a hundred yards from
hese pens, on the side away from the river, were posts. To each of
hese posts would repair a gun, together with his loader, and thence
would at a fixed time make his way to his appointed pen as silently as
ossible. The loader had his eye on his watch whilst they were
crouching down in the pen, and when five minutes had elapsed after
eaving the post would touch the gun on the shoulder. The guns
hen all stood up simultaneously and fired at any duck within range.
A wild five minutes or so then ensued, as duck would be flying in all

directions and the *battue* would continue until they rose out o
shot.

When the Duke of Cambridge had been shooting there a week
or two before, an unlucky youth had got up and opened fire before
the appointed moment, thus spoiling the whole of the *battue* and
getting terribly into the black books of his somewhat irascible althougl
at heart very kindly host.

One day when we were out shooting, I was standing in a field a
the side of the covert. No guns or stops were at the end of the wood
Lord Normanton was walking down with the beaters and killed a
low pheasant which was flying straight towards the end of the covert
a quite justifiable and normally a perfectly safe shot. One pellet
unfortunately *ricocheted* from the trunk of a tree and struck me on the
bone which runs between the eye and the temple, where it luckily
lodged. Had it been a shade more either to the right or to the left
the consequences would have been serious. For the moment it felt
as though I had been struck by a heavy stone, but there was so little
pain that I was able to continue shooting. It was the last beat of the
day and as we were driving home it began to hurt. Lord Normanton
apologized, not on his own account but on behalf of his agent, Colonel
Baird. When I afterwards told Baird that I knew that he had not
fired the shot, the Colonel, who was naturally rather nettled at Lord
N.'s accusation, said: "Oh! that's all right. His lordship always says
that it is me when he hits anybody!" Curiously enough Lord
Normanton had himself lost an eye in the same way earlier in life.
The pellet is still there and has never given me any trouble.

On leaving Somerley I witnessed an instance of great self-restraint
on the part of Lord Malmesbury, who had been Foreign Secretary in
Lord Derby's Government. I was accompanying him and his charming and talented wife to the station in a four-seated brougham. The
last to get in was Lady M.'s French maid, who was unfortunate enough
to plant a small and narrow heel full on Lord M.'s big toe, which was
badly inflamed by the gout. The girl turned pale and we all expected
an outburst, but although he must have suffered agonies, he only
smiled and never said a word.

A bye-election was in progress at Ipswich in the early part of
December, where Mr Henry West, Q.C., whose wife was a sister of
Lady Granville's and who was Sir Algernon West's brother, was
opposed in the Conservative interest by Sir William Charley. Mr

West invited me to go down and speak for him and I accordingly addressed a large meeting. My speech was lucky enough to elicit the following very flattering letter from my Chief:

"Hawarden Castle,
"Chester.
"Dec. 24, '83.

"MY DEAR G. LEVESON,

"I have read your speech at Ipswich with even greater pleasure than former speeches have given me, and it gratifies me exceedingly to think that the political succession in your family is already so well provided for.

"You pass from grave to gay with a genuine lightness of touch, and sacrifice neither to the other. Sound in argument, eloquent in language, balanced in statement, it really seems to be all that your best and nearest friends could desire, and I trust that what you have done is only to operate as an incentive to what you have yet to do.

"Wishing you this and many a happy Christmas
"I remain, sincerely yours,
"W. E. GLADSTONE."

Mr West won the election, receiving 3,286 votes against 2,816 given to his opponent.

About this time Mr Haweis attracted considerable notice as a popular preacher. He was a little, dark, energetic man with an excitable manner, who chose sensational texts and subjects for his sermons. When it was the fashion for women to pile enormous chignons on to their heads, he gave out as his text an arresting abbreviation, "Top (k)not come down." The full context being, "Let her that is on the house-top not come down." This may be thought irreverent but it certainly attracted attention. He was devoted to music and published a book called *Music and Morals*. After the birth of his little daughter he used to ask his friends to write something in an album which he had started for her benefit. One day he rather importuned Matthew Arnold who was engaged in an interesting conversation; at last Matt. complied and this is what he wrote:

"Little baby Haweis, playing with your corals,
    Papa will teach you music . . . but who will teach you morals?"

Father Bernard Vaughan of the Farm Street Chapel and brother to

P   215

Cardinal Vaughan, a man with a fine presence and a preacher of high repute among Catholics, once preached a sermon against the evils resulting from high play at cards at country houses. He instanced cases where young girls of good family and reputation had been placed in positions of great danger through losing large sums at high stakes at bridge, which they were unable to pay. "Pray understand," he went on, "that I should be the last to object to a little innocent amusement such as might be provided by a family game of bridge at nominal stakes; sixpenny points, for instance." The last suggestion was unfortunately too much for the congregation's gravity.

Rodd and I used often in those days to drop in on a Sunday morning to see Jimmy Whistler at his studio as he was kind enough to encourage our visits. Once he was not dressed and called out to us from his bedroom, which was separated by a portière from the studio, to make ourselves at home till he was ready. Presently a voice with a strong American accent came from a corresponding bedroom at the opposite side of the studio: "Say, Jimmie, can you loan me a pair of scissors?" 'What do you want them for?" "Why, to trim my cuffs, of course!"

In later years I saw something of him at the house of the late William Heinemann, the publisher, and he sometimes dined or lunched with us, but he was then dejected and embittered and only the shadow of his former self. Occasionally a flash of the old mordant spirit would show itself, as happened when an egregious, conceited and semi-educated young man, held forth on Art in a pompous and dictatorial manner. He also was an American, but from the North, which did not diminish the heinousness of his offence in the eyes of Whistler, who was a Southerner. When he had gone, Whistler blazed out in choice vituperation; after a compendious and unflattering *résumé* of his fellow-countryman's ancestry, upbringing, intelligence, manners and appearance he wound up: "And a fellow like that dares to preach to me about Art! What is he, after all? Nothing but a damned Yankee!" using that epithet as though one of all-embracing condemnation.

Oscar Wilde, who was a few years my senior and who was at Magdalen, was very slightly known to me whilst I was at Oxford. My chief recollection of him there was how on our return by boat from a large picnic at Nuneham, he held forth in his favourite paradoxical style on the character of Nero. That Emperor, he declared, was a much misunderstood and maligned man; he was one of the very few Romans who appreciated Art. It was in order to undermine the prejudice existing against Art and Artists (with a big A) that he had acted and played in public and not from motives of personal vanity. As for the burning of Rome, Wilde proclaimed this as a master-stroke. Nero wished Rome to be rebuilt in a manner worthy of the Empire and of himself. This he could not do, as he would have been hampered by religious superstitions and the obstructiveness of vested interests. He therefore concluded that it was only by forcible methods that he could get his way. "And then," his apologist continued, "think what a stroke of genius it was!" Nero accused the Christians of starting the fire, knowing that the hatred which this charge would arouse amongst the populace would go far towards destroying them. He himself detested the Christians as people who were indifferent to Rome's greatness and who were hostile to Art. At one blow he planned to rebuild Rome and to wipe out Christianity! It was sublime!"

Rennell and I and a few others occasionally visited Wilde in his house in Tite Street, Chelsea; as his conversation was always amusing and often stimulating. Several of us were there one winter morning after there had been a heavy fall of snow. He was at work on an article on the Italian Renaissance when his servant came in and announced that snow was coming through the roof in several places. "Now, my good Johnson, do please try to be reasonable. How in the world am I to finish my article and correctly to apportion the share which Eastern and Western influences exercised in moulding the Renaissance, if you come in to interrupt me with idle talk about snow and roofs and similar trivialities?" "But that don't prevent the snow from drifting in, sir," muttered the unconvinced Johnson. "Why don't you take off your coat, Oscar, and get a spade and go on to the roof and shovel it off yourself?" I suggested, half in the hope of our witnessing what would doubtless have been an amusing sight. He looked at me with pained reproof and answered: "My dear Leveson, I consider that a man who could take off his coat, get a spade, go on to the roof and thence shovel snow on to the ground . . deliberately denies the immortality of the soul!"

Another time I met him coming out of a hairdresser's just opposite the St. James's Theatre and asked him whether he had been having his hair cut. "Waved, my dear fellow, waved, not cut," was his answer. I then inquired what he had been doing and he said that the night before he had dined with the ex-King of Serbia, "and a very good dinner it was," he added. With complacent reminiscence: "I am told that it cost £20 a head." This, I maintained, was a sum which no self-respecting man ought to spend or allow to be spent on his dinner. "Well, perhaps you may be right, although I'm inclined to doubt it. But"—with a wave of the hand—"I wish to be broad-minded. I'll tell you what! I'll engage never again to eat a dinner worth £20 a head, if you will guarantee me against ever having to eat one worth less than £2." After a pause he thoughtfully resumed: "I have missed my vocation. It should have been that of the ex-King of Serbia. I should like to be paid £50,000 a year in order not to be a King!"

Once I met him at a party at Wilton House. He was full of anecdotes of his two small sons, who, he said, did not treat him altogether well. "I listen with respectful interest to amazing adventures with tigers in Hyde Park and lions in Kensington Gardens; but when, in return, I casually mention an ogre of my acquaintance or one or two fairies with whom I happen to be on friendly terms, they only roar with laughter. I really think they might allow me a giant or so now and then!"

Near Wilde's house in Tite Street was the home of Sir Percy and Lady Shelley. He was the son of the poet, and they were fond of private theatricals and had a small theatre attached to their home. I have often seen plays there, although I never took part in one. Later on I visited Lady Shelley, when she was a widow, at her home at Boscombe Manor, among the pinewoods near Bournemouth. It is now a girls' school.

Until I got into Parliament I heard a good deal of music, and for several years Shoobridge and I had two permanent stalls for the Monday Pops, held at the now demolished St James's Hall. Richter was conductor. His English was elementary. During a rehearsal he was vexed by a charwoman's noisy activities and called out to her: "Wife, wife, do not care!" to her no little amazement. It may be explained that he had tried to translate the German "*Weib*," which might be properly rendered as "Woman"; and that "*Kehren*" is German for "to sweep." At another rehearsal he was dissatisfied with the rendering of a pizzicato passage and admonished the orchestra "You shall not touch the strings with the nail but with the meat." Amongst the numerous good private concerts one may mention those f Frank Schuster, Pandeli Ralli and Lord Northampton. The house f the Blumenthals (he was always known as "Monsieur") just eyond the Albert Hall was a well-known resort of the musical world, nd their really excellent concerts and no less pleasant dinners made it most enjoyable social centre. Mr Dannreuther also gave extremely greeable concerts of a semi-public nature at his house in Orme quare. You paid a moderate sum for your ticket, but it was much nore like a party of friends, especially as there was an interval with ight refreshments, during which you could move about and chat vith anybody whom you knew.

As previously intimated, I withdrew from my candidature for Much Wenlock early in 1884, and in February of that year was dopted as second Liberal candidate for North Staffordshire. That onstituency was then represented by Mr W. Y. Craig, a well-known oal-owner, as a Liberal, and by Mr Hanbury, a Conservative, who vas at one time Post Master General. It was a difficult and expensive onstituency to fight, especially in those pre-motor days. It was of arge extent, very hilly, included a big agricultural area, many coal-nines, iron and steel works, and potteries, whilst at Leek on its north-eastern side were extensive silk works, mainly the property of he firm of Nicholsons. It also included the freehold voters of the Potteries, the Five Towns since celebrated by the works of Arnold Bennett, and of the ancient borough of Newcastle-under-Lyme, which had been represented in Parliament some two hundred years earlier by my ancestor, Sir William Leveson Gower. It was indeed a formidable task for a young man to undertake, who was a stranger, and was by no means wealthy and standing for the first time. One had to live in the discomfort and bustle of an hotel, and to do all one's correspondence, preparation of speeches, etc., without the help of a secretary; whilst especially in the winter evenings, the long and tedious drives on dark nights to distant places of meeting with in-different horses, a coachman who often did not know his way, along rough country roads and up and down steep hills were anything but pleasant. On the other hand the hearty sturdiness of my supporters, combined with the high standard of intelligence, public spirit and sense of fairness generally prevailing did much to reconcile me to what otherwise would have been a trying as well as a difficult under-taking. Although several of the great houses in the neighbourhood, besides Trentham, were occupied by blood relations, the doors of every one of them were closed to me an account of my politics, whilst even at Trentham, the head of my family only received me on non-political occasions as he was at heart opposed to the cause of progress, although, like so many others, he only openly proclaimed his hostility to Liberalism when given an opportunity by the inauguration of the policy of Home Rule for Ireland in 1886. All this of course made my campaign far more arduous as well as more costly, although I gratefully recollect the kind hospitality which I received from many of my supporters in all parts of the Division. As this campaign had to be conducted in the time which was allowed me for my holidays from my work at Downing Street, the years of 1884 and 1885 proved to be a period of pretty strenuous exertion.

On May the 10th of 1884 Lord Rosebery addressed a large meeting at Hanley, one of the Pottery towns in the centre of the Division, on the occasion of the opening of the Liberal Club of which I was President. I was in the Chair and reminded the audience of his descent from the great Lord Chatham. Lord Rosebery made, as usual, an excellent speech, although he was much preoccupied, as I have noticed him to be on other occasions, before the meeting.

Early this summer Shoobridge and I had a pleasant boating expedition. After seeing the ruins of Kenilworth and Warwick Castle, we went down the Avon. The boat which we hired at Warwick had been recently repainted, and as the paint was not quite dry, and as during our trip we often had to get out to push our craft through shallows, towards the end of our journey we presented a most disreputable appearance, our flannels having become an artistic scheme in which green and brown largely predominated. The upper reaches of the Avon were barely navigable, the weirs and locks being mostly out of repair, whilst the latter we had to work ourselves. We were further much delayed by strong head winds. Stopping at Stratford, which I fancy was less overrun than it is now, we made our way to Pershore. Thence we went by train to Ross on the Wye, where we again hired a boat. Our progress down this delightful river was sheer enjoyment; we stopped at Hereford and Tintern, concluding our little tour at Chepstow.

After speaking at public meetings at Dorking and Guildford, as well as conducting an intermittent campaign in North Staffordshire, I managed on the first of September to get a month's holiday with Shoobridge in Germany.

Within a few days of my return in October a political campaign in North Staffordshire was inaugurated by a succession of mass meetings, culminating in a big demonstration at Hanley, where Mr Chamberlain was the principal speaker. It was on this occasion that he so annoyed Conservatives by comparing them to the drones in the political hive, the lilies of the field that "toil not neither do they spin."

By now the country was thoroughly aroused on behalf of the third Reform Bill, the safety of which was threatened by Lord Salisbury and the House of Lords, and a long series of enthusiastic meetings in North Staffordshire during this autumn and winter showed that here, as elsewhere, the Government's measures for extending the County Franchise were evoking hearty and increasing support.

I was blackballed for the Travellers Club, not long after the death of General Gordon at Khartoum, presumably because I was Mr Gladstone's Secretary, about as logical a proceeding as though my blackballers had kicked his butler had they met him in the street. I was chiefly annoyed because of the pain which this gave my Father, who was an old member of the Club. One of his acquaintances with more good will than tact said: "I suppose it was not for any personal reason?" "No," answered my Father, "I don't think that he has robbed the till as yet." At that time two blackballs were enough to exclude and a good deal of feeling existed in the Club owing to the fact that every candidate connected, however remotely, with the Horse Guards, was invariably pilled. This was attributed to a Colonel Dawkins, who had some obscure but very rancorous grievance against that Department, and who was generally suspected of being, at any rate on that subject, rather unbalanced in mind; but to effect his purpose it was obvious that he must have had an accomplice in the Club, so the rules of the ballot were altered and it was made rather more difficult to pill a candidate; whereupon this particular scandal ceased. My own blackballing had a rather comic epilogue some thirty years later. One of my Clubs, Brooks's, and the Travellers open their doors to each other when either is temporarily closed. I mentioned at home that, during one of these periods, I had been lunching at the Travellers, whereupon one of my little daughters expressed surprise that after my blackballing I should have been admitted. I explained that I went there in my character of an invited member of Brooks's, and not as a previously blackballed candidate for the Travellers. She then said: "I would not have gone into the horrid place!" and was not satisfied by my answering her that probably none of the existing members knew anything of my having been pilled and would care even less if they did, whilst it was likely that my black-ballers were by now no longer living.

To revert to Gordon. My Father when he first heard a rumour that he might be sent to the Soudan, personally implored every Cabinet Minister who was in London and wrote to all those who were not, entreating them not to take this step, since he feared (as it proved, only too justly) that Gordon's religious hallucinations . . . as they might be termed . . . coupled with his marked independence and insubordination might lead to a catastrophe. It was explained to my Father that Gordon had been repeatedly and specifically instructed that his commission was merely to extricate and bring back to Egypt the various garrisons scattered in the Soudan, whilst if he found this task impracticable, he was himself to return forthwith, and that he had definitely promised to conform to these orders. When he got to Khartoum he seems to have either forgotten or ignored these instructions, as well as his own previous assurances that he would comply with them, and to have gone blindly to his fate. After his death much political capital was made against the Government in the most discreditable way, malice making a catspaw of emotional sentiment, for their alleged "failure" to "rescue" him. An expedition was despatched for this purpose at the very earliest possible moment and came within a hair's-breadth of success, but that any such expedition was necessary was due to the General's previous deliberate disregard of definite orders which he had announced himself prepared to obey. Whatever blame may be attached to the Government in this sad matter must be confined to their sending out such a man at all in spite of the urgent warnings conveyed to them by my Father and other experienced and competent advisers.

I think it was in the winter of 1884 that I went to shoot in Norfolk at Lynford, the estate of Mrs Lyne Stephens. She had been a renowned *première danseuse* at the Opera at Paris in the Second Empire, of the name, if I remember aright, of Mademoiselle du Vernais, and had married Mr Lyne Stephens, who on his death had left her his beautiful house and fine estate, which has recently become an Agricultural College for the instruction of prospective emigrants to Australia. She was a charming, vivacious little old lady and a delightful hostess. She contributed largely to the building of the

Catholic Cathedral at Cambridge. At Lynford I was laid up with another diphtheritic attack, due, I believe, to the bad drains of Downing Street previously alluded to. I was attended by Dr Joy, a local practitioner. One day when he asked on arriving, what sort of night I had passed, I quoted: "Heaviness endureth for the night but Joy cometh in the morning." At which liberty taken with his name he was, as it appeared to me, somewhat unreasonably annoyed. At least I know that if I had been in his place, I should have been pleased (I had nearly said "over-joyed"!) at my patient being able to make any sort of a joke, even a bad one and although at my expense.

The estate of Lynford was managed by the late General Sir Edward Stopford Claremont, a very handsome man, whose father was connected with the Stopford Sackvilles of Drayton previously mentioned and whose mother was a French lady. He was a life-long friend of my Father's, as they had been fellow pupils under Mr Berry, a Nottinghamshire clergyman to whom my Father went after leaving Eton and before going to Oxford. Claremont was appointed chief liaison officer during the Crimea, where he was attached to the French G.H.Q. As he had been brought up in Paris and spoke French like a Frenchman, he told me that now and then some of Marshal Canrobert's staff, with whom he was on terms of the greatest intimacy and cordiality, would momentarily forget his nationality and criticize or make fun of their allies and of our military dispositions. Then suddenly remembering that he was an Englishman they would subside into embarrassed silence. He performed some perilous exploits in carrying despatches and behaved generally with great gallantry throughout that campaign. He was subsequently our Military Attaché at Paris. During the war of 1870–71, he thought that he would have time to slip over to England to see his wife and family before the siege isolated Paris; but he was mistaken, as the Germans advanced more rapidly than he had anticipated. He was thus, to his great chagrin, unable to return to the French capital. For this he was adversely criticized in Parliament, but my Father amply vindicated him in a spirited defence, wherein he referred to his numerous acts of bravery as a sufficient refutation of the attacks on his old friend.

Early in 1885 North Staffordshire was divided into two, the North-Western Division and the Leek or North-Eastern Division, by the operation of the Redistribution of Seats Act. The Liberals of both Divisions were kind enough to wish to have me as their candidate,

and left the choice to me. I tried to persuade Lord Stafford (the late
Duke of Sutherland) to allow himself to be nominated as candidate
for either Division and said that if he selected one I would fight the
other. He preferred, however, to stand for the County of Sutherland
(for which he was eventually returned). I then elected to stand for
the North-Western Division, Mr Crompton, a distinguished barrister,
being chosen candidate for that of Leek.

In the early summer of 1885 the Government resigned after a defeat
on the Budget on a question relating to spirits and beer. I wrote
some lines on this event, which appeared over my initials in the *Echo*.
The only person who guessed my authorship was Mr Stokes, an old
friend and supporter of my Father at Bodmin. I cannot lay my hand
on a copy, but give as much as I remember.

"As I was walking down the shady side
　Of sweet Pall Mall, in meditation wrapt
On all the ills that threaten this fair realm,
　A voice discordant, jubilant and loud
Broke from the portals of the Carlton Club
　In tones most inharmonious, and fell
To some such purport on my 'wildered ear. . . .

"The Rads are defeated and flying,
　　Old Gladstone is piping his eye,
　Though for Office we long have been trying
　　We have smitten them now hip and thigh:
Votes of censure have failed by the dozen,
　　Of our motions the House would not hear,
So proclaim to each far country cousin
　　That we've won upon SPIRITS and BEER!

"Then with Randolph at India installed
　　And the Markis made snug in F.O.[1]
'Rule Britannia!' all day shall be bawled
　　As the rivers of alcohol flow.
Free Trade far too long has been borne,
　　For we hate all their damned foreign stuff,
So five shillings we'll clap upon corn,
　　Or more if that isn't enough.

[1] Both of these predicted appointments were verified after my lines appeared.

"On the Bible we'll keep a sharp eye,
If C.B.[1] at the Bar should appear,
To the country we'll go on the cry
Of 'Bible and Spirits and Beer!'"

Mr Bertram Currie, the well-known banker, lent the Gladstones his beautiful house, 1, Richmond Terrace (that nearest the river) for the short remaining time of the Session, the business of which was being wound up by Lord Salisbury's Government, the "Stop-Gap" Administration, as it was called. I continued my secretarial duties as a volunteer. These were naturally far less heavy than when my Chief had been in Office, so I had plenty of time to explore his host's most interesting library, which included, amongst other treasures, a number of the finest 18th-century editions of the French classics, exquisitely bound and often adorned with superb illustrations.

[1] Charles Bradlaugh who, having been elected for Northampton, claimed his right to affirm, instead of taking the Oath, previous to taking his seat. The denial of this claim led to violent scenes, during which he was forcibly expelled by the Police, his clothes being torn in the struggle.

CHAPTER XX

THE SUNBEAM, M.P. AND ROME

Sir Thomas Brassey (afterwards Lord Brassey), who had been Financial Secretary to the Admiralty in the last Administration, very kindly asked me to join the party which was to accompany Mr Gladstone on the *Sunbeam* for a cruise in the Fiords of Norway. We were a large number, consisting of our host and hostess, their three daughters (the two younger of whom were still children), Mr, Mrs and Miss Mary Gladstone, Sir Andrew Clark (Mr G.'s doctor), Arnold Morley (Chief Whip in the next Government), Loulou Harcourt (Sir William's son, the late Viscount H.), and Mrs Bridge, the musical wife of Admiral (afterwards Sir Cyprian) Bridge. We sailed on August the 9th from Tilbury, being seen off by a number of friends, including Lady Stepney, Professor Stuart, M.P., and Clinton Dawkins. The second mate kindly lent me his cabin, the only disadvantage to which was that a cupboard was fixed some three inches above the pillow of my bunk, so that for the first night or two I got resounding cracks on the skull every time I turned over. It was curious how quickly one learnt caution from experience, even when sleeping; indeed for a week or two after the cruise I never awoke in bed without putting my head out sideways with much precaution.

Sir Thomas was an expert navigator and enjoyed sailing the *Sunbeam*, although of course there was a captain. We sailed to Stavanger. Here and wherever else we landed the Norwegians received Mr G. with quiet enthusiasm, hailing him as "Mistar Glad-sto-ô-one!" One of them excitedly alluded to him in a burst of perverted eloquence as "the Big Old Man." The people were hardly distinguishable in appearance from the sea-faring population of our own northern and eastern coasts.

I was surprised to find Sir A. Clark a pronounced High Churchman; he was a kindly man but rather too fond of engaging in theological discussion and was not over tolerant of disagreement.

Mr G. was in great health and spirits and thought nothing, at the age of seventy-five, of an 18-mile walk, a 6-mile row and 2,000 feet climb to see a waterfall which fell a sheer 600 feet. But he had a bad head for heights. I remember his insisting on taking my arm before crossing a rough plank bridge over a river, although the bridge was some twelve feet broad, because there was no hand-rail at the side, whilst the sight of the rushing torrent between the ill-joined planks made him giddy.

Our host had got into some trifling muddle over Admiralty finance shortly before the late Government's fall, and seemed rather unnecessarily preoccupied on the subject. He was anxious that I should explain to Mr G. that the error was not as serious as was supposed and entered into lengthy and rather unintelligible details. I resolutely declined to trouble my Chief with the matter, alleging that he had come on a holiday and adding that it would be presumptuous in me to try to explain what Sir Thomas could elucidate so much better than I. I finally persuaded him to leave it alone.

We followed the Norwegian coastline, going up each fiord in turn to its furthest limit, often a considerable distance, and always, except for an occasional hour or so, when there was a bit of open sea in going from one fiord to another, in absolutely smooth water. The scenery was marvellous and the life very pleasant. We often landed to climb neighbouring heights, to visit towns which we passed or to make expeditions up the valleys in the primitive little native carriages called "carrioles" or "stolkjaere," which were made to take either one or two people. The Norwegian peasantry had charming and simple manners. If you gave a child a small tip for holding a gate open, he or she would always thank you by shaking hands. We enjoyed a pleasant day at Bergen, where we saw an interesting old church and a large and ancient country house, of which last there were very few, belonging to a member of the former nobility. Molde was our extreme point northwards. Here a deputation presented Mr G. with an address in which they welcomed him as the friend and defender of liberty in his own and every other country. We had one or two readings and concerts on board which were attended by the crew. At one of these Mr G. retired to his cabin to write but left his door ajar so that he could listen to anything that he wanted to. I had to read the scene of the Trial in *Pickwick* and before long the old statesman's laughter dominated that of the rest of the audience.

We landed at Inverness, thus terminating a most enjoyable four weeks' voyage. Before leaving, Mr Gladstone, although pressed for time to catch the train, insisted on shaking hands with every member of the crew from the captain to the cabin boy.

By the Redistribution of Seats Act, the Borough of Bodmin, for which my Father had sat uninterruptedly since 1859, and that of Liskeard, which was represented in the Liberal interest by Mr Leonard Courtney (afterwards Lord Courtney), were thrown into what was thenceforward known as the Bodmin Division. A meeting of Liberal delegates from these two boroughs and from the country districts was held to decide whether my Father or Courtney should be nominated as candidate for the new constituency. The delegates from each borough voted for their respective Members, but the majority of the country voters, no doubt actuated by the fact that Courtney was a Cornishman, supported his candidature; and he was subsequently elected at the General Election of 1885.

There was then some question of my Father standing for the Western Division of Staffordshire (which bordered on the North-Western, for which I was candidate); but he was luckily not selected, as if he had been, he would probably have failed to win the seat whilst the family resources would have been depleted still more seriously.

From the moment of my return from Norway at the beginning of September I started electioneering in North-West Staffordshire. The campaign went on without a break for three months until polling day. I spoke practically every evening, except Sundays, sometimes at two or even three meetings in a day and occasionally at out-door meetings, which were trying to the voice. One of my chief aims was to avoid repetition, and although this made preparation more laborious, I believe that the variety of subjects which one had to deal with not only prevented one from getting stale but added to the vigour of one's speeches and increased the interest of one's audience. I can never be thankful enough to Leonard Shoobridge for his indefatigable and cheerful help during this trying time. His Father had inherited property in various parts of the constituency and Shoobridge remained with me the whole of the time. A cousin of his kindly lent her little house to us, it was at a place called Hartshill between Stoke-on-Trent and Newcastle-under-Lyme. She only made one stipulation, that we should not have a late dinner on Sundays, as her cook was walking out with one of the under-gardeners at Trentham. We of course complied, although it was rather hard as Sunday was the only day in the week upon which we could have indulged in such a luxury, and, worst of all, the walking out never culminated in matrimony. Occasionally we got away for a Sunday's rest: once to Rudyard Lake, a picturesque spot which has given Mr Kipling his Christian name, as it was there that his parents became engaged; once to an inn on the outskirts of Hawkstone Park, Lord Hill's place, celebrated for its beautiful scenery and breed of black rabbits. I remember that it was here that I read the Introduction of George Meredith's *Diana of the Crossways*, and found it so difficult to understand that I feared that my hard work was bringing on softening of the brain; I asked Shoobridge to read it and tell me what he thought of it. My relief was great when he said that he could not understand a word. Another time we went rather further afield, to Llangollen, and were much refreshed by its lovely surroundings.

Amongst those who kindly came down to speak for me were my two recent shipmates, Arnold Morley and Loulou Harcourt, my Father, who received a warm welcome from many who had voted for him when he was M.P. for Stoke twenty-six years previously, Lord Wolmer (the present Lord Selborne), Willie Compton, who at the same election won the seat of South Warwickshire, and Professor Thorold Rogers, the Political Economist and the author of a remarkable work on the History of Prices. The last was anything but mealy mouthed. When my Father told someone that he had been talking to "Dr Rogers," his friend asked whether this was "Dr Rogers of Bishopsgate." "No," he answered, "Dr Rogers of Billingsgate." The other Dr Rogers was incumbent of Bishopsgate in the City, an intimate friend of Lord Rosebery's and a most agreeable companion. Thorold kept up his reputation for putting his foot in it when he spoke for me. I met him at Woodall's, then M.P. for Hanley, and, hearing that we were both going to a meeting of mine at a village called Hanford, not far from Trentham, he very good-naturedly offered to come with us and make a speech. I could not very well refuse although the cordiality of my acceptance was accompanied by inward fear lest he should make a hash of it. My apprehension was unfortunately justified. He made a capital speech, but unluckily said: "*If* the farmers were fools enough to believe" (whatever it was) "then, etc. etc." My opponents of course fastened on this, omitting the all-important "If," and said that the farmers had

been called fools at one of my meetings. I believe that this slip of the
Professor cost me several score of votes. Such is life!

The polling day was on the first of December. It was a great
scramble to get round the extensive constituency and visit all the
polling stations during the twelve hours that the poll was open; by
starting at 7.30, we just managed it by means of relays of post-horses,
getting home rather late and very tired.

On the following day the poll was declared, the figures being:

$$
\begin{array}{lr}
\text{Gower (L)} & 5757 \\
\text{Heathcote (C)} & 4720 \\
\hline
\text{Majority} & 1037
\end{array}
$$

All the five North Staffordshire seats were won by the Liberals by
substantial majorities, and throughout the country generally a sufficient
majority was secured to ensure their return to power. In some ways
it was a curious election. The Irish voters in Great Britain voted,
according to their leader's instructions, solidly for Conservative
candidates, not from sympathy with that party but because the Irish
Nationalists were shrewd enough to foresee that the Liberals would
probably poll more votes than the Tories and that the best chance of
Ireland's claims being considered and her grievances redressed lay in
the two English parties being as evenly balanced as possible, so
that, at the best, the votes of the Irish Party might hold the
scale and thus maintain in Office whichever party was prepared to
give them the better terms, or, failing this, that either party should
have such a slender majority that they would find it difficult to remain
in power without Irish support and would thus be more amenable
to pressure. In the circumstances it was intelligible and probably,
from their point of view, justifiable strategy, although not a specially
broad-minded or dignified policy. The Conservatives found no
difficulty in accepting Irish support, although a few months later they
affected to be horrified by Mr Gladstone's attempt, with the help of
the Nationalists, to change the basis of the administration of Ireland
from one of coercion to one of self-government effected by mutual
consent. The general result of the election was that the Liberals
returned numbered exactly half the House of Commons, the Conservatives and Irish constituting the other half; the Conservatives won
a few borough seats, but the Liberals carried everything before them

in the Counties. One feature of the election was the lukewarmness (to say the least of it) of a certain section of Whigs, who for some time had been gradually undergoing a process of ossification of their political systems. They based their growing disaffection upon the increasing influence of Mr Chamberlain and of the advanced principles which he then entertained and advocated with much vigour and growing acceptance. I was more than once asked during my candidature whether I regarded Lord Hartington or Mr Chamberlain as my leader, to which I answered that neither was my leader, but that I was a follower of Mr Gladstone, as were both those statesmen. One obstinate heckler persisted with an inquiry as to which of the two I would follow if Mr G. resigned; to which I replied that the proper time to ask that question was when such a resignation had taken place. It was a curious comment on this rivalry between two of Mr G.'s chief lieutenants, that within half a year they united in joining the Tories in deposing their old leader. But more of this anon.

After the declaration of the poll I went to Chatsworth, where the contest for the Division of Derbyshire for which Lord Edward Cavendish, Hartington's brother, was candidate, was still in progress. On the polling day I walked with Hartington to the village where he recorded his vote in his brother's favour. He told me that he had read a speech of Chamberlain's a few days earlier that had "made him sick." I said that I supposed that he spoke metaphorically. "No," he said. "Literally, physically sick." He then gave a half-humorous, self-pitying account of certain circumstances in which he had delivered a recent speech, including how he had had to stay with a teetotal host and had barked his shin badly on ascending the platform. He narrated these various *contretemps* in a perfectly quiet and unemotional voice, more as though they had happened to somebody else than to himself.

After leaving Chatsworth I went with Shoobridge to Rome for a few weeks' well-earned holiday. We did much sight-seeing and went out a good deal into society, where I renewed many old acquaintances and formed many new ones. Amongst the latter was a Marchesa di Rocca Giovane, whom we disrespectfully christened the Young Rock; she was connected with the family of the Bonapartes and belonged to the Black, or Clerical, section of Roman society. She lived in a house looking on to the Foro Trajano, but when I said what a pleasure it must be to look out of one's own rooms upon such splendid relics of antiquity she only answered: "*Pour ma part, j'avoue que je ne m'intéresse pas beaucoup à toutes ces vieilles pierres, mon fils s'en occupe beaucoup plus que moi.*" ("I confess that I am not much interested in all those old stones, my son is much more taken up with them than I am.") At one of her receptions I found a good deal of excitement prevailing, which was occasioned by a recent pronouncement of the Pope, as to the significance of which there was some difference of opinion. The Marchesa declared that, not being a Catholic, I could give an impartial judgment and asked how I understood the pronouncement. I had not read it or even heard of it and had not the remotest idea of its subject, but as a confession of such ignorance would have put one quite beyond the social pale I merely said: "It is very difficult to decide as His Holiness's pronouncement may be interpreted in more than one way." This platitude happily proved a sufficient answer and they again fell to discussing the difficulty.

At an evening reception of one of the greatest of the old Roman families some hired waiters were employed in the cloakroom and stole a silk scarf, a silver cigarette-case and a pair of gloves out of the pocket of my overcoat. I did not complain as I did not wish to upset my host over such a trifle, but in future I took care not to leave anything in my overcoat when I went to a party in Rome.

I had the honour to be presented to the great actress, Madame Ristori; she had married a Marchese, I think, del Grillo; she was a stately old lady with beautiful manners.

I also heard Liszt play, quite informally, at an afternoon reception. He played, as might be expected, exquisitely. When he had finished all the ladies crowded round him to kiss his hands. He was then very old; he had a massive head, strongly marked features and long white hair. As a young man he had at Paris been music-master to my aunt, Lady Georgiana, then a young girl at the time that my grandfather was Ambassador.

Countess Apponyi was another prominent member of Roman society at that time. She was Russian by birth and very proud of the confidence reposed in her father by the Emperor Nicholas. She told us with quite unconscious satisfaction that her father used to relate all that he heard in Russian society to his august master and it never seemed to occur to her that what was a source of so much pride might strike others as the activities of a spy. I am not sure whether it was this lady or a namesake of hers who was, a long time ago, Austrian

Ambassadress at London and noted for the overpowering sweetness of her manner. When her husband was succeeded by another Ambassador, somebody said to M. Tschann, then Swiss Minister, that he heard that the wife of the newcomer was rather brusque in her manner. "*Si elle est brutale cela sera rafraîchissant*" ("If she is brutal it will be refreshing"), was Tschann's comment.

The Marchese Lavaggi and his wife and their two charming daughters, one of whom, Donna Maria, had married a Grazioli, also showed me much hospitality, as did Mr and Mrs William Story in their apartment at the top of the Palazzo Barberini. Their son, Waldo, who married a beautiful Miss Broadwood, was also a sculptor. He told me how once when he was in Sardinia shooting moufflon, a species of wild sheep found in the mountains and very difficult of access, his beaters returned home to their village by what seemed an unnecessarily distant and circuitous route; on his asking the reason they said that they were at feud with a neighbouring village who, they heard, were lying in ambush for them on the road by which they had come in the morning.

I returned to London in time for the opening of Parliament, and found Mr Gladstone without a secretary, Spencer Lyttelton having gone to India. Mr G. had cabled to him to come home, and I resumed my duties during the few weeks that intervened before his arrival.

The Conservative Government was promptly challenged by a motion of Mr Jesse Collings, one of the Birmingham group, on agriculture, advocating the adoption of the policy generally known as that of "Three Acres and a Cow." A good deal of lobbying went on, to which I have before alluded, on the part of discontented Whigs who preferred that Lord Salisbury should remain in power, but though some thirty of them voted against the motion it was carried by a substantial majority and Lord Salisbury resigned.

Conservative speakers in this debate missed a great opportunity for making a happy quotation from Virgil's First Eclogue, with reference to Mr Gladstone's choice of Mr Collings to move the above-mentioned Resolution. They might have quoted:

> "*Ille meas errare boves qua libet et ipsum*
> *Ludere quae vellem calamo permisit agresti.*"

("He allowed my cows to wander where they would and permitted me to play what tunes I chose upon my rustic pipe.")

To which a subsequent speaker on the Liberal side might have replied by a quotation from the same Eclogue, alluding to the newly enfranchised electors:

> "*Libertas, quae sera tamen respexit inertem,*
>   *Respexit tandem et longo post tempore venit.*"

("Freedom, who although late yet looked back upon the helpless, looked back at length and after a long time she came.")

But even then the happy days of apt quotation from the Classics in Parliament had passed, whilst now I suppose you might as well quote Choctaw or Swahili for all the meaning which would be conveyed to the great majority of members.

CHAPTER XXI

IN AND OUT OF PARLIAMENT

On the formation of a new Government early in February Mr Gladstone was so kind as to offer me the post of one of the Junior Lords of the Treasury, which included the duties of a Whip. I was very grateful for such an honour, especially considering that I had no parliamentary experience and had not even opened my mouth in the House. Labouchere made a savage onslaught in *Truth* on my appointment, with caustic remarks on the assiduity of the old Whig wolves in providing for the young Whig wolf cubs, who would grow up into wolves later on and provide in turn for yet another lupine generation. On this particular occasion he perhaps hit the mark rather nearer than he had suspected as the wolf happens to be our family crest. One of my friends good-naturedly remonstrated with Labby, saying, I believe, various kind things about myself, adding that it was hard luck to damn me, so to speak, unheard. "Not at all, my dear fellow, not at all; you don't understand. I rather like the young fellow and thought that it would be a way of giving him a good send off." "Rather a queer sort of 'send off' to abuse him up hill and down dale!" "That's just where you're wrong. If I hadn't mentioned him in *Truth* nobody would have thought or said anything about him; whereas now all his friends will be up in arms saying what a shame it is, and what a beast I am and what a decent chap he is. It will be a splendid piece of advertisement for him!"

The old established idea of a Whip was that his duties were comprised by "Making a House, keeping a House and cheering the Minister." Whilst this was a part of his work—although the "cheering" was not insisted on—there were multifarious other obligations. During one debate Harcourt was thundering away, denouncing the Opposition in his best style. The House was empty, as was usual at that hour, it being immediately after the dinner interval, the Front Bench being particularly sparsely occupied. One of my fellow-Whips suggested that I should sit there during the speech so as to make it look less bare. I had had a very tiring week and unluckily fell into a doze, from which I was awakened by my colleague, who said that if I wanted to have a nap I had better take it in the Whips' room. A Junior Lord's duties in connection with the Treasury were almost nominal, consisting in signing a certain number of documents, chiefly Warrants; but inside the House one had to make oneself useful in a number of ways besides the three specified obligations. One had, in the first place, to get to know by sight not only all the M.P.s of one's own flock, but also those of other parties. I learnt them in the following manner. One of our Messengers had a little book containing small photographs and short notices of all the M.P.s; he used to stand behind me near the entrance to the Inner Lobby, whilst I had a Vacher's Parliamentary Guide containing a similar alphabetical list. When I had definitely identified a man I scratched his name through in my Vacher, thus gradually diminishing the number of the "unknown quantities"; when I was not sure of a man or did not know him at all the Messenger was often able, with the help of his book, to supply his name, and so in a few weeks I got to know them all. One had also to remember, if possible, the constituency for which the Member sat, and if you could recollect the approximate amount of his majority so much the better. By degrees one got to know something of the particular views of the various Members, which I fear we sometimes thought of privately as "fads" or "hobbies." Then one had to learn the names, faces and jobs of the staff of attendants on the House from the highest to the lowest; also the names of the Pressmen and of the papers which they represented, particularly those on one's own side; and further to supply them from time to time with such items of news as could be imparted, or sometimes to set the current of their ideas flowing in a desirable direction. As to the M.P.s themselves, one had to act as a sort of liaison officer, at stormy times as a lightning conductor, between Private Members and Ministers; the former having sometimes to be placated or encouraged, the latter forewarned or enlightened as to the movements of opinion or the fears, hopes and even susceptibilities of the rank and file. With this object in view one had to be "all things to all men," and occasionally to "suffer fools gladly." Indeed when we were on actual duty at the Whips' seat leading out of the Inner Lobby and charged with the obligation of seeing that nobody went away unpaired we were fair game to whoever chose to have a shot at us. It was a unique opportunity for the bores, to have a victim provided who was officially bound to listen to whatever was said to him and who could not get away, however much he might want to do so. "*Une véritable aubaine*." One old Member in particular was my bugbear. He was addicted to prolix and tedious orations, which it was his deplorable custom to rehearse to me, beginning with, "I am thinking of saying something of this kind," or some similar exordium. My friends derived more entertainment from these performances than myself.

I was occasionally mistaken by Members of the Opposition for Akers Douglas, afterwards Viscount Chilston, the chief Conservative Whip, to whom I bore a superficial resemblance. One old gentleman, a Conservative, who had spoken to me under this misapprehension, on discovering his mistake thought he was being civil when he said: "You have too honest a face to be a Radical." I could only answer that I could hardly feel flattered by a personal compliment which was coupled to an insult to my Party. A more amusing episode was that furnished by an Irish M.P., who, whilst one of the older brand of Home Rulers, viewed Parnell's followers with distrust and dislike. He was a little in his cups and wished to impart some secret, involved and probably impracticable scheme to Akers Douglas. Mistaking me for him, he engaged me in confidential, alcoholic and quite unintelligible conversation. For some time, what between his brogue and his mysteriousness, I could neither make out the drift of his talk or whom he was taking me for, but, as soon as I discovered the latter fact, proceeded to set him right. He rose with some difficulty from the seat beside me, moved a step or two away and balefully regarded me. "Ah! So ye'ed be wur-r-ming me secrets from me! Do ye call that the conduct of an honourable gentleman, now? If it had been forty years ago, I'd have sent me friends to call on ye." A friend or two of his coming up, presumably with the object of getting him away, he asked them, pointing a trembling forefinger at me: "Do ye see that man setting there? 'Phwat is he?" They informed him. "Liberal Whip, is he? Why didn't he say so at wance? I'll tell ye what he is." A pause for dramatic effect. "He's a low blaygyuard, and to-morrow"—with immense dignity—"I'll post him in the town as a villain!" By this time the scene had attracted several of my friends, who, as may be supposed, were quite delighted with this gratuitous entertainment.

The same gentleman on another occasion, being in the same condition, was advised by some of his friends to go home: "Is it home ye'll be wanting me to be goin'?" A pause to sum up the suggestion dispassionately—a slow shake of the head. "Ah! ye'll not be knowin' Julia. . . . !" (his wife).

He had some obscure, hereditary feud with the Redmonds, of whom, the elder, John, was a real statesman and later on became leader of the Nationalist Party, whilst the younger, Willie, died on the field of honour in the Great War. The latter was once the object of the old M.P.'s attack in the course of a debate, when he alluded to him as "The young say sarpint from the County Clare," their father having, for some unknown reason, been known as the "Sea Serpent." The Speaker pulled him up for this unparliamentary form of address, and later on Willie Redmond, coming across him in the smoking-room, remonstrated with him in dignified terms. Now Willie had an enormous mop of curly hair, so gazing earnestly at him, and taking a shilling out of his pocket, the old gentleman thus addressed him: "Do you see this shillin', Willie, me boy? Take it and go and get your hair cut, and when ye come back, looking more like a dacent Christian than ye do just now, maybe I'll do ye the honour of kickin' ye out of the room!" A strange form of *amende honorable*!

My relations with the members of my Party were nearly always agreeable and harmonious; but very occasionally one came across an awkward customer, who professedly on a public, though more often in reality on a private grievance, would try to make himself disagreeable by adopting a hectoring tone and by threatening to withdraw his support from the Government at a critical juncture on this or the other ground. In nine cases out of ten, or probably nineteen out of twenty, he would be acting entirely off his own bat and would only be promptly disavowed by his supporters in his constituency; so, instead of shouting back at him, I found the more effective way was to simulate concern and say "Really! Is it as bad as all that? I suppose before taking so serious a step you have already assured yourself of the concurrence of the Association in your constituency?" This nearly always acted as a perfect sedative.

Outside the House there was also a good deal of work for a Whip. You had to keep in touch with the main political organizations of the Party and their leading Members and officials, both in London and in the provinces, to act as intermediary between constituencies and their candidates, to keep up relations with the provincial as well as the London Press. Indeed by the end of my second term of office (1892–1895) the Whips each had a district allotted to them, which was to be their special province and for which they were to be individually responsible. It was nearly as trying a situation as that of St Paul, who had "the care of all the Churches." Another of our duties was to provide M.P.s as speakers at public meetings, and it required some little thought and trouble to get the right man for audiences widely differing in character and composition.

We had also to attend political gatherings of a social nature, not only the big evening receptions or garden-parties given by leading Liberal hostesses, who often invoked our help in the preliminary arrangements, but gatherings held to welcome provincial delegates, whenever some occasion brought a number of them to town. Now and then one of us was told off to act as showman to a party of country cousins who wanted to see the Houses of Parliament. Once I had to take charge of no less than 240 Liberal ladies, and to deliver a kind of peripatetic lecture on the various points of interest. On taking leave, as they filed out of the Inner Lobby, each one of them on shaking hands named the constituency from which she came: "Thank you for Bristol; Thank you for Leeds; Thank you for Dover, etc. etc." Further, we had to keep in touch with the paid agents in the various constituencies, and to speak at breakfasts or luncheons where they were assembled in conference from time to time.

In the Outer Lobby a constituent once gave me his card and said that he would like to speak to his Member. I came back and said that he would come out to him presently, whereupon he kindly tipped me a shilling, as he mistook me for an attendant, since I had no hat and wore a short jacket as was the Whips' custom.

I was entrusted with the business in the House of the Office of Works, the First Commissioner being then a peer. The Earl of Morley (not to be confused with John Morley who much later became a peer) first occupied the post. He was a Devonshire man, who had been Under Secretary for War in the 1880 Government. He and I were on one occasion guests of the Duke of Cleveland at Battle Abbey. The Duchess had a Visitors' Book in which you had to inscribe answers to a number of perplexing questions. One of these being: "Why did you come here?" Morley answered: "To get away from W.O." (the War Office); and I followed suit with:

"To get away from W.G." (Mr Gladstone), which scandalized my Father, who lectured me on "want of respect," etc.

Lord Morley I found an excellent chief, with a special knack of getting at the heart of things. I went to the Office of Works, then a dingy old building in Whitehall Place, every morning, and together with him and Barty Mitford,* the secretary, went over any questions relating to the Department of which notice had been given by M.P.s and which had to be answered in the House. We would then draw up the replies which I should make, and, as far as was possible, anticipate whatever supplementary questions might be expected and decide on the best line to be taken. When the Home Rule split took place, Morley resigned, together with other Members of the Government, and was succeeded by Lord Elgin, afterwards Viceroy of India.

A more ticklish job was that of preparing the departmental Estimates, which I had to carry through the House of Commons single-handed. As I had never even heard Estimates debated and had not yet opened my mouth in the House, this was a formidable task. I carefully considered what questions I would put if I were a hostile critic, and would then get my answers ready after consultations with my Chief and the officials. Further, I read the Debates on the Office of Works Estimates for the previous ten years, in search of knotty questions, and noted whether there were any similar pitfalls in the Estimates of the current year. I found that a good many points came up every year, like hardy annuals. The actual Debate lasted eight hours, during the whole of which time I had to parry, as best I could, questions and criticisms of every kind. The Estimates got through all right, after a serious hitch over the Vote for the London Parks. Here we were "wounded in the house of our friends," as Labouchere headed a number of newly-elected Liberal M.P.s who were eager to show their zeal in defending their constituents' pockets. They argued, and as it seemed to me, quite fairly, that it was hard that country tax-payers should be mulcted for the maintenance of the London Parks, which Londoners enjoyed gratis, whilst all the provincial parks had to be paid for solely out of the rates. In my reply, I suppressed my feeling that there was some justice in what they urged, but laid stress on the fact of London being the Capital not only of the United Kingdom but of the Empire, that the beauty of its parks was enjoyed by people who came to London both from the country and from the

* Afterwards Lord Redesdale.

Colonies, etc. etc. But my pleas were all of no avail and the Government was beaten in Committee, the vote being reduced by £50,000. The victors were so delighted at their success that we had no difficulty in putting things right again at the Report stage; but Herbert Gladstone could not resist poking a little fun at me: "A nice chap you are! My Father gives you a post as soon as you are elected, and the first thing you do is to get beaten on the Estimates!" He knew, of course, as well as I, that the young hounds had to be blooded!

Lord Morley, who was not a wealthy peer, married one of the charming daughters of Mr Holford, the father of the late Sir George. When he was engaged, he was discussing the question of settlements with his future father-in-law, who regretted being prevented making these on a very ample scale because of the heavy expenses which he had recently incurred in building Dorchester House (in Park Lane) and Westonbirt (in Gloucestershire). Morley is reported to have murmured the quotation: "A plague on both your houses!"

Mr Holford, like his son, was a great collector of rare plants and shrubs. It is said that when he had a shooting-party he used to accompany the guns, although he did not himself shoot. When they were in shrubberies near the house he would often call out, if he saw a guest aiming at a rabbit, "Don't shoot! Don't shoot! That's a . . ." (the scientific name of some valuable specimen) "right in the way!" being much more solicitous for the safety of the plant than for the size of the day's bag.

Barty Mitford was known as "the Japanese Swell," from his intimate knowledge of that country and from his always being perfectly dressed. He published a good many years ago a delightful book called *Tales of Old Japan* and made the gardens and grounds of his home at Batsford beautiful by the judicious way with which he adorned them with oriental shrubs and trees. I remember once when, as a youth, I was at a very big party at, I think, Longleat, his luggage had miscarried. His perfect ease at dinner impressed me, whilst I realized how awkward I should have felt had I been similarly situated and determined never to be embarrassed in the future, if I could help it, by any external happening of so little importance as not having on the right clothes for the moment.

Another of my Office of Works experiences was when I was put on to a small House of Commons Committee which had to deal with the Bill settling the proportion which the different parishes had to pay for the recent improvements at Hyde Park Corner. I represented the Government on that Committee and at last got a compromise agreed to, on condition that the Office of Works would undertake to maintain the various islands between the different roads. I had no authority to undertake this responsibility and no means of communicating with my Chief, the First Commissioner; but I gave the undertaking as I realized that the cost would not be large and that the important thing was to get the Bill through the Committee.

I then had to pilot it through the House. It was my first speech and I felt nervous, but my friends were very indulgent and the thing went through all right. I remember trying to lighten my speech a little by saying that all the different parishes were in agreement; they were all unanimous that the money should be found and equally unanimous that somebody else should find it. Sir William Harcourt wrote a kind note to my Father about my maiden effort.

I give a first impression of Office and the House in a letter to a friend dated from the House of Commons.

"Feb. 23, 1886.

"So here I am now a Junior Lord, and pretty stiff work it is too. On one's legs all the night in the Lobby and one's stool all day in the Office is about the form. I answered my first questions for the Office of Works yesterday and they gave me a pleasant cheer when I got up.

"The House is a funny place, rather like a grown up school; with plenty of jokes and fun under the upper current of serious business. Many of the new Members seem possessed with an earnestness and a dullness which is quite appalling; but we must hope that the former, if not the latter, will wear off in time.

"We had our lower windows at 14, South Audley Street smashed by the Socialists the other day: my Father and I were both away, but the footman put up the shutters like a brick, so that nothing else was damaged.

"We are not so busy to-night as it is not a Government night, but as a rule we all squash about the Lobby to prevent sleepy or hungry men going to bed or to dinner. It is like the demons who get no rest themselves but make up for it by letting no one else get any."

The troubles of the Government began as soon as their Home Rule policy was announced. Mr Chamberlain gave a big dinner to a number of Liberal M.P.s, including myself, and made a little speech explaining his difficulties in accepting the Home Rule Bill and announcing his determination to oppose it. He then invited each of us to give our opinion; which we did in turn. Some agreed with him, some shilly-shallied, whilst others, including myself, said that we meant to continue to support the Government. Defections were both numerous and influential both within the Government itself and amongst private M.P.s. A certain number of Whigs (including those who had voted against Mr Jesse Collings' motion which had turned the former Government out), headed by Lord Hartington, declared against the Government. Many of them were actuated by dislike of their general policy, which they thought too advanced, as well as by their distrust of the Irish scheme. Chamberlain carried Birmingham (hitherto a Radical stronghold) with him and its group of Members; whilst Mr Bright's defection had much effect with those who had long looked up to him as a powerful and convinced exponent of Radicalism. I think that his action was, very likely half unconsciously, influenced by the very bitter attacks which had been made on him in the last few years by Nationalist M.P.s, and that his hostility to Home Rule affected the political attitude of a certain number of Free Churchmen, who could not divest themselves of the fear that Irish Self-Government would be unduly dominated by Catholicism and so become subservient to Rome.

Sir George Trevelyan, although he rallied not long after to the cause of Irish self-government, was also an opponent of the Bill, and the fact that he had so recently been Chief Secretary to the Lord Lieutenant, together with the secession of Lord Cowper, who had held that responsible post, drew many away from their allegiance. On the other hand, Lord Cowper's brother-in-law, Lord William Compton, who had been his private secretary at Dublin and who was now M.P. for South Warwickshire, was a staunch advocate of Home Rule.

Altogether the split in the Party was formidable, and became more and more pronounced as the debates proceeded. The danger of the situation lay not only in the number and influence of the secessionists, but in the fact that many of them were amongst the wealthiest men in the Party and the largest contributors to the Central Party Fund and to those of the local Associations; whilst the constituencies, especially the newly enfranchised voters, were bewildered and dismayed

by this new departure, which was as startling to them as it was unexpected.

The Government were further handicapped by the Irish Land
Purchase Bill which they had thought necessary to bring in side by
side with the Home Rule Bill. Its financial provisions were exploited
to their disadvantage and huge posters were stuck up all over the
country displaying long trains bearing trucks full of British gold to
be shipped away to Ireland.

As soon as I became aware of the Government's resolve to bring in
a Home Rule Bill, which of course was not so soon as would have
been the case had I still been Mr Gladstone's Private Secretary, I was
impressed by the gravity of the crisis and the slender chances of the
Bill's success. I saw men falling away daily, almost hourly, and
became more and more convinced that both the Government and their
policy would be defeated, largely owing to the precipitancy of their
action. Although I felt the responsibility was heavy, especially in
view of my youth and of the very short time which I had been in
Parliament or in office, I thought it my duty to do my utmost to use
all my influence, such as it was, to induce those Members of the
Government with whom I was well acquainted, especially my uncle,
to adopt what seemed to me a slower but a surer way to success.
What I tried to impress on them was as follows: I argued that the
novelty of the proposal, and its seeming one-sidedness in favour of
Ireland, combined to prevent many people supporting it who would
be willing to concur with a more comprehensive scheme. I further
pointed out that the new electors in Great Britain who had so recently
and so largely contributed to place the Government in power, had a
right to have their own claims considered and that if nothing were
done for them they would naturally be disappointed if not discouraged
or even actually alienated. My proposal therefore was that a declaration should be made by the Government, in general terms, affirming
their adhesion to a policy of self-government for local purposes not
confined to Ireland but including all parts of the United Kingdom,
and stating that a measure to that effect would be introduced in the
following year. Having thus assured themselves of the support of
the Nationalists, and of the consequent tranquillity of Ireland, the
Government might then employ the Session in introducing and, as
far as the House of Lords would let them, passing two or three much
needed measures of Reform for Great Britain which would consolidate

their position in the constituencies, whilst in the following autumn a great campaign would be started with the cordial co-operation of Nationalist M.P.s to explain and popularize their scheme of federal self-government which would be introduced in the following Session. Such a scheme would provide an Imperial Parliament, smaller in size and with larger constituencies than that in existence, on which should depend, as at present, the Imperial Government. This Parliament and its Government, being freed from the pressure of purely local questions, would be able to devote more time and thought to imperial matters, including, of course, foreign and colonial affairs. All local matters on the other hand would be dealt with by federal legislatures with their respective administrations, each representing a few great sections of the country; Ireland being, possibly, divided into two provinces, Northern and Southern. One advantage of this scheme would be that persons desirous of entering politics would have the choice of becoming candidates for either the imperial or one of the local parliaments, according to whether their natural interests and inclinations were more attracted by imperial or local problems. Again the duty of the elector would be simplified and his interests stimulated, as he would no longer, as is sometimes the case, find himself in the position of preferring the imperial policy of one of the candidates and the local programme of another. Nor would the imperial policy be occasionally endangered, as now, by the overthrow of a Government upon some purely subordinate or local issue, bringing about, together with a change of Government, a change of international policy which may not be desirable or even desired.

I still believe that if some such scheme could have been adopted at the beginning of the Session of 1886; a policy such as that given in outline might have been carried in 1887, and the Government have remained in power for its full term of office. But, what is far more important than this, Ireland would probably have been pacified many years earlier, and, since it is known that the belief entertained in Germany that Irish disaffection would prevent Great Britain from engaging in hostilities was not one of the least causes which led Germany to plunge into war in 1914, the German Government might have hesitated before doing so; whilst even if they had continued on their course of violence, a pacified and loyal Ireland would have added enormously to our strength, especially in the early stages of the conflict.

Speaker Peel had a trying time during this tense period of strong emotions and violent antipathies, but, as always, bore himself with a dignity and impartiality which won him universal respect and admiration. He had a tall and commanding presence, great readiness and power of quick decision and of prompt action, together with fine and impressive diction. His only defect was, possibly, a quickness of temper which he occasionally found hard to keep under complete control. I always remember the positively awe-inspiring manner in which he rebuked the directors of the Cambrian Railway, one of whom, Mr McClure, was a Member, when they were brought to the Bar of the House and were there reproved for contempt of Parliament, in having dismissed one of their employees for evidence given by him before a Committee of the House of Commons. They came up to the Bar as if they thought it a good joke, but left it after the Speaker's short but crushing castigation in a very chastened spirit.

One less serious incident recalls itself to my memory. I was standing by the Speaker's Chair, not long after I had been made a Whip, one afternoon when the daylight was bad and before the artificial light had been turned on. A Member rose to his feet, rather under the Gallery and at the further end of the Chamber. The Speaker, before calling him by name, asked me who he was. I thought it was a Mr Leicester, an excellent working man who sat for a London constituency. "Mr Leicester," called the Speaker in his resonant voice. The man remained silent. "Mr Joseph Leicester," repeated the Speaker. The silence continued. By this time I realized that I had made a mistake and that it was somebody else and incontinently fled to the lobby behind the Speaker's Chair. I never asked how the episode terminated.

On June 7 the blow, which I had so long expected, fell and the Second Reading of the Home Rule Bill was defeated by a majority of thirty. At the General Election in the following July I lost my seat on the 10th of that month, the numbers being:

Heathcote	.. ..	5252
Gower	.. ..	4459

Conservative Maj. 793

Only three incidents in this election remain in my remembrance. The first was being heckled at one of my meetings by my own

Chairman, a thing which I have never heard of before or since. What made it more ludicrous was that I had got him made a J.P. shortly before and had received from him a fulsome and effusive letter of thanks. He was a pompous and conceited individual. The meeting had gone off very well, my speech being excellently received. At its conclusion, the Chairman made the usual inquiry whether anybody wished to ask me any questions, which he repeated more than once (as I thought quite unnecessarily). "As nobody wishes to ask the candidate any questions, I now propose to ask him some myself"; which he proceeded to do, pulling out a long roll of papers from his pocket. I did not spare him and made him look pretty foolish before I had done with him.

The second incident was, I should think, also unparalleled. My opponent had the audacity, or shall I say the impudence, to advance, as one of the reasons why I should not be re-elected, that if I were defeated the country would be saved £1,000 a year, the amount of my salary as Junior Lord. After the election and the formation of the Conservative Government I was at first inclined to issue a challenge to him in the local paper offering to pay £100 to any local charity if he could prove that one of the Conservative Junior Lords was not drawing his salary, on condition that my opponent should do the same if he failed to adduce the required proof. My friends, however, induced me to leave it alone, saying, and indeed with truth, that he had already covered himself with so much ridicule by his preposterous suggestion that it was not worth while rubbing it in.

The third was as follows. Colonel Hollins, the head of Minton's well-known china manufactory, was one of my staunchest supporters as years ago he had been one of my Father's. He lived at a beautiful place called Whitmore Hall, a few miles westward of Newcastle-under-Lyme. He told me that he had never nominated a candidate who had not got in, but in 1886 I am sorry to say that I was the means of breaking this proud record. His daughters were also zealous Liberals. Colonel Ingram, who had lent Shoobridge and myself his house at Hartshill, as previously mentioned, was a Conservative. He was Adjutant of the Volunteers and was a great friend of the Misses Hollins, who one day pinned a big blue poster of mine with "Vote for Gower" on it on to his back as he was driving them in his dog-cart, much to the amusement of those whom he met on the road. He was a very pleasant and popular man, and died in India from wounds inflicted by a panther. His only son, Edward Maurice Berkeley Ingram, is one of our leading diplomatists.

On June 21 I wrote to a friend from the House of Commons with reference to the turmoil which succeeded the defeat of the Government and which preceded the consequent General Election:

"I am overwhelmed, submerged and annihilated in the sea of politics and wire-pulling in which I have been so suddenly plunged. Candidates wanting constituencies and constituencies wanting candidates and both of them wanting money, such are the main features of the daily waking nightmare of a Whip just before a General Election. I have to stick on here to help to wind up the business of the House and more or less to neglect my constituency, contenting myself with an occasional dash down there, whilst my opponent is working away day and night. In addition to this I am worried to death, as I said before, with helping to fix things up in other constituencies, whilst all the time I am longing to get to work on my own.

"I have had a few meetings, both crowded and enthusiastic, but influential supporters keep falling away in a most discouraging fashion."

After my defeat my old Chief wrote me a letter, which seemed to me important as it practically pledged himself and the Liberal Party, or that portion of it which still regarded him as its leader, to persevere in the attempt to confer self-government on Ireland. With this in my mind I asked Mr Gladstone whether he would object to its publication, and accordingly when he said he would like it to be published and when this view was corroborated by two such experienced politicians as my Father and my uncle, I sent a copy of it to the daily Press. It runs as follows, being taken from the columns of *The Times* of Saturday, July 17, 1886.

"MY DEAR GEORGE,—I am sadly and sorely grieved at your defeat; but you will suffer in a noble cause. It will be some consolation to you to observe how, even at the moment, the whole civilized world is with us. You have, I hope, very long years before you; and I do not think many of them, though probably some, will have passed before you receive your vindication. I advise you to take resolutely to the study of Irish history. I have done in that way the little that I could, and I am amazed at the deadness of vulgar opinion to the blackguardism and baseness—no words are strong enough—which befoul the whole history of the Union. It is an open question in my mind whether if this folly lasts, the thing may not in the end contribute to repeal, which I should greatly regret. Time will be the great instructor, and, in truth, when we consider all things, much has been done in a very limited time. I am so glad you have had your share.

"Yours faithfully,

"W. E. GLADSTONE."

The publication of this letter was received with much indignation, real or simulated, on the part of the victorious Conservatives, who were particularly incensed by the reference to the "blackguardism and baseness" which attended Pitt's methods of bringing about the Union. In my opinion, and I should think in that of everybody who has taken the trouble to make himself acquainted with the details of that infamous transaction, the words are not a bit too strong and are nothing more than a plain statement of fact. But whilst this letter aroused the ire of political opponents I have more than once been assured by Nationalist leaders that it greatly confirmed the belief of their own followers in the sincerity and persistency of Mr Gladstone and his adherents and did not a little to discount the assurances of the party of physical force that all English statesmen and parties were equally untrustworthy and that Ireland could never obtain justice by constitutional means.

Fourteen years after when I was staying at a big hotel in New York, I was touched when the Irish lift-man said that he knew my name and remembered this letter and refused to take any tip from me. The Irish have certainly long memories and warm hearts.

After a fortnight's well-earned rest at Holmbury I paid, amongst other visits, a particularly pleasant one of several days on July 26 to the Speaker at his house at Sandy Lodge, in Bedfordshire. He was very kind to me, urged me not to be downcast by my defeat, which he said was a thing one must expect now and then in a political career and prophesied that I should soon be back again. I thought this was specially gracious of him as he was politically opposed to Mr Gladstone's Home Rule policy, though, of course, as Speaker, he maintained an attitude of strict impartiality.

I see from my correspondence that I must have taken his good advice to heart, as I wrote to a friend from Holmbury:

"For the first time within the last seven weeks I have a few hours to myself. Well, I've done my best and like other men not done well enough; but I am content because I know that I fought hard and fair, whilst the others . . .

"After all defeat is annoying but nothing more; it is not like some other disasters which time cannot repair. Life, as a fact, is very good, only there are some bits of it which are very bad. If one is wise one tries to prevent the bad parts turning all the rest sour."

APPENDIX

The Masque of Balliol

Master.
I come first, my name is Jowett:
That which is to know, I know it.
I am the Master of this College:
That which I know not is not knowledge.

Fellows.
J. L. Strachan Davidson.
I'm Strachan Davidson, the lean
Unbuttoned, cigaretted dean.
Brother numismatists, you see a
Historian in a dahabiah.

The Rev. T. K. Cheyne.   (Chaplain.)
I am Cheyne: I confess
That I love a deaconess;
I can wed without misgiving
Now I've got a college living.

R. L. Nettleship.
Roughly, so to speak, you know,
I am the Junior Dean, or so.
I think you're gated after Hall:
That's all—at least, that's nearly all.

R. G. Tatton.
Here am I, the often sat on
Dancing don; my name is Tatton;
Like old wine in a new bottle
Is my talk on Aristotle.

E. Abbott.
I am Abbott: where I go
My man Tom must go also,
He on foot, I in my chair,
But that's neither here nor there.[1]

W. H. Forbes.
O, I say,[2] I once was Forbes,
Me the Master now absorbs;
Me and many other mes
In his new Thucydides.

A. C. Bradley.
I'm Bradley, and I bury deep
A secret that no man can keep.
If you'll not let the Master know it,
Nor Forbes, I'll tell you: I'm a poet.

F. de Paravicini.
What an oddity am I,
Little cynic Paravi,
Virgil can I shrilly render
Cock-a-hoop upon the fender.

Tutors and Lecturers not on the Foundation.
A. L. Smith.
My name, my friends, is A. L. Smith,
I'm somewhat hard to struggle with.
Who'd have looked for so much vigour
In so very small a figure!

A. Toynbee.
What finance and trade and coin be
Learn of me, for I am Toynbee:
Green and I our faith have plighted
To a sepulchre re-whited.

[1] A favourite phrase of his.
[2] Also a favourite phrase of W. H. F.

A. J. Grahame.
Grahame am I, so calm, so bright,
The scholar's peer, the don's delight.
"I have developed no defect
Of either" but their grace elect.

H. E. Boulton.
Waifs and Strays I, Boulton, edit,
And my ballads do me credit;
I'm in everything that's going,
I know everyone worth knowing.

The Honble. G. N. Curzon.
I am a most superior person;
My name is George Nathaniel Curzon;
My cheeks are pink, my hair is sleek,
I dine at Blenheim twice a week.

C. A. James.
I am Truthful James, whose bent
Brows express astonishment.
James and eyebrows you may sever,
James and anecdotage never.

P. E. Matheson.
Upright and shrewd, more woo'd of fame
Than wooing, Matheson's my name.
I'm not what you would call intense,
But I've uncommon common sense.

J. A. Hamilton.
I am Hamilton; my mission
Is to be a politician;
Judicious love of Art refines
The paragon of Philistines.

C. A. Spring Rice.
Can story-telling be a vice
When you're an "uncle" like Spring Rice?
My versatility is such
None likes me little or loves me much.

253

Lucius F. Smith.
I am Lucy; when I play
Bliss[1] and Dawkins flee away.
Art and orthodoxy wait
On my Archdiaconate.

J. B. B. Nichols.
Mark the subtle smile that trickles
O'er the sphinx-like face of Nichols.
My hair is black, my china blue,
My Botticellis' forty two.

A. C. Grant Duff.
I'm Grant Duff, with much misgiving
Whether life be worth the living,
But there's balm in Gilead, should a
Friend be brought to talk of Buddha.

G. and C. L. Sclater Booth.
Brothers twain, yet single hearted
Rarely will you see us parted,
Sclater Booth and Sclater Booth,
Leviathan and Behemoth.

B. Mallet.
Spoken jest of Strachey, shall it
Not arouse a smile in Mallet?
Thro' my eyelids softly peeping
Like as one that walketh sleeping.

R. W. Simpson.
Could you by feeding tea and shrimps on
Ever become as lean as Simpson?
No, but you might by trying to defer
So very obstinate a questioner.

C. J. Jessel.
Out of the way, for I am Jessel,
You'll find you are the weaker vessel;
But as I occupy the ground
You have the choice, so which way round?

[1] Bliss, his scout.

254

Abdul Kassim.
I am Abdul Kassim Khan,
In my grave sweet way I scan
Western life. My thoughts would fill a
Book if written out. Bismillah.

Leonard Huxley.
I am Huxley, blond and merry,
Fond of jokes and laughter, very.
Laughed I but at what is witty,
I'd laugh less—which were a pity.

G. G. R. Repton.
Faultless I from brim to sole,
Coat and gloves and buttonhole;
High-souled Brummel, touched, had wept on
Seeing me, for I am Repton.

S. Brearley.
No poor Britisher is nearly
Half so fine a man as Brearley;
But I cheerfully acknowledge
Harvard's whipped by Balliol College.

C. E. Dawkins.
Positivists never talk in s-
Uch an epic style as Dawkins;
Creeds are nought and Man is all,
Spell Him with a capital.

Honorary Scholar.
J. W. Mackail.
From Dawks and Chitty at my tail
You'll syllogize that I'm Mackail.
In all I do I'm sure always;
In all I say, *à l'écossaise.*

255

Exhibitioners.

A. N. Cumming. (Snell exhibitioner.)
I am Cumming, I inveigle
Everyone to talk of Hegel;
Mr Ruskin would have sobbed on
Seeing the motto of my Cobden.

—Montague. (Jenkyns exhibitioner.)
Old tips come out as good as new
From me, for I am Montague;
With head aslant I softly cram
The world into an epigram.

H. C. C. Macleod. (Open exhibitioner.)
An anti-everything-you-list,
Insipid epigrammatist,
Of eccentricity I'm proud,
A human artichoke, Macleod.

H. C. Beeching. (Open exhibitioner.)
I am the apostle Beeching,
Busby and Burne-Jones my teaching.
I write poems; but one saith
My poems are a form of death.

Minor Exhibitioners.

J. M. MacKay.
Red my head, and blue my tie,
Soft my speech, for I'm MacKay;
Aphrodeety may be dead,
But we've Nicholson instead.

G. H. Battersby.
Like the gurgling brook that patters by
Flows my speech, for I am Battersby.
Never swan nor yet giraffe
Had so GRAND a throat by half.

S. E. Lee.
I am featly tripping Lee,
Learned in modern history,
My gown, the wonder of beholders,
Hangs like a foot-note from my shoulders.

Two others may be added, which although not belonging to the
Masque itself, are also of the same period.

The Regius Professor of Greek.
For Pyramus cannot be Thisbe
Though one Bottom their substance absorbs:
But oh! could thy scholarship his be,
Or thine his translation, O! Forbes!
What a sanctity super egregious
Would attach to the words you would speak,
· O! incorporate Forbes and the Regius
Professor of Greek!

(See Epigram 7.)

This last has nothing to do with Balliol, but refers to the Dean and
Mrs Liddell.

I am the Dean of Christ Church, sir;
This is my wife; pray look at her;
She is the Broad and I'm the High;
We are the University.

INDEX

Place names in small capitals